The Wrong Way to Wright

A NOVEL BY

D. Adiba

The Wrong Way To Wright
A NOVEL

Copyright © 2017 D. Adiba

All rights reserved. This book or any portion thereof may not be reproduced or used in any manner whatsoever without the express written permission of the publisher except for the use of brief quotations in a book review.

This is a work of fiction. Unless otherwise indicated, all the names, characters, places, events and incidents in this book are either the product of the author's imagination or used in a fictitious manner. Any resemblance to actual persons, living or dead, or actual events is purely coincidental.

ISBN 978-1-7750009-4-5
Ebook ISBN 978-1-7750009-0-7

Second Edition
Manufactured in Canada

Edited by Tanis Nessler @ www.revisionediting.ca
Cover Design by Kozakura @ fiverr.com/kozakura
Interior Design by Kozakura @ fiverr.com/kozakura

Published by

To learn more about D. Adiba, go to www.theadibaspot.com and follow @theadibaspot on Twitter.

The Wrong Way to Wright

Chapter 1

Thirty-three hours. Aya Daniels was actually counting down until she could take her few belongings and sneak away to begin a very different life. For she had said yes without reservation, even if it was spoken so softly that she had to repeat it. And now she needed to act quickly in order to be ready in time.

She took advantage of the noise her aunt and her aunt's friends were making, cackling like the hens they became when they got together to gossip. Preoccupied as they were in their own dramas, they would not come to investigate the shuffling sounds coming from Aya's dingy room.

She pulled her suitcase from the bottom of the wardrobe and started sorting through her clothes. She was pleased to see that most of them had become too big for her in the year since she had relocated to the Caribbean. She took her most professional pieces and stylish casuals as she wanted to make a good impression.

She packed the creams and ointments she kept in her wicker drawer to treat her heat rash and unabating mosquito bites. Then she raised her hands to place the tiny twists of her black shoulder-length locks into a high ponytail to keep them out of her sweat-soaked face. She wiped her brow and turned on the wall fan, which did little other than blow the hot air around her confined quarters.

Aya looked at herself in the mirror above the wicker dresser. Would she be able to live up to his expectations? She turned to the right to review her profile from that angle. Her generous bosom was still perky and much of the bloat of the previous years had left her midsection.

Her behind was a little flat, but she hadn't known him to be like most island men in that regard.

She moved in closer to scrutinize her face. She was almost thirty-six years old, but she had yet to feel like her own woman. She plumped her full lips, tipped her chin down, and smiled when she remembered how often he complimented her on them. Observing how the relentless sun had toasted her complexion to a healthy-looking caramel tone, she was satisfied. She then squinted to examine the dark circles under her expressive deep-set eyes. The climate had failed to hide the stress and worry of the past couple of years.

Aya turned away from the mirror to examine her mail, which consisted mostly of credit card bills with large balances. She slid the envelopes into the front flap of her case and then sifted through what remained in her drawer. Among the several articles about how to write your first novel was a picture that hit her like a kick in the guts. It was him.

Her aunt Bea walked by her bedroom on the way to the bathroom next door and invited Aya out to join the meal she was serving her friends. Aya held the picture to her breast, mumbled a curt refusal, and lowered herself onto her twin bed. Her body tensed as she remembered the end of a conversation she had overheard her aunt having with her mother on the phone only the day before.

Bea had returned home from the grocery store, talking on her cell with the speaker on as she unpacked and put away the groceries. She didn't realize Aya had come home early from work and was writing on her laptop in her room.

"I don't think she's ready to come back to you in Canada yet, Pearl."

"Why not? You can see she isn't happy there," her mother said frankly. "She left her job, her few friends, and her family to get a fresh start but is still doing the same nonsense. She's not getting any younger either. There's no time to waste."

"At least she has that good job I got her doing the accounts at the hotel. And she's taken off all of that weight."

"I didn't send my daughter to you to be shut up in her room every night."

"Well, I try taking her out with me, but she always refuses. I introduce her to all the young men I come across, but nothing ever comes of that either. I can't even get her to join me at church. I don't know what else to do."

"I curse the day she ever met that blasted Bradley! Do you suppose she's still depressed?"

Bea took a moment to respond, breathing heavily as she lumbered her wide body about the room. "She don't say too much to me about anything, really. She has a girlfriend from work who calls sometimes, but they don't do much together. I hoped Nicola would be here for her until she up and went off to England to do her Master's. I know Aya was really counting on her cousin and very disappointed that when she finally pack up and come, her closest relative up and leave."

"Is she still overeating?"

"I told you, she's slimmed down nicely. I doubt she can find half of the junk she used to gorge on down here anyway."

"She doesn't talk much to me after I told her she needed to forget a career as a writer since she has so much debt to pay off. I don't know why Nicola put that idea in her head. She's not still shopping, is she? It boggles my mind to think of all the money she wasted on rubbish that's now crammed into a storage unit."

"No. No more mindless spending. She gets the bills you forward to her, and after making the payments she doesn't have funds to play with, so she doesn't go out much. I offer to help—"

"She can't stay with you for free, Bea. I know you can afford it, but I've told her time and again that she cannot spend her way out of a broken heart."

"Well, I feel bad. She must be lonely, always stuck in that room. I wish I knew how to help her. What do you expect her to go back to Canada and do?"

At that moment, Aya's cell had started ringing. She had stumbled about trying to silence it while Bea had quickly ended the call.

Aya was incensed. They were always trying to run her life. Depressed? She wasn't depressed. She was in pain due to a festering wound that had been rubbed raw for nearly a decade. She raised the picture she was holding to her tearing eyes.

The photo was taken at a family picnic. The very striking Bradley was smiling at the camera, his muscular arm draped around her shoulders. Her face was beaming as she looked up at him. She had loved this guy from afar for three years in university, where the popular athlete had the run of all the girls on campus. A year after graduating, the new financial advisor had crossed paths with Aya when she was working as a teller at one of the top banks.

Aya thought it was a dream come true when they started dating and thanked the heavens that love was still alive, which she had doubted after living through her parents' nasty divorce only a few years before. She was deliriously happy with him for eight months, until he got his first promotion. Once he started making a lot more money, he became too busy with clients or company events to extend her an invitation.

Aya had already envisioned taking his name and planned their entire future together when he started being seen with other women. He became distant with her and would only make time for sexual encounters. Aya was not prepared to have actual intercourse with him unless he proposed. She excused his dalliances with other women because she was silly enough to believe it was her he really wanted.

Their romance was off far more than on during their second year, but Aya could not give him up. She was desperate to keep some semblance of joy in her life, especially since her father was angry and distant while her mother was manipulative and clinging. She remained hopeful that the man she had fallen so deeply in love with would return. Until his son was born to the girl he had gone steady with during most of those university years. Then Aya had to face that she may never have had the man at all.

She blamed herself for not giving in to him physically, no matter how hot and heavy their sessions would get. Although not religious, Aya could not find it in herself to be with a man who did not desire her enough to make her his bride. She had gambled that holding out would make him commit, and lost.

Aya crumpled up the picture and wiped her eyes. She would not shed one more tear over Bradley Wentworth. Then a flash of memory that she had long repressed came through. A moment from the night her mother was out working and Aya thought she was home alone. She had cried so hard over him that she wanted to end her pain and die right there on the family room couch.

Unbeknownst to her, Mr. Franklyn, a long-time friend of the family, was visiting and had fallen asleep in the basement TV room. Aya was horrified to feel him lay his clean-shaven head next to hers while she sobbed, but he continued to hold her when she tried to push him away. Eventually, she grew weary and let him. Desmond Franklyn could guess what had happened to devastate her so as he had cautioned Aya several times over Bradley's immature ways.

Once Aya was able to compose herself, the tall, dark, and handsome man gently wiped her tears, stroked her face, and put his arm around her hip as she leaned her head on his broad shoulders. They sat together, saying nothing, and she relaxed under his caresses.

The jolting sound of the garage door opening brought them out of their stupor and Aya abruptly sat up, getting ready to flee the room as she did not want her mother to see her destroyed. Mr. Franklyn's dark lips smiled gently when he took her face in his hands and kissed her fully on the mouth, his clipped goatee tickling her face until they heard footsteps coming up from the basement. He got up and had kept Pearl talking in the kitchen so that Aya could get into bed. They had never spoken of it again.

Sweat rolled down Aya's neck and she jumped up to get back to the matter at hand. She reorganized her belongings so nothing looked amiss and returned her case to the wardrobe. She would pack her toiletries from the bathroom as soon as the coast was clear.

Now all she could do was wait. If only she had known that morning, while waiting for the stifling, crammed bus she took to work, that it would be her last day. He hadn't asked her to resign, but she knew it was expected, and she more than welcomed it.

She had stunned her supervisor when she informed him that she was leaving. Her abrupt departure could hardly come as a surprise to the ruddy British national, who knew that his escalating lust for her was not lost on Aya, nor most of the people in the office. Someone had spilled the beans to his venomous wife, who was making frequent unannounced visits to thwart what she believed to be inevitable. Her spies in the building were also fanning the flames and making Aya's life miserable. Her boss had made one last attempt, hoping that Aya would relent and let him get at her now that she would no longer be his subordinate.

Aya found herself coming up against such experiences often, as plenty of carnal attention was directed her way in this sizzling land of libido, rum, and Carnival. She would have been flattered if the advances were ever from anyone suitable. Unfortunately, they were always either too old, married, or attached to any number of other women. They looked at her parts with no thought or care for who she really was as a person.

Not giving a damn anymore what people would say about her decision, Aya squared her shoulders and scowled. For she was now certain that she was doing the right thing. An opportunity that had miraculously become available when she was beyond all hope. She was leaving tomorrow evening to become Mrs. Desmond Franklyn, as she had promised him she would.

Chapter 2

Mr. Franklyn made a habit of coming by to check on things around the house for Aya's aunt, and then they would sit on her balcony to shoot the breeze. Aya hated bugs and never joined the pair outside. She would remain in the sitting room behind them, watching her shows.

Lately, Mr. Franklyn started visiting a lot more often. Whatever the reason, the six foot three, soft-spoken gentleman would sit his gangly legs on the couch and make polite conversation until he asked, as he always did, why such a pretty girl was home alone by herself. His needling would irritate Aya, but then he would present her with the dessert that he had picked up from the local bakery and she would end up offering him a beer. They would finish eating and he would clean up and head to the balcony so Aya could return to watching her programs. It was an odd situation that she had never bothered to question as it made her feel somewhat less alone in the world.

So, there he was outside the door again last night. The air conditioning and refrigeration technician had been working on a job down the hill for the past few weeks and liked to come watch the night action of the bay from Bea's house.

Bea was out with her friends and so Aya had just come out of her room to make herself comfortable on the couch. It was a humid November evening—too hot for underthings—and so she wore only an oversized white T-shirt as she turned the fan up to high so she would not stick to the couch while watching her favourite detective series. Then she heard the knock on the door and Mr. Franklyn calling her name. She cringed, cursing herself for blasting the noisy fan and having the television volume so loud that he would know she was home and awake.

Aya hissed and promised herself she would be short with him so that he would get the message and leave. However, Mr. Franklyn paid her no mind. He talked endlessly about his work and how proud he was of his boys while Aya rolled her eyes and feigned sleepiness.

Aya informed Mr. Franklyn that it was late and she was going to bed. He had other ideas. He slid closer and turned her to face him so that she had no choice but to look into his protruding dark brown eyes. He bent down to meet her gaze, rested his long arm on her shoulders, and spoke gently.

"You know how much I care 'bout you, right?"

Aya staggered back, her eyebrows raised. "Yeaaahh," she answered slowly.

"Well, I want you to come be with me. You wasting away here," he whispered, smiling.

Aya squinted, trying to understand. "Go where? Mr. Franklyn, I—"

"Desi," he corrected. "You call me Desi. I ain't a stranger to you. I been loving you for many years."

Aya's eyes grew large and she started to feel faint. He couldn't possibly be saying what she thought she was hearing. *The dirty dog!*

"Now, don't be thinking I'm tryin' to take advantage of you, because that ain't so. I been waiting for you to be ready. I know how unhappy you were back home, especially once you and him split up."

He grinned and the light caught the gold cap on his front tooth. His chains and bracelets chimed as he repositioned his arm. They combined with his long, curled eyelashes; short, pointed nose; and full, dark lips to give him something of a swarthy pirate look.

"I was so happy to hear that you come back here to live, Ay, you wouldn't believe," he continued. "I wanted you to get accustomed to me before I had this talk with you. You see, I know you very well, and understand you even better."

Aya could think of nothing to say and didn't believe a word of it. She fidgeted with the bangles on her wrist.

Mr. Franklyn leaned in, put his arm around her, and pulled her closer to him. His body was lean and his workman's hands were wide, thick, and a little scruffy. She could now taste his overbearing cologne and winced at the thought of what he might do next.

"You feel misunderstood, don't you, Ay? That you're always the odd one out? Here you are, as beautiful as ever, and still lonely. I'm telling you, I've known for some time that I'm the man for you and we can be so happy together. Life's too short to waste. You gotta grab joy when you find it."

Aya looked away, surprised that Mr. Franklyn was so aware of her anguish.

"Listen," he said, trying to regain her attention. "I am dead serious. I wanna committed relationship, not monkey business. I'm ready to make you my wife. Maybe even give you a child to cherish."

Aya wanted to gag, finding the very idea beyond vulgar. *What is he thinking? He's like family, and much too old for me!* She could never let him get any closer than he was now, and at that thought, she pushed him back.

"Don't look at me like that, Aya," he said sternly. "I've thought this over a long time. You need a good man, and I know what you like. Yes, I'm older, but no geezer in any way, and you nearing forty. I'm a lot younger than your father, you know? I have my own business, a lot of land and interests. You won't want for nothing. You can work for me or do your own thing, whatever you like. You could even write that book."

Aya's head snapped back as her mouth dropped open. She had forgotten that she had told him about that dream. "Mr. Franklyn—" Aya stammered.

"Desi," he repeated, smiling.

"What do you want with me? I have nothing to give anyone, and on top of that, I'm leaving soon."

"Oh? I know you not going back already."

"No, I'm going to try my luck somewhere else. I haven't decided where yet."

"That's the thing, Ay. You running 'round trying to find yourself, and I'm telling you it is here with me. It's no coincidence that we both find ourselves here at this time, you know? We can take care of each other and live the good life. Don't worry 'bout the boys, they're my responsibility. I got a woman who looks after them and the house, so you won't have to lift a finger. We got plenty of room, and you'll have your own car. And I'll see to the bills. You don't have to spend one more minute at that dead-end job. Don't you see, you'll be set?"

Yeah, Aya thought, *and I'll have to spread my legs far and wide to reap those benefits.* She clenched her teeth. "Mr. Fra— I mean, Desi. I could never marry a man I don't love. I don't even know you!"

At that, he laughed aloud. "You know me better than you think, it's just you haven't been paying attention. I been 'round you most of your life, and we have a strong connection. You would'a noticed if you weren't so broken over that boy. This a great thing happening here. You got nothing to lose."

Aya could not believe his gall and got up to walk away. *Wait until I tell my Father!* "I don't know what you think I am, but I'm not suited to you at all. You can have any woman, go take up with one of them. What do you want with me anyway? You better leave."

He rose, grabbed her by both shoulders, and pulled her into him once again. She tried to back away but only ended up cornered against the wall. He gave her a deep, passionate kiss while rubbing his hands up and down her lower back. Stunned, Aya went limp. Her lips were damp with his when he released her—much like that time years before.

"I do love you, Aya," he said slowly. "If you don't believe me now, trust me, you'll see soon enough. Why you think I'm always coming 'round here finding things to fix? I wanna be with you is why, and you kinda like that. I wanna come home to you every night and sit just like we do and spend time. We can go out to dinner or movies or wherever on an evening, you don't need to sit home all alone. I have and always will look after you. I'm the only man who has never failed you your whole life."

Still feeling lost, Aya remained in his embrace, falling into a trance as she looked deeply into his eyes. She slowly began to realize that she somehow was no longer repulsed by him. Before she could act, Auntie Bea and her friends came strolling in, giving them a curious look as they walked by.

The couple quickly parted. Aya went to her room while Mr. Franklyn gave excuses to make a hasty exit.

Later that restless night, Aya tossed and turned on her sweat-soaked sheets. She pulled her pillow down over her head. Unfortunately, these discomforts failed to disguise the real reason behind her unrest. Desi Franklyn had proposed to her! He was offering her everything she wanted on a silver platter—other than the fact that she would have to actually share her life with him. She had never given him much thought over the years, even though she had seen his purplish manhood once when he'd left the bathroom door open while urinating in her family home many years ago. And had never forgotten it.

While she was growing up in Canada, Desi had flown in for all of their family functions, and he was always the one to pick them up at the airport when they returned to the island for summers. During her parent's divorce, his time in Alberta was supposed to be temporary, yet he had stayed on for several months after her family had separated and she ended up with her demanding mother. He had come to her mother's place quite a lot, fixing whatever needed it and having a drink on the patio, much like he did now with Bea. Except that he would stay late into the evening. Her mother had clearly desired him, while he seemed distracted or uncommitted at most. She was aware he was frequently in trouble with women over one thing or another, only she never cared to know the details.

Aya could not remember meeting his children despite being at several functions where they had been present. On these occasions, Desi would give her a hug, ask about her schooling and plans, then give her a treat.

Aya knew his divorce was worse than that of her parents and he was supposedly finished with women, so why was he propositioning her in such a manner? What could she do? Who could she tell? Aya tossed, turned, and perspired. Her mind simply could not rest, and her body ached with tension: sexual tension and frustration.

As she lay there breathing heavily, her mind wandered to the kiss and the intensity she'd seen in his eyes. She had to admit that it felt nice to be held by him in that way. It had been so long since she had been close to a man, and the astonishing fact that she was still a virgin on this sexually charged island was a constant source of shame and insecurity.

He had cast a spell on her and she could not reason it away easily. Desi was somewhat attractive—arresting even. What's more, he had succeeded in planting a seed of desire in her where so many others had failed.

Aya could not believe she was even entertaining the notion. Nonetheless, by the early hours of that morning, Aya had convinced herself that Mr. Franklyn was right. Not only would she marry him, she would do it right away.

When he called to follow up on his request a few moments later, she noticed he wasn't the least bit surprised by her acceptance. He would pick her up the following evening without a word to anyone. They would stay at the secluded Shady Dayze Hotel until they married.

Chapter 3

Bright and early that Tuesday morning they were joined in matrimony at the registrar's office. Aya, trembling and feeling anxious, wore a simple white slip dress that covered her heels. Her locks were pulled back into a side braid to display the three-karat necklace, earrings, and ring set that her betrothed had bought for her.

When it came time to sign the license, Aya became light-headed and weak in the knees. The registrar furrowed his brow as he waited for her to regain her composure. A hot minute went by with Aya unable to move until her groom, dressed fashionably in a crisp silver tux, came up behind her and guided her hand down to sign. He whispered soothing words about their exciting new life and made a lewd joke that put a puzzled smile on his bride's face. Aya gulped and created her new signature.

Desi's sons Junior and Carlton were away on a job, so he brought his youngest along. Ricky was very excited and had even dressed up in a grey suit much like his father's. The eight-year-old boy was every inch his father and followed him everywhere like a puppy. He had the same skin tone, facial features and disposition. Unfortunately, he also had his father's odd short, square teeth in gums that were far too dark.

Tears had come to Desi's eyes as he made his vows to his bride, and the depth of his emotion pleasantly surprised Aya. Unfortunately, it did little to alleviate her concerns about making love to the man that evening.

Aya paced around her cabin constantly in her black satin nightie. She had thrown back a few brandies while waiting for her husband to come out of the bathroom. Their honeymoon suite on a catamaran was a romantic idea, but the sea was not helping her queasiness.

The king bed had half a dozen pillows propped up on it, and a large heart made of red rose petals was laid out in the centre. When she heard the toilet flush, she started ringing her hands. She looked out the large window to the deck with the desire to escape through it. Her mind was racing, trying to come up with suitable excuses not to consummate things now. Her period was still twelve days away, and a headache would seem pitiful. Although she was not as put off by him anymore, she couldn't fathom wrapping her legs around him either. She had never gotten comfortable next to the immense heat of his body at the hotel in the days before their wedding.

Hearing his approach, she dashed to the bed and carefully positioned herself at the side. He came out with just a towel wrapped around his waist, and when he saw her, he got down on his knees at her feet, took her face in his hands, and started kissing her tenderly.

He rose and placed her gently on the bed, then lay down on top of her. He took too long kissing and fondling her when she just wanted him to get on with it. He fumbled with her breasts, squeezing them much too hard, and then he began to suck on her nipples for far too long. Although she felt the occasional tingle, Aya was far from aroused.

Desi made his way down to her tender spot and began to fiddle around. Every now and then Aya would gasp when he stabbed her; however, he eventually succeeded in making her moist enough to penetrate.

Aya braced herself for the initial impact, holding a knot of sheets in her fist. It was tight, really tight. But he went into her gently, making his way little by little, and then she felt an easing. It wasn't awful, although his sloppy kisses were annoying. She would not recall the experience as being pleasurable.

It seemed like forever before Desi, breathing intensely, finally climaxed, remaining in and on top of her. His body trembling and spasmodic, they remained locked in that embrace until he caught his breath.

When he finally rolled off her, Aya shot up to clean herself in the bathroom and noticed Desi's disappointed look. After washing, Aya plopped herself down on the toilet lid, and that's when she realized she had never even considered birth control. After a lengthy period of resting her face in her hands, Aya decided she couldn't hide any longer. Upon her return to the bed, Desi held his arms out to her and she went to him.

"You okay?"

"Yeah, I'm fine. It's just ..." She paused, carefully choosing her words.

"It will get better, you know, hon."

"Oh, I know. It's just, we didn't use any protection, and—"

Desi let out two loud yelps. "That ain't nothing to worry 'bout. I ain't sleeping with anyone else. Are you?"

"Obviously not, just, I don't want to get pregnant."

"Well, I took care of that. I had myself snipped before Ricky was born."

She frowned. "You said you wanted us to have a child!"

"Well, you always said you didn't want kids, only now you have a husband and the means to support them." He shrugged. "Besides, I can have it reversed."

"There are also STDs to consider, and—"

"Now wait a minute"—he leaned in close to her face—"I ain't got no diseases." He sighed and rolled onto his back, staring at the ceiling. "We can get tested once we get back home if you like."

"We? I've never had sex before, and you—" She stopped herself cold. She had not meant to blurt that out.

Desi whipped around to look at her. "What? How is that possible?" She didn't answer him. "You mean you never? Not even with Bradley?"

"No, I did not!" she said. "You better wear condoms until this gets sorted out."

Desi whistled and rolled onto his back again, where they remained in silence for quite some time. Not the best way to start a honeymoon. After a while, Aya started to feel guilty. She really was not being nice to him, and she knew she would have to remind herself to do so as she had so little patience for most people.

"Des," she said. "I didn't mean to seem like ..."

"Oh, I understand. I understand," he said quietly while crossing his legs.

"It's that so many women, Black women in particular, get these diseases, and we have to protect ourselves."

Aya knew he was still processing her lengthy abstinence.

"You've been with so many women," she continued.

"Not that many, I ain't my father," he said. "My first was my wife."

"What happened with her?"

Desi rolled over. "She wasn't you," he said simply. "We married too young, and only because she got pregnant. It was over as soon as we came together, only we didn't do nothing 'bout it. Neither of us knew 'bout such things, so we kept along. I focused on building the business and she on raising Junior. We were sure to separate before he turned two, then I started making real good money, so she stuck around. We led different lives. She only left when I forced the issue."

Aya looked at him quizzically.

"I got another girl pregnant and everybody knew. Carlton's mother had quite a mouth on her, much like you." He winked. "She told everyone 'bout us. To save face, the ex left me and tried to take my business."

"Oh," Aya said. "You must've really hurt her."

"Naw, we didn't even share a bed anymore. She had someone else too, you know? Anyways, it went bad. It took years to get settled, and I ended up starting a new business. I was still angry when I got with Carlton's mother. I shouldn't'a gone there, that one is on me."

"What happened there?" Aya asked.

"There wasn't much money coming to her with the divorce proceedings going on. She wanted this and needed that, and I was living on my last reserves. She plumb wore me out. I knew I could never commit to her, so I let her know it. Except she kept holding on."

Aya noticed that Desi never mentioned any names; still, she would not bother for those details now.

"She gave me a lovely boy though. Carlton is something else. Well behaved and always willing to help. I kept him with me, especially since the ex had Junior wrapped around her finger. She turned him against me, you know?" he said, frowning.

"Really? Aren't you setting the business up for him?"

"It's for all three of them. Although Carlton wants to go overseas to study and will probably not come back for a while. Yeah, Junior and I are good now, only we were strangers until he was nearly thirteen. Once his mother got serious for her man, the boy was in the way. Fortunately, he didn't wanna raise another man's son, and I owe him for that. She got two girls for him now and that is her real family. Now, Junior wasn't happy to be pushed out. His mother is not much in his life, too busy with her girls and her man, who won't marry her no matter how hard she tries." Desi smirked.

"So how did Ricky come about?"

"Carlton's mother and I were 'bout through. She brought the boy to me when he was a little over a year, thinking I wouldn't be able to manage and would send for her too. She would come 'round all the time to care for him during the day, but I wouldn't never invite her to move in or stay the night. I didn't trust her anymore neither, so there wasn't much hanky-panky. I couldn't catch another child from her.

"She kept trying to force the issue of marriage and her living in, so I hired a woman to help take care of the house and the child so she would ease up. Her name's Marva Beccles, and you'll meet her when we get back. She comes in four days a week and every other Saturday. She been with me near sixteen years now, and she ain't ever been married or had children of her own.

"Anyways, from time to time she would bring in a helper when the windows needed cleaning and such, who she claimed was some relative of hers. A tall, fine young lady I'm certain she had in mind for me."

Desi turned to Aya and pulled her in close.

"Now I wasn't messing with no women at this time. The business was taking up all my energy, the money starting to come in fast and furious, and I was finally fixing my finances. But, you know, a man has needs, Ay. After a while, she and I started up. She was convenient and didn't ask for nothing and pretty much left me alone. She just made herself available. Yeah, I realize I was basically paying for it, but I wasn't studying that. Then she got pregnant and—"

"You keep saying that," Aya interrupted. "Like you had nothing to do with it. Couldn't you have worn a condom, or pulled out? I mean, you went through all of that with Carlton's mother."

"Yes, yes," he said, nodding. "You don't understand, nothing is foolproof. We did try, me especially. I was thinking 'bout getting the snip, even then, only I didn't wanna swear off getting married for real. Anyways, I love my son and I'm glad he's here."

"Where's his mother?"

Desi looked down and did not answer right away. "She died," he said finally.

"Oh my God, Des!" Aya said and bolted upright in the bed. "How?"

Desi cleared his throat. "An accident. A terrible accident. I don't like to think 'bout it, she was so young and Ricky only five. She would come and go between her family and us. She never moved in, she would stay only a few days here and there."

Aya wanted details but would not press him now. She would wait. "So, you've been single between now and then? For four years?"

Desi cocked his head at her and curved his lips. "You mean if I've been fornicating, don't you?" He laughed. "I always get my needs met—even still, I am clean. I get a full physical every year and check my pressure and sugar every four months as it runs in my family but hasn't caught me yet. As you can see, my member is a fine specimen, and I don't have no STDs."

Aya couldn't help bursting out laughing at that remark. She laid back down into his open arms.

"If you want condoms for now, I'll do it," he said. "For *now*."

With that, he ended the conversation by closing his eyes to sleep.

Chapter 4

Aya was relieved to return to shore, even though she knew she was going to have to face the screeching music. Auntie Bea had too many friends, and she was certain that she'd recognized one of them observing her marrying at the courthouse.

The Franklyn estate was a mere fourteen-minute drive away from the seaside parish that Aya had been living in. "Frankly Fine" was a three-acre ranch nestled upcountry in the lush rolling hills of the small village of St. Clements, which, at nearly 900 feet above sea level, would receive the cooling Atlantic breezes that brought frequent rainfall. The climate was perfect for the abundance of fruit trees, plants, shrubs, and tropical flowers on the southern expanse of the property that ran up to the back patio.

A large dilapidated barn toward the eastern side bordered something of a rainforest. Additionally, there were three chattel house–style sheds spread about the back bluff of land that faced the sea. A hundred meters below, the jungle continued for a mile until the main road.

Aya arrived at her new home to find the black-skinned Marva sweeping the front hall. Aya thought she looked to be middle-aged, and she was five feet of fit and slender. Along with her gorgeous colouring, she had tiny eyes obscured by thick glasses, a broad flat nose, large protruding lips, and a three-inch-long afro. She carried herself in a mannish way. Perhaps there was a reason she had never married or had kids.

"Morning, Mrs. Franklyn," Marva mumbled. "Welcome home."

"Oh, you don't have to be so formal. Call me Aya."

"Mm-hmm." Marva kept on sweeping. Somehow or other, she would never get around to calling Aya anything other than the Missus.

"So, you got yourself a new wife at last," Marva remarked to Desi while he was out in the car park.

Desi put his arm around her and pulled her in close. "Now, don't you start taking on. She's not after your job. She'll be mostly out back."

"Why?" Marva grumbled. "She not working?"

"She's very hard-working, a real business woman. She's starting up her own thing and managing the books for me."

"Mm-hmm."

Marva did not like the sound of that at all. Somehow Desi was always getting wrapped up with conniving women who would take him for his money. She had thought that he'd finally seen sense until he brought this one home, marrying quick-quick before she could find out anything about the girl. Worse still, he loved the Missus as that was written all over his face. She had never known him to take on so for anyone other than his kids. Marva was certain that another son must be on the way.

"Don't you start nothing," Desi said. "It's no extra work, Marv. Aya's real clean and tidy. She'll probably be of use to you. She'll help around the house."

Help me outta a job, more like, was all Marva could think.

Aya was cheered by the pleasant welcomes of her stepsons. She presented them with the gifts that in reality had been picked out and purchased by Desi, and they were well pleased.

Junior was nineteen years old. He was brown-skinned and built much like his father, only he had the feline eyes and tightly coiled hair of his mother. Carlton, on the other hand, was of a high yellow complexion and had the sturdy build of his mother. He had soft curly hair, light brown eyes, and he dressed his muscular body immaculately. Though not as tall as Junior, the sixteen-year-old was not much less than six feet. He spoke softly and with purpose, and he had impeccable manners.

As Aya made her way through the modern two-story home, she realized it had been built piecemeal, which accounted for its unusual floor plan. The nearly black hardwood floors on both levels did not complement the stark white interior, whose ground floor consisted of a master ensuite, laundry, office, library, storage, kitchen, sitting room, dining room, and bathroom.

The kitchen had a large screened sliding door, which was kept open out to the yard. Although large windows were plentiful, there was a presence of gloom about the place. The staircase faced the large wooden double-door entry and went up to three more bedrooms, two washrooms, and a large family room that faced the sea behind the house.

Aya unpacked her clothes, which included many new items that Desi had bought for her—a pink negligee, in particular. She despised the colour; nevertheless, Desi had delighted in seeing her in—and then out of—it on the last night of their honeymoon. The sex had gotten a little better and, although she was yet to orgasm, Aya was now able to actually relax some.

Once she had everything put away, she focused her attention on handling Auntie Bea, who could be tearing up the highway to strike her backside this very moment, for all she knew. What was done was done. She was married to a successful small businessman, lived in a lovely home, had no bills to pay, and would be compensated well to do Desi's books. She would be able to settle her debts by the end of the year and start saving again. She would stay out of the way and make appearances as needed. Even better, she would have enough free time to finally work on her novel.

Chapter 5

"Your mother wants to kill me! How could you do this? Was it so bad at my house?" Bea cried while patting her wispy grey curls, which she wore slicked back and cut short on all sides other than the top. She then crossed her arms over her large droopy breasts.

"This has nothing to do with you or her, Auntie," Aya said. "This is my life, remember?" Bea noticed that Marva was taking an awful long time to circulate around the family room chair as she and her niece sat talking at the kitchen table.

"How long has this been going on?"

"Please lower your voice, we don't need the whole neighborhood in my business!" Aya snapped, making full and direct eye contact with Marva, who was obviously taking in everything with delight.

"Listen," Bea said in a hushed tone. "I am fond of the man. He has helped me and your mother many times. You realize he has three children that you are now going to have to raise? And you've quit your job? To do what?"

"I'm doing the accounts for him, Auntie, and working on my own projects."

"So, you are completely dependent on him? Why would you put yourself in this situation?"

"I'll be making my own money separate from him soon enough, Auntie. Stop worrying! I am fine. I'm not some schoolgirl, I'm creeping close to forty! I know what I'm doing. And he is in charge of the children."

Bea raised her eyebrows. "Oh? Do you know his history with women? He hates his father, even if he has more respect for him than his mother or most women. We are only objects to him—more like subjects! He gets what he wants and then he loses interest, much like his horny father. Don't tell me you're pregnant?"

At these words, Marva jerked her head around to face the conversation.

Aya sighed. "Marva, do you mind dealing with the upstairs now and leaving this for later?"

Marva, although clearly out of line, scowled at being ordered away. Then a satisfied smile settled on her face. "I'll finish the laundry," she said. Sure enough, she went to the clothesline, which was right outside the kitchen window and in clear earshot.

"Do not speak about him like that. Auntie, I know all about his three baby mommas. He married me! Don't forget that."

"Yes, he did," Bea said. "That's the only way he could get you, I suppose. I've noticed him eying you over the years. Now I see that's why he was coming over all the time." Her eyes narrowed. "You never answered me."

Aya sighed. "I'm not pregnant. I don't want to have children, you know that. Besides, he already has his boys, so he's not bothered."

"And how long has this been going on?"

"Long enough."

"You know, I really don't think so." Bea shook her head. "Your daddy and everyone think this has been going on awhile. Not me. I would've known if you two had been at it. I would've been able to tell, believe me. He was lusting after you because he wasn't getting it. You didn't give him the time of day, and not because you two were hiding anything either. Something else must've happened!" She wagged a finger. "Probably that day I came home to find you and him pressed against the wall. And you never wanted to marry anyways! So many young men I brought to you and there was always something wrong with them, and him you marry?"

"What difference does it make?" Aya said. "We're well suited."

"You see, when I cornered him out in the driveway he went on and on about you. About how he feels and how happy he is and what he'll do for you and more. Yet you haven't once said you love him."

At that, Bea noticed Marva nod through the window.

"I see no point in discussing that with you, Auntie. You've all made up your minds about us without knowing anything. I'm not wasting my time trying to convince you, or anyone. If you're concerned for me, there's no need to be. I'm quite happy here with him, and you'll see that in time. Now eat your food, it's getting cold."

Bea stared down at her uneaten plate of rice and peas with plantain and a fried chicken thigh. She had no appetite at all. She knew that something was up with her niece, only she couldn't figure it out and Aya was standing firm. She had no answers to give Pearl, who was dumbfounded, especially since her own daughter was not returning her calls. She decided to switch tactics.

"Did he tell you about Lucinda?"

"And who is she?" Aya rolled her head to loosen her neck.

"She is the last boy's mother."

"Oh yeah, she died. He told me."

"She was murdered."

Aya's head whipped back and she raised her hand. "It was an accident. He—"

"It was no accident!" Bea interrupted. "He kept playing the fool. Not letting her stay over most nights when the woman deserved to be with her child! He wouldn't let her stay the evening it happened, and she was out on the street trying to catch a late bus when she was attacked. He couldn't even take her home at that hour of the night? The mother of his child?"

Bea watched Aya shrink back and take deep breaths. Knowing that she was on the right track, she continued.

"It was all very suspicious. He wanted her gone, he as much as told me so. I teased him about marrying this one, and he couldn't have been more appalled. He only wanted the child and just kept her around because the boy was still nursing and needed his mother. Nursing at almost five years of age? He was angry with her for refusing to stop, figuring it was her ploy to stick around. He thought she was making the boy a sissy and was downright cruel to her. Even in passing I witnessed some ugly scenes. I will not have that happen to you!"

Aya looked bewildered. "Attacked?"

"Yes, dear," Bea said. "She was found in the ditch days later. There was this awful stench and all these flies, and there she was, bloodied and bruised. Some people still think that he—"

"He did not kill her, Auntie!" Aya shouted. "Come on."

Only Bea thought Aya no longer looked quite so sure.

"Well, the police report said she must've been struck by something while she was crossing. Many people aren't believing though. He is guilty just the same for doing her like that. Wouldn't help pay for or come to the funeral, nor let the boy. I'll never forgive him for that. Ever!"

An enraged Marva clenched the linen she was folding.

That ol' bitch spreading lies!

Marva was tired of people blaming Desi for the accident. He had been very good to her over the years, and she was not one to ever forget. He had been the only man in her life who, although he spoke crassly to her, treated her with respect and made sure to provide anything she needed.

Marva had loved Lucinda as she would her own child and had practically brought her up from young. She had been in love with Lucinda's father in her girlhood. He'd taken her virginity, and they'd shared many warm nights together and many days humping out in the cane fields. Sadly, she was too ugly for him to do anything else with, in her opinion, and he had married another.

She had been happiest while carrying his secret child for those fourteen weeks before she had miscarried. She did not tell a soul. It was her rotten luck, being born poor and the unwanted child of the county whore and whoever her father was, and then looking the way she did on top of it all. She would never escape her rut. Somehow, loving Lulu, as she fondly called Lucinda, had brought a measure of grace to her life. She had spoiled the girl rotten so that she would continue to come to

Marva's lonely house, where Marva lived with her now-invalid mother and the trail of men she was forever screwing.

Witnessing so much sexual activity all her life along with her defeated pregnancy had put Marva off intimacy. In fact, she'd given up on life. No one ever really paid any attention to her, and she felt like she was on the outside of things. She did not finish beyond grade school and instead took to cleaning people's houses, happy to get away from her mother. She found it interesting to see how other people lived, and she was all up in everyone's business so that she could live vicariously through them. She developed a trained eye for gossip, and if anyone was messing around, she knew it first. Marva would often report a pregnancy before it was even confirmed, and she became the 411 of the district.

So her body flushed when hearing something so false about her sweetheart. Everyone knew that a minibus had come by and run Lulu over, throwing her body into that ditch. Desi didn't have anything to do with it. He had a right to have who he wanted in his own house.

Marva believed Lulu had no business trying to keep him the way she had either. Marva had warned her that he had still not gotten over his divorce, nor the woman who followed it, and would not make her a good match. If she wanted to sleep with him and get extra cash in hand for it, that was her business. She should not have gotten pregnant—and to do it on purpose! Now that he finally had a woman he loved, this old broad was trying to frig it up for him. Marva wasn't having it. She would make sure to talk to the Missus about it the first chance she got.

Marva heard raised voices and came out of her reverie.

"Well, that didn't stop you from having him over countless times to fix things around the house for free, did it?" Aya said.

"And I knew his wife very well," Bea continued unabated. "Imagine getting the babysitter pregnant? All the time she spent at the house supposedly to help out, and she was whoring around with him, in their very house!"

"They were living separate lives," Aya tried to interject.

"They had no shame! Of course, she took him for everything he had. I don't blame her. Fine if he wanted to have an outside woman, at least have the decency to keep her outside! And that silly tramp telling everyone that she was the true Mrs. Franklyn and badmouthing the wife to anyone who would listen to ease her conscience. Funny thing, though—Desi dropped her not long after."

Aya shook her head vigorously. "He could have ignored the children, but he's raising them, Auntie. He's setting them up in his business. He keeps them close all of the time. He's a wonderful father. Considering how he grew up—"

"What do you know about that? His father—although tall, tan, and lovely—was the biggest son of a bitch around, and his own father disowned him. He would leech off women, doing just enough work to pay his bar tab. A true bastard! Ruined so many lives and scarred all of his children. He has dozens of boys by many counts. Died drunk and penniless while pissing in an alley."

Bea went on without waiting for a response. "His mother was crazy. Never left the house. She had mental problems after Levi kept passing her over. Yes, that was his name. Levi. She couldn't cope. She was a nice fair-skinned woman, with long hair and eyelashes, much like Desi's. Her mind went blank. She would stay in her room and look out the window, waiting for her man to return."

Bea was not yet finished. "Desi's grandfather was a good man, very prominent in the community. I can remember his contempt for Levi. I understand he took over raising Desi and even left him all his land. Your grandmother also adored him as a child and kept him with her a lot."

"He still talks about Gran and considers her his true mother," Aya added. "He loved her very much. Still does."

"Yes, that is probably true," Bea said with a nod. "Believe me, though, he is an angry man. And he is practically your uncle, Aya!"

"He is no more than ten years older than me."

"Try fifteen. He's turning fifty-one, Aya. Fifty-one! Yes, he's not blood, and maybe didn't change your diaper. But it's just wrong, so wrong. He's not the man for you. I've come to take you back home so that you can see sense."

"I am not going anywhere now, Auntie." Aya locked her hands and rested them on her lap.

Bea did not press the matter further and left shortly after Desi and the boys returned from a job. As Desi came in, Marva tried to warn him that there was trouble, but with Carlton looking on, she didn't get a chance to elaborate.

It was a tense dinner, with Desi trying to coax conversation from his wife, who had little to say and would not look him in the eye. Her mind was swirling with all of her aunt's revelations. She would crucify her husband when she got him alone. She felt like a damn fool.

Aya pushed her pasta from one side of her plate to another. She thought the older boys could tell there was trouble in paradise already, but energetic Ricky was not fazed. He clearly missed having a mother and seemed to like Aya. He talked about his day at school and told her all kinds of jokes, which she pretended to laugh at. She had to admit that he was rather sweet.

Desi had the boys clear the table and was trying to usher Aya into their room to talk when a phone call came in from her mother. Choosing the call as the lesser of two evils, Aya took the phone outside to the front porch, sat on the steps, and braced herself.

"Why? Aya, I can't believe you've done this."

"Mother, I don't want to argue about this, all right? We've known him for years, he's no stranger."

"He's practically your father's brother!" Pearl shrieked.

"That didn't stop you from going after him when you divorced," Aya snapped. She had not meant to say that, only she was tired and pissed off with the world right now. Who were they to think that they could run her life? She was happy to be away from them all. She was certain the only reason she had not heard from her father was that he had chosen to stop speaking to her again. Like she gave a damn.

"Don't talk to me like that, Ay. That's not true, I was never interested in him like that. And that is not the issue. Why can't you find someone your own age? And his three sons? How are you going to manage that? I have half a mind to fly right out there and slap his face for dragging you down with him."

"If you're going to go on about this, I'm just going to hang up. I know what I'm doing," Aya said, knowing full well that her mother was more hurt by Desi's rejection than by anything else.

Aya knew Pearl had previously thought the highest of Desi. Thought it was wonderful to have him around when they were both going through their messy divorces. Loved how he continued to check on her even when her ex-husband had cut him off for doing so.

"Aya, I know you're a grown woman and can make your own decisions. I understand that you're fed up with things not working out for you, but you have to be patient. He's not the man you think he is, trust me. He's not a bad man, I'm not saying that. You simply can't be married to him."

"He's not my father, is he?"

"That is not funny. Won't you listen to me and take this seriously? None of his relationships have ended well. In fact, they've ended horribly! I have such a terrible feeling about this. I can't sleep, I can't eat. I am so sick with worry."

"Don't try to use guilt against me, Mother. It won't work. What's done is done. We are married. Whether it works or not is between us now. This is our business."

"Ay, you're going to need support. You can't turn your back on everyone and rely only on him. You now have three kids, and don't tell me that they're not yours because they will most certainly end up being so."

"Mother, two of them are practically grown. There's only Ricky, and he's fine."

"Didya hear what happened to his mother?"

Aya rubbed her temples and grimaced. "Yes, and we're not discussing that now either."

"Please don't get pregnant for him. That will be the end of you if you do, you know."

"I thought you always wanted grandchildren?"

"Not like this, Aya. Not as a detriment to you."

"Well, you have three step-grandchildren now, so stop complaining. Go rest yourself and stop fretting. I'll call you later next week once I'm settled."

Aya put down the phone while her mother whimpered on the other end. She could not deal with this. She was good and furious now.

Aya rushed right by Desi as she walked through their bedroom to the bathroom and got into the shower to think. He followed her in and tried to talk, and she ignored him until she finally had to tell him they would talk when she got out.

Desi was troubled by this side of Aya. He could not have another marriage fall apart before it got started.

Lord, please let this work.

He changed into a T-shirt and briefs and sat down to rest on the cream lounger in front of the bay window. He sighed as he listened to his happy boys playing video games upstairs. He hoped that would occupy them so as to not hear any argument.

Initially, Desi was concerned that Aya was not being sexually fulfilled by him. He knew it would take time; unfortunately, he didn't have long to use their lack of familiarity as an excuse. He was willing to buy her whatever she wanted, no questions asked, and give her the run of the house if need be. But he would not be disrespected, especially in front of his boys. He would nip this in the bud and set the precedent that her behaviour was not acceptable. It was going to be a long night.

"You were very foul at dinner," Desi said when Aya walked into the room. "What's the matter with you?"

"You lied to me about everything! You're fifty?"

Desi threw his head back and sighed. "So your family got you all worked up?"

"Ricky's mother was murdered? Carlton's mother was the babysitter?"

"All right, all right. Just a minute. Won't you hear my side of things?"

"I asked you first but you didn't tell me everything! I had to sit there and listen to Auntie go on and on, and I didn't have a clue. Do you know how that makes me look?"

"Listen. Ricky's mother—"

"Lucinda!"

"Yes." Desi nodded. "She did die. But it was an accident, and that is the truth."

"Why didn't you give her a ride home?"

"You don't understand, it wasn't like that. We were not in a relationship. She lived with her family and Ricky stayed with me. She and Marva would watch him during the day, then when I got back in the evening, she would go home. We would eat together often and she would put Ricky down to bed and then either go or …"

"Have sex if you wanted," Aya said tersely.

"When the mood allowed," he corrected her. "And, yes, she would sometimes spend the night if things ran late or if I was leaving early in the morning. It wasn't a regular thing. I didn't encourage that at all. And Marva? She liked it even less." He stretched out his legs as if to avoid a cramp.

"I ain't sure what Lucinda told people the nature of our relationship was. She was a sweet girl, but I got the impression she was letting on it was more than it was on account of the child. She didn't want me going by her house or her family. I think she didn't want me answering their questions. She always took the last van when she stayed late, that was nothing new. There wasn't any danger neither. She would call and let me know when she reached home safely, usually within forty-five minutes."

"And when she didn't call that night?"

"I'd already gone off to bed and sleeping some," Desi explained. "Then my eyes popped open 'cause it was breaking dawn and I hadn't heard her yet. Later on, my phone was beeping, which meant there was a message, so I figured I'd missed her and went back to sleep.

It wasn't until she didn't turn up the next morning that I knew something was wrong."

Desi wrapped his hands around one of Aya's and tried to reassure her. "Listen, I wish I'd realized earlier that it wasn't her leaving me a message. I wish she'd reached home safely. But it ain't my fault she got ran over! That's ridiculous! I'd never put that on no one."

"Why didn't you go to the funeral?"

"Her family didn't say nothing to me 'bout it. They wouldn't talk to me, although I did call. I tried to bring the boy 'round, they just weren't interested—never were. They'd only recognize us if I married Lu, and that wasn't happening. I wouldn't have my son by those people calling him a bastard to his face. They were that nasty!"

"They blamed you," Aya added quietly.

Desi nodded. "It took some time for me to come to figuring that out. Marva filled me in slow. Even though she was clearly struck by a large vehicle, they think I did that to her to get her outta my life and keep my son. But Lu was never trying to take our son. She was okay with the arrangement."

Desi pulled Aya down to sit on the lounger next to him. He noticed that a lot of the fire that had been flashing through her eyes had now faded.

"Yeah, I know she would'a liked me to commit to her even though when she told me she was pregnant, I made it perfectly plain that I'd never marry again. I took responsibility for the child, made sure she got decent care and a job with cash in hand. I made sure she ate well too. How was I to know her parents had put her out?"

Desi noticed that Aya had opened her mouth to speak, but she must have changed her mind about whatever she was going to ask or say, and so he went on.

"I learned a lot after she died. Once she was showing and wouldn't tell them who the father was, they made her leave. She was staying with Marva, so her father became furious at both of them for shaming the family. If only he knew the things Marva told me 'bout him, the blasted hypocrite! They only found out I was the father when Ricky started staying with me. Then they began trashing my name. Imagine that? For taking care of my kid? So no, I wasn't at the funeral, and they don't know my son by *their* choice, not mine."

"Carlton's mother was your babysitter?" Aya asked slowly, studying his face.

Desi threw his head back and rolled his eyes, tired of this story. "Yeah, she was. We were together for a couple of months, actually. Not a proper relationship—raw sex. My ex and I were not together in any real sense, like I told you. We were meeting our needs. I was working all day and most evenings and she was convenient. I didn't expect ..."

"Desi, how could you? I mean, why didn't you just divorce?"

"I tell you, we weren't thinking like that. We figured that's what marriage was, we didn't know better. I was paying the bills and the business was doing good. We were coming up. She had a good government job so we were able to convert the house from wood to wall. She had a nice car, home, everything paid and lived her life. We were fine as long as we didn't spend much time together. We kept up appearances, and she had other men, you know?"

"Even still, Des," Aya said. "You kept getting these women pregnant. Why? I'd think you'd wear triple protection with your history. You keep acting like it's something that they've done to you, even though you were equally culpable."

That stung him. He did not want her to look down on him. A large part of his rushing Aya to the altar was to prevent this knowledge from turning her against him. "You right," he said softly. "Every time I thought it wouldn't happen again, it did. I couldn't understand it. Still, I took responsibility and looked after my boys and their mothers to the best of my ability. Always! She didn't divorce me when she found out 'bout the pregnancy, you know? She called it quits once the word got out and everyone else knew, especially at her work. She loved to run her mouth 'bout other people's business when she needed to mind her own. Anyway, that was when she got angry. She didn't give a damn before." He clicked his tongue and rubbed the hairs on his greying goatee.

"Oh yes, she was miffed when she found out 'bout it at first, though it didn't disturb her much. She fired the girl and got her sister to watch Junior. Yeah, she gave me dirty looks and barked at me a little more than usual, except she wasn't going anywhere then. Only when she thought it'd reflect badly on her, that she could have the house for herself and put me outta business, did she go.

"She forgot my Dadad wasn't dead yet. No, sir! He lived to a hundred and six years, so the land was still his and not mine, therefore she had no claim to it. She had already moved out before she learned that one." He laughed.

"And yeah, I suppose she did deserve something for helping get the business off the ground. She didn't have to shut me down. Talking my name to valuable customers to make them uncomfortable. Showing up, and making a scene. Trying to suspend my license or any operations until ownership was established by the courts. She put me through hell!

"We were both earning good money, but since she didn't have a home of her own, I was willing to give her reasonable support. And I never stopped paying for the boy, even if it meant I went hungry. I thought we could go our separate ways, divide things up, and move on. Then all of a sudden, she felt humiliated and wanted me to suffer. Especially when Carlton come out a boy. She got real vicious then, and the case dragged on. I thought I'd lose my mind."

Desi thought the look on Aya's face was softening, so he elaborated further.

"Not to mention Carlton's mother on me all the time too. Wanting money or wanting this and that. It was all too much. Your dad invited me to come visit him for a few weeks, and I stayed near six months. I got some advanced training and certifications up there and let the other business go, which was long gone anyways.

"Your parent's divorce was getting real bad too around that time, so I thought it best to go. I didn't like how your dad was getting. Too much like my ex—angry and bitter. How could I not spend time with you and your mother? I'd always looked in on you all. You in particular," he said cheekily. He leaned in close to Aya, who was also smiling. The battle was almost over.

"Did you always fancy me? Or was it my mother?"

Desi pulled his head back so he could see her clearly. "I always liked your spirit, Aya. There's something 'bout you. Always has been. I could never figure out what it is. You get to me, is all. And you done got me now," he said, slipping his arm around her again.

"Where is Carlton's mother?"

"She's in Trinidad," he said. "Living with her mother while studying for yet another degree, as she could never set her mind to one. He visits once a year and she calls on occasion. She's not allowed back in the country too long as she was here illegally the last time. This is why she was pushing the pregnancy and marriage thing, hoping to be able to stay. I could'a helped her except she was way too much to handle.

"I'll be honest, I was glad to see her go. She didn't care 'bout our son neither, she basically saw him as the means. Once he didn't get her what she wanted, she was angry with him. Like it was all his fault, the mad woman. At least she's arranged for Carlton to stay with her family in the UK when he goes there for his studies." He picked Aya up and put her on his lap, hoping she could feel what direction he wanted the evening to go in.

"There are always two sides to the story, and I'm sorry I didn't give you the benefit of the doubt," Aya said. "Yes, you showed poor judgement, but you did the best you could in each situation." She grasped him by the chin and made him look in her eyes. "If I'm going to get past this, I need to know the truth. Why did you marry me?"

"I knew you were the one. I always wanted someone like you. I know you very well, you know? Very, very well. I got you figured out. And I knew that once you understood me and what I been through, you would know that I was the man for you. You've picked a few doozies yourself, you know? That Bradley was absolutely the worst—"

"Let's not bring him up," Aya interjected.

Desi laughed and kissed her roughly. He started to undress her, but Aya held him off.

"You didn't tell me about your mother," she said coolly, and he froze as if she had poured a bucket of ice water over him. "What happened with her? And your father?"

It was a long time before he spoke. "Do we need to talk about this right now, Ay?" He became irritated, believing she would not succumb to his advances.

"Aren't we talking about everything now? I don't want to ever have someone tell me things concerning you that I don't know about. Can't you do this for me?"

"Fine. You know my parents never married. My father went from woman to woman. We discussed this already," he said with a moan.

"What happened to him?" Aya pressed.

"He died. They both died. He didn't have any more women or money. It was too late to try to lean on his sons as none of them would have anything to do with him. He was a drunk. Died of some attack, or his heart probably wore out. Could'a been his liver, I don't know. He wasn't anything to me. I had my Dadad," he said calmly.

"I know you don't like to talk about your mother, so help me understand. It's important that you tell me about her," Aya said soothingly, rubbing Desi's back and kissing his cheek. He picked up that a delay was not a denial, and that sex was back on the table.

"She really loved him, the best that I could tell. Vena put him first, even before me. She thought she had done something wrong that he kept leaving. That was the problem. He wouldn't stay gone. She'd get good and happy again, then he would come back like clockwork to mess with her head until she couldn't take it. She was real soft-hearted where he was concerned and lost herself, is all," he said softly, relaxing under his wife's touch.

"How'd she die?"

"She was living dead for many years. In the end, she had a breakdown. Well, she had several, and the last one took. Dadad did not want me more shamed than I was already, so he wouldn't let her go off to the mental. She lived in her room and we had a helper. I stayed away. I was by your gran or Dadad, or playing in the fields or sea with your father and his brothers. I liked running with them and was grateful they let me stick around since I was so much younger than them. I think your gran had something to do with it, she knew my Dadad well."

A strong gust blew open the curtains to signal the beginning of a downpour.

"Ma died peaceful in her sleep at fifty-five. She wasn't crazy, you know? No ranting, raving, or carrying on. She got real quiet and still, barely living. She was so beautiful too," he finished.

"Are you still angry with them?"

"I'm working on it," he said simply.

"Be open and honest with me and we'll be fine, Desi."

Desi lifted Aya off him and placed her on the bed, happy to finally begin his work.

Chapter 6

When Aya came into the kitchen the next day to make herself breakfast, she was confused by all the food spread out on the counter before her. Marva was not responsible for feeding Aya, yet she had prepared her fruit salad, hard-boiled eggs, fish sticks, rye toast, fresh pineapple juice, and peppermint tea. She had also left several healthy boxes of cereal out on the counter, along with almond milk.

Aya thanked Marva graciously, curious to see where this was all going. They made small talk until Marva put out the bait. "That woman you mother who come the other day?"

Aya remembered that Marva had probably heard the whole discussion and was actually interested in hearing her thoughts. Now that she knew all the details, she was more comfortable having the conversation. She also figured that Marva, having been in the house for many years, would have all kinds of insights.

"No, she's my auntie. I used to live with her."

"You close to her?" Marva asked.

"I only really got to know her over the past year I've been living here. I spent limited time with her during my childhood summertime visits since I was always off with my cousin."

"Well, be careful a what she says."

Aya laughed. "You certainly heard it all. I understand you practically raised Lucinda."

"Lord, I loved that girl." Marva pulled out a chair and sat down, and Aya smiled and poured her some juice. "She was dear to me. Loved me like her mother when her own was so mean and nasty! Dunno why she that way with her, she wasn't like that with her sons. Lulu stayed sweet regardless though."

"What about her father?"

"That so-and-so!" Marva spat. "Had no balls! Excuse my language, Missus. He let his wife run him, he was so terrified a that woman. She kept him on a short leash. He made me sick. I think he loved Lulu best, so that why she treat her so bad. When she got pregnant …"

"You brought her to work for Desi?"

"I know what you thinking." Marva crossed her arms. "I didn't bring her here for that. I needed help, and she needed work. Desi said he would give her a little something. I didn't know it would be a child! I figured out what she was up to when it was too late. They was already at it."

"What was she up to?"

"Trying to get him, that's what! Lulu a smart girl, and I wanted her to stick to her books. But she saw how he was living and thought she'd go the easy way. I told her he not the marrying kind— I mean back then, Missus. But she don't wanna hear. She got all kinds a foolish ideas in her head. I told her and told her she too young and—"

"How old was she?"

"Nineteen."

"Nineteen!" Aya shrieked. "You've got to be kidding me!"

"Yes," Marva said reluctantly. "She look more like twenty-five though," she added quickly, clearly trying to reduce the damage. "Real tall, near tall as Desi. Big ta tas like you and long legs too.

"She young and like screwing, and that normal. Then she lie and say she taking the pill, so I warn him. I tell him to use rubbers since she looking to be the mistress a the house. I dunno if he listen. I know Junior like her real bad. He want her for himself."

It was obvious Marva enjoyed having a captivated audience, so Aya leaned in for more.

"She loved riding him, going on 'bout how good he do her, as you well know."

Aya felt herself blush.

"Lulu bragged 'bout the money he would give her, even though she never asked him for it directly. She had a way a letting him know she needed things, and Desi would always help out." Marva hit the table with the heel of her hand. "And he trusted her 'cause a me! I felt guilty. I kept telling him, but he wouldn't listen. He couldn't see it. He think I jealous. Me?

"When she come up pregnant I didn't say nothing. I wiped my hands. He so mad knowing I was right all along he could spit. He didn't say nothing, but he raging. I could tell. Even Lulu feel she in trouble. She real scared 'cause he finish with her so sudden, stopped sleeping with her although the damage done, and wouldn't say much to her neither."

Marva took a sip of the juice Aya had poured for her. "But I knew he wouldn't run out on the baby. I had a long talk with her and she finally seem to listen. She wouldn't make any demands on him and take whatever he give her. When her family put her out, I didn't tell him a thing," she continued. "I had to take her, mad as I was. She a foolish girl gone dick crazy. He gave me money to make sure she saw the doctor and got the right food. He took care a her through me."

"What happened when the baby was born?" Aya asked.

"He came to the hospital when Ricky born. He proud a his son and even named him. He look just like Desi, and he never put him down. He let both a us stay with him that first week to tend to the boy since he didn't wanna be away from him. He real sweet.

"I think Lulu fall in love for real then." Marva wiped a tear from her eye and adjusted her glasses.

"'Cept he don't want her. He sent us home and we come back and forth. She didn't complain. I was proud a her for that. It worked out good. I thought they might even start back again." At that, Marva stopped short and looked worried.

"It's okay, I know they kept having relations from time to time," Aya said.

"Well, she good and happy. She had her son and her man sometimes and nuff access to this nice place. Desi supported her. She had some money. Though she not living here, she happy. Believe it. It nuff for her. Even if she had to walk all the way home, she'd'a done it. Gladly.

"Then the minibus hit her and she land in an out the way place, so we didn't find her right away." Marva wiped tears from her eyes. "She loved that boy. She loved Desi. She still a child. It not all Desi's fault. That what I want you to know. Don't put it all on him. Lulu played her part. That all I wanna say 'bout it." Marva wiped her glasses and pushed out her bottom lip as if to say, *Now what do you think about that?*

"Thank you for telling me," Aya said. "Seems like she was not the only one who loved him."

Marva fumbled in her seat and looked uncomfortable. "Me? That ain't true. Not true at all."

"I mean that you love Desi, not that you are *in* love with him, Marva. Look how protective you are of him even though he's made a lot of mistakes that most women would find unforgivable." Aya smiled and took Marva's hands in her own. "Don't worry, I'm glad he's had someone in his corner all these years. He thinks the world of you. I doubt he would've made it without you around. Not like he listened, but you were always there for him—through the good, the bad, and the worse!"

Aya let go of Marva's hands and took a sip of tea. "I know you must be wondering if I'm going to change things around here, and I have no intention of doing that. This family needs you too much."

Marva smiled. "So, you really don't want children? You still young."

"It's far too much work and I don't have it in me. Nor do I have the patience or want the hassle. Besides, you don't have any children of your own either."

"No, but I raised many children. The Lord didn't see fit to give me one a my own, and he know best. I love kids. I hope you do have one. I don't see how you can get away from it, being married to him."

Marva laughed and Aya joined in.

"Not going to happen! His three are enough, and Ricky's still young."

"Yes, but Junior grown and Carlton going away to school next year. Desi always wanted a girl."

Aya got up to clear the table and end the conversation. "Franklyns only get boys, and three is enough."

"You gonna catch one soon nuff," Marva said under her breath.

Chapter 7

"Oh Lord, Glenda," Marva said to her long-time friend over the phone the next Sunday evening. "I so glad you back from America. So much go on while you away, girl, I dunno where to begin. I can't believe things could happen like this in barely six weeks, but listen—Desi got married! ...

"No, no. She young, younger than him, she in her thirties. Looks real good though, I didn't think she was as old as that. Her name Aya Daniels. Well, was Daniels ...

"It happen too quick for me to tell you before you gone. He turn up early one afternoon saying he bringing his wife to live with him soon and need me to give the place a good cleaning. So I ask, 'What wife you talking 'bout? You can't mean the ex, Sherrie?' So he tell me it the woman he should'a married ever since and wouldn't say no more. He real happy, singing and moving things 'round his room ...

"I keep trying to find out, but he won't give me no name. Even the boys dunno, he only just tell them too. They say they seen her before and know her a little ...

"So I getting real worried now, Glenda. Desi ain't got no luck with women at-all, at-all. He hate marriage so much that I can't believe he actually done it with someone no one know a thing 'bout ...

"Yes, I know he been messing with that girl from his shop, but that ain't serious. He done closed that up and fire her now that she threatening him so. Then Junior step in and take his father's place, if you know what I mean, and things seem quiet for now. Dunno how the Missus would take that if she know! Desi know how to play his cards though. He transfer the office to his home garage. He extend it well beyond the ackee trees now. Double the size from before. And the Missus handle all the office work so he saving some money. And he need it too 'cause she can't be cheap!

"So, I been saying I worried 'bout this girl coming in and taking over. Junior not much interested in anything but sexing and don't mind his father getting a permanent supply. Carlton don't take on much 'bout nothing but his studies, and he know he don't got long to put up with her so he not bothered. And Ricky seem to think she gonna be the momma he never had. It had me scrubbing and scraping so hard I thought I'd wear through the walls. The house had to be perfect since I sure she would find any excuse to get rid a me.

"So, she turn up the next weekend, just married, and I see her. Not what I expect, but I remember her mother from when she visited last year, and she a lot like her. Brown-skinned and busty the way he like, with tiny dreadlocks down her back. Her lipstick too dark for her mouth though. And she always got silver bangles on her right hand, three earrings in her ears, and lots a silver rings on her middle fingers that don't go at all with her wedding ring.

"She even got muscles! She like yoga and eats healthy. No macaroni pie for the Missus! She like all that Western food I dunno much 'bout ...

"She come with lots a new things he bought her for sure. None too expensive though. She dress simple nuff. Only jeans or those khaki pants. Everything in cream or tan or black. She don't wear no other colours. Every time in those fedora hats like you daddy used to wear too. And Glenda, the ring real simple. I'd'a thought she'd go for something more flashy, but you hardly see it. She real like that, not wanting to stand out. Keeping back or out the way. Like she don't want anyone to notice. But I see everything! She keep to her room or the cabin out back, which Desi make into a studio for her. She always in there type-typing some book. She only come out to the TV room when she think no one 'round ...

"I have to say, she trying now with the boys, but she not much interested in motherhood. She even tell me so. She don't want no kids.

Me knowing Desi, there ain't no other way to go. She gonna have a battle on her hands …

"Funny you ask, I ain't so sure if she love Desi really. He adore her though. Aya this and Aya that. He always talking her name. He whipped sure nuff. I found out some things 'bout her though. The Missus born here and raised up in Canada. Her family come every summer and stay down the south coast. You know some a the Daniels down there, right? … Yeah, them that live by the rum shop. She got an uncle real high up in government too, that minister on the news in those flashy tops all the time. Remember, Desi come up with him. He was real close to the Missus's father too … Yes-yes, that's right. That her grandmother who brung him up …

"Ooh, Glenda, you terrible! Desi sure do like them young. To me it seem more like he had the mother though. She constantly calling here after him when he come back and he'd take the calls in his room. For what? She don't call 'round here no more though! …

"It seem the Missus did well at school and was working and doing okay, but there's some trouble over a man and the mother told her to go stay by her sister up there in Jackson for a while. You know, she up here as soon as they got back from their honeymoon talking nonsense 'bout things she know nothing 'bout. Her name Beatrice, more like *Bee-yotch*! …

"All right, all right, I gettin' to it, Glenda! So, she come up here for a few months and end up staying. The mother didn't expect that, and figured she'd come back soon nuff. Not likely now she married. She had a good job down by that big hotel over the cliff until she quit as soon as she become a Franklyn …

"Oh no, Desi want her to. He don't want his wife working for no one. He got airs now that he got that contract to do the wiring for that fancy mall. He working day and night to get it all done on time, but his boys work well and it coming off good. He gonna be rich nuff if he keep getting that kinda work …

"Oh yeah, he see the Missus nuff for her. She don't complain. She happiest by herself. He looking thin though, like he not eating nuff.

I keep warning him he has to take care a himself or the sickness will come back, but he say he will rest when the project finish.

"Back to the wedding from outta nowhere though. They been seen together a few times in the months before, but it didn't look like anything. He scoop her right outta her auntie's place anyhow. No one could believe it when they come back married. They didn't tell or invite anyone. No one even knew they were together—and I don't think they were neither. I just can't figure why she marry him like that. None a her family happy 'bout it …

"True-true. None a his women's family ever cared for him much. But this one practically family! I haven't soused out the true story, but I gonna get it, Glenda. Something not right 'bout this. He happy nuff though. And she settled in fine now, even if her auntie still making trouble.

"She make me real vex when she bring up my Lucinda. She outta order on that, and confusing the Missus's head. The poor girl didn't know if she coming or going. She tried to act like she knew it all, but she breathing so hard it clear she didn't. She real sharp when Desi got home, so they must'a had it out. It all smoothed over by the time I come the next morning. I dunno how he do it. Well, I sure he gave it to her real nice all night so she wouldn't be thinking 'bout no other women. She as sweet as pie and he happy again. His eyes all big and loving like a puppy looking at her. He thinks he so lucky. We'll have to see …

"Anyway, I figure I need to check her out proper, so we have a talk later and she seem all right, for now. They always start that way, then they get to treating me like a slave sure nuff. She not what I thought though. I can't put my finger on it. She smart and good looking and could get any man 'bout here. Dunno why she go for Desi 'cause she don't love him, I can tell. I'll have to see what she really wants …

"She stay out the way and even helps me, which a first. She don't seem to have much friends 'cause no one really calls for her. She talks mostly on the computer to people overseas and locks herself up in the cabin, type-typing."

"The Missus already got the Franklyn books organized so she don't spend long dealing with them. She answers the business line and sets up orders, but she mostly has her time to herself. She does everything real quick-quick, it gives me a headache. Always rushing. Makes me wonder what she thinks gonna catch her.

"She real clean and tidy though. Real organized too. She even cook for herself and the rest a the family now and then. She asked me to show her Desi's favourites so she can make them, but I haven't got 'round to it yet. She real friendly to me though. Like she want me to be her buddy …

"Me? No, I ain't worried 'bout that lady. I been round too long to let anyone put me out. She gotta have a weakness, everybody got one. I'll find it out. You see, she just acting. The Missus ain't being her real self yet. My eye will be on her, and when I catch her, she won't be able to get rid a me! …

"Too right! Men so foolish. Thinking with their crotch! If it money she want, she may get it this time 'cause the cash be rolling in. Desi owns the house now too. He didn't have her sign any papers neither. That's why he buying up everything in sight for her and working himself into an early grave. As you say, he pay now or he pay later …

"No, my mother and me still not agreeing. She like to work me like a dog when I get home. 'Marva, do this. Marva, get that! Marva, you not doing it right. Marva, why can't you act right? Marva, Marva, Marva!' She driving me crazy. Glenda, girl, the other night she couldn't get her medication down her throat and I hoped she would choke on it. I asked the Lord to forgive me, but I want her out my life. She make it a misery.

"None a her men come 'round much anymore neither so it just me. Serves her right, losing her leg and foot to diabetes! Always supping on sugar. One night she coughing so much she lost her voice and I finally get a good night's sleep! She vexed that she on her way out and won't be able to torture me no more. So she holding on with her few real teeth to stick 'round. I hope she go soon …

"Oh yes, I do mean it. You know how hard it's been, Glenda. I ain't never really been her child, just her servant. Use me to get support from the government or her men. Taking money supposed to be for my school fees for her drinks and smokes. That ain't right. That ain't right.

"You always telling me she dunno no better and to forgive her. How come no one knows much 'bout her family? On this small island? What, she just sprung up out the ground? I know my father bought her this shack, but he didn't know her real name. She paint herself up and wear those red wigs so no one'd recognize her, but one day the truth'll out. Every now and then she slip out her backcountry sayings and think I don't notice. She think she smart …

"I dunno why you keep asking why I so angry. Me? She not worth it. Truth is I wanna know. I deserve to know my people. All my life I walking 'bout here and could be passing them on the street and wouldn't know it. Just 'cause she hate her family, she take mine away from me. And I know she hate them, she always tell me how wutless they are. That I should be happy to have a mother like her. Me?

"She used to be so pretty, and now looking as ugly as she truly is. Taking other people's men between her legs instead a getting herself a proper family. I could'a had a decent life …

"No, Glenda. You wrong 'bout that. The past not over and done with if it living in me every day. And I gotta deal with her and act like I give a damn when I don't. You keep telling me to let it go, let it go. That easy for you to say. You was brung up right. You had you mother and father and grandparents with aunties and uncles. You got dozens a cousins. You family loved you and told you all the time. They took up for you so you never had to fend for yourself …

"No, I not getting myself all worked up again. Me? You the only one who nice to me back in school. You didn't make fun a me. Even when I had to stop going you still checked up on me, so you is the family I never had, but don't push me. You can't act like what been done to me ain't been done …

"Yes, I know the Lord, so stop reminding me. I do my duty. I make sure she eats and sleeps and shits on time. I do that. When most every night I don't even wanna come in the door. I could just keep walking …

"Wha'? Who you fooling? I don't need no man at my age. I damn near sixty! I don't need anyone else messing up my head or my bed, thank you! I too ol' to get myself a fine husband like you got. But I good, girl. I good …

"Once she dead, I wanna fix up the house proper and sell it. I don't wanna live here no more …

"And do what? I dunno. Desi got a lot a space and I'd like to live there full time. He never wanted it, but I getting older now and I think the Missus would go for it in time. When she get pregnant, I'll use it to my advantage …

"Come live with you? I don't need you looking over everything I do! I know you feel lonely now you kids grown and gone overseas and Marshall always on the golf course, but you don't want me hanging 'round …

"You son getting married? Oh, Glenda, how nice. To that girl he went to school with? …

"'Course I'll be at the wedding! …

"Stop being like that, she a lovely girl who respectful. She never done you nothing! You should be happy he like girls at all, unlike our Carlton. The boy as much a woman as could be. Desi blind to it, he don't wanna see. Even the Missus asking me questions to find out. I dunno what Carlton gonna do. I sure Junior know, and he don't like it 'cause it looks badly on him. It good he going to England. It can't come soon nuff 'cause if his father knew what I saw him doing with his *friend*,' he'd have a conniption …

"Oh no, Desi dunno. He praise Carlton to the sky. He always call him the best. Desi too busy with his women and his business to look too much at his children. He keep them with him 'cause his own father was never 'round. I don't think he even know them really.

"Carlton's mess gonna catch up with him sooner or later. And I love the boy anyhow, so I not telling what I know. That the Lord's business. I don't want him to lose his family. I know too well how that feels …

"Well, yes, I told you, but that don't count. The Lord shouldn't'a made me so nosy! But you right, the Franklyns my family too. I seen them through a lot a things and they count on me. Can always depend on Marva. 'Marva, where this? Marva, where that?' They nearly died when I gone with you that time on that trip to Miami. Oh Lord! They beg me to never leave again …

"Yes! Yes! When we got so drunk and so sick. I never been so sick! You so malicious! I dunno what I'd do without you, Glenda. I miss you like crazy when you gone. I had no one to talk to. It was so hard to keep it in so long, so forgive me for letting it all out. I got lonely. No one know me like you do, and if anything ever happened to you …

"Now, don't talk like that. You gonna live long. You only got a little sugar. Just stay on you medication and stop coming off and on. We got a lot a living yet, girl, you wait and see. At least you retired and don't have to be working long hours like me. At least you secure. I don't grudge you none as I secure with the Lord. He gonna take care a me. He gonna right all the wrongs done me …

"No, I ain't feeling sorry for myself. The Missus make me see that Desi the only decent man in my life. She figure I love him. Me?

"Even though he complains I move too slow and sit 'round as soon as they leave. I don't sit near as long as he say! And that time he nearly caught me sleeping in his bed! Oh Lordy! I so lucky Ricky come in the house so loud and wake me in time …

"So what if I get my own groceries with the household money? I live there most a the time anyway, you! I don't take more than I deserve, just my tip! …

"I do my work when I get 'round to it. They can't say it's dirty, not that …

"He don't mind me using the phone to make my calls. I gotta keep up with what going on. He got a business line then, didn't he? …

"Stop talking 'bout those things and laughing at me. I make up for everything. Whatever he lost by me, I make sure he make back. So don't you talk …

"I don't love him like that, I got him figured. I'm 'bout the only one. He can't help himself. He keep setting out to do right with the wrong person. He just don't see what's as plain as day when it come to it. Whether it 'cause he don't wanna see it—like Carlton—is beyond me.

"The Missus is the best one, though, by far. She reasonable. She don't want more than her share. But let's see if he keeps his dick in check, that where the problem is. I don't sense the fireworks in the bedroom with her either. She not trying to get him alone to get at him all the time like the others. Maybe she playing innocent for now, but I waiting for her …

"All right, Glenda, I hear you yawning. I'll let you go now I done talked you ear off. I so glad you made it back safely. I miss this bad! …

"No, I ain't working tomorrow. The Franklyns gonna be home all day as Desi finally taking time off. I'd love to be there to know what go on. I'm sure he'll just be sleeping and she'll be off type-typing …

"Good night, then. I done talk."

Chapter 8

Marva could not believe how quickly the time had gone by. She had to admit that despite the Missus's strange ways, she did make Desi very happy. No one had thought they would last, and now here it was nearly a year and a half later, and with no pregnancy in sight.

Desi was working himself very hard, and it was showing; he was looking spindly. Carlton had graduated with top marks and would be leaving for England by the weekend. Junior was finally doing some jobs on his own to take some pressure off his father, and he had started making very good money. He had bought himself a large sporty truck that used a fortune in gas. His father had long since removed his gold cap, so he got one for himself and he wore a thick rope necklace and a huge diamond stud earring in his left ear, along with a large pinky ring on his right hand. He bathed in expensive cologne and had a different girl every other night.

On the other hand, Ricky was in need of ever more discipline. He simply could not sit still. His teachers were exasperated; however, Desi was always able to smooth things over. He would play the mother-died-on-him-young card, and it would buy him time until the next incident. The extra tutoring was of no help to the boy, so the Missus suggested he get involved in some sports to use up some of his energy. He was good at track and field and sufficient at basketball, which kept him out of the house a few nights a week. Desi registered him in Scouts to give him some discipline because as hard as he tried, he truly could not do it. He would send him to his room or take away his toys and games, only to give into the boy's whining before too long.

The Missus cautioned him about this, and Desi told her to leave it to him as it was just a phase the boy was going through. Neither the Missus nor Marva agreed; however, as long as they didn't have to deal with him, they would leave Desi to it.

Things had fallen into place within a couple of months of the marriage, and they were now settled into their routines. At first Bea frequently showed up without notice, although she soon gave up. She had her own life to live and was tired of the unwelcome way she was made to feel after all she had done for her niece.

Besides Bea, the Missus had no family or friends at any event. Nothing was heard from her father other than that he was disgusted by the union. Her mother did return to the island and stayed with Bea, but the Missus met with them there. The one friend the Missus had made from the job at the hotel was never invited over. There was only Nicola, who would return to the island from time to time over breaks in her studies in the UK. Marva figured the Missus would be very lonely if she weren't always locked up in her cabin working her manuscript.

Desi picked up on this too and would take his wife out to dinner for a date night once a week and to the movies at least once a month. She went overseas with him to get supplies, and they would spend occasional weekends away at the nicer hotels on the island when he was trying to entice her to have relations.

That, Marva could not understand. Desi was a respectable-looking man, and his sexpertise was well known and admired. He could work magic with that stick, yet the Missus didn't seem interested.

Several comments had proven this. Once, Desi had arranged for them to have the house to themselves. He had spread a luxurious blanket sprinkled with rose petals on the ground of the upstairs TV room, opened the patio doors to expose the full moon, and put champagne on ice on the balcony table, along with a beautiful bouquet of tropical flowers. Marva had to admit it looked incredibly romantic. Desi had left to run a quick errand before the Missus got home, so when she came in, Marva took her up to show her. The Missus could not hide her annoyance. She told Marva she really wanted to finalize a few chapters that night and wasn't in the mood.

Put off by her attitude, Marva asked what woman did not want a hot night with her husband, who worked such long hours most of the time? When the Missus told her that it was more like a lukewarm night, Marva was shocked. Desi not able to satisfy a woman? That was not possible! There had to be something wrong with the Missus if her only satisfaction could be found within the walls of a studio.

Other than that, Marva and her Missus were getting along quite well. Even though she couldn't understand the Missus's way of thinking, Marva had come to like her a lot since she left Marva alone. She kept to her quarters so that Marva was still able to watch her soap operas, make her calls, and doze off when needed. There was no added pressure or demands. If the Missus saw something that needed doing, she simply did it herself.

Other than linen and towels, the Missus did all of the laundry for her husband and herself. She also wiped down and disinfected the kitchen and the dining table every evening after dinner. The cupboards were all tidy and organized. She even maintained order in the once unruly fridge.

The Missus was a creature of habit, and Marva had her schedule down pat. She would rise at 7:30 a.m. as Desi was getting his coffee to sit and drink tea with the family while they ate breakfast. Once they were out the door, she would go to the upstairs TV room to exercise. At around 9:00 a.m., she would come down to eat fruit with yogurt and take her vitamins while watching her morning comedies. Marva came to like some of these shows and would often be invited to come and sit with her. Then the Missus would take the Franklyn business calls, make work orders, pay the bills as well as herself, and deal with the paperwork.

So she would not be interrupted, the Missus would bring her lunch and Franklyn business with her and be holed up out back by 11:30 a.m., where she would stay until 7:00 p.m. Desi or Junior picked up Ricky from school by 3:00 p.m. so she never had to bother. Everyone would sit together as a family for dinner. More often than not, Desi and the older boys would have to go back out to do some more work and not come home until nearly 10:00 p.m. Ricky would play his video games until they returned, while the Missus would enjoy her bath and watch TV in her bedroom.

Marva teased her about not getting suspicious over Desi's frequent absences, only the Missus didn't seem to mind. Desi had a history of working hard, but he seemed obsessed about acquiring money lately, and Marva couldn't understand it since the Missus wasn't shopping. He had set about expanding his enterprise with an established legal team to oversee the finances, leaving the Missus to her book. He worked like a madman, telling his wife that his current job would set them up and swearing to rest when he had finished. But he could never turn down a large job, no matter how all-encompassing it was. He asked the Missus to hold on, saying he was putting their finances in order so he could be semi-retired by fifty-five, when he would oversee tasks from home and leave the actual work to others.

Little did he know that his wife preferred him working. Marva knew that even if Desi stopped, which was completely against his nature, he would find the Missus busy in her office. Hopefully she would be over her writing fanaticism by then.

Although the Missus had told Marva to wait for her to help clean up after Carlton's graduation party, Marva saw it was now creeping up to noon and they were all still in bed. And what a party! It was nice to see the house full of cheerful people, and Marva had to admit that the Missus had a talent for entertaining. She had arranged incredible appetizers, which looked a lot fancier than they were and cost even less. She had made simple decorations, which looked incredibly elegant, to Carlton's delight. It was a classy event, with champagne to boot. Marva was happy enough to be a guest and not the help, even though she had to clean up after it today.

About fifteen of Carlton's classmates had shown up, not including the one Marva had once seen him giving fellatio. She was relieved that he kept those friends away. The Missus kept to herself as usual, while Desi was beaming at her side for most of the night. Marva had never known Desi to drink so much since becoming sober years before. He kept going around the room offering everyone liquor, as proud as a father could be. The evening went very well, although Carlton's Trini mother, Carlotta, had the nerve to show up and try to make trouble. Marva knew that, in reality, she had come to see what woman Desi had chosen to marry over her, which had made for a very interesting evening. She kept flirting and touching up on Desi and acting as though she had something to do with the successful student Carlton had become. She drank too much, loudly talking about this fancy house and these fancy things. She was trying to unnerve the Missus, who seemingly wasn't paying her any attention, although she looked clearly aggravated by the end of the evening.

Nonetheless, the party had been a success, and Desi and the Missus were a handsome couple, looking every bit the flourishing family.

"Oh, Marv, I'm not up for anything today," the Missus groaned when she finally got up and came to the kitchen for tea.

"I'll get it done," Marva said, knowing full well that the Franklyns had already put most of the house back in order before going to bed early that morning. Even the first batch of dishes was clean and ready to be unloaded from the dishwasher.

"No, don't worry about it for now. Leave the drinks and snacks as they are so the boys can polish them off later. You were there until the last, how come you're up so early?"

"I get up by six every morning no matter I got to sleep nearly at four," she replied while pouring the tea for the Missus, who had her eyes closed and her head resting in her right palm. Marva had succeeded in spending the night due to the party, but thus far she had failed at making it permanent. She liked being up before the others so she could make herself at home in the kitchen and play as if it were her own. She'd already had two hot cups of coffee spiked with some of the liqueurs left over from the party. She'd also helped herself to the finger foods and warmed up a full plate of lasagna. She felt like a queen and thanked the Lord for the blessing to be in a lovely home with a loving family and no worry about food or unemployment. Although life had shortchanged her in most respects, Marva was very grateful.

"Well, then," the Missus said, "make sure you get a good rest in later or go home early. I know how you must want to get to your own bed."

Marva decided to test the waters again. "Me? I wouldn't care if I never went back!"

"Oh, still having problems with your mother?"

"You dunno the half a it. I wish I could just sell the place and put her away 'cause she too much to handle now. She need constant care."

"Well, Desi and I are willing to help. Do you need some time off?"

"No, Missus. This the only place I get a break! Don't want no more time with her. The land in her name so I can't sell it 'til she go. I don't even know for sure if she leave it to me, the miserable b—"

"I see," the Missus said slowly. Over the past year, she and Marva had discussed their tricky relationships with their mothers. Marva knew she had helped the Missus see her own mother in a more positive light, even though there was still distance between them. She would now spend time with Pearl when she visited and would touch base on occasion. "Do you have any savings? I mean, what will you do if you get put out?"

Marva had put a lot of thought into that. She would go stay by Glenda, whose husband was most definitely having an affair that kept him away most of the time. She had saved up nearly twenty-five thousand dollars by using a relatively small portion of the Franklyn household money as her own. Unfortunately, that was not enough to own anything.

"I got some money there for emergencies and to bury me," she said slyly. "It not nuff to live on by myself. I gonna be working for the rest a my life."

"What if you get the title to the house?"

"Yes, but she gotta be dead first. And that woman fighting hard even though she barely living. She as stubborn as shite! She won't never give in. And I won't get nothing much for an ol' run down board house neither."

"Maybe you could rent it out once it's tidied up. That would give you some cash in hand. Land, no matter how bad you think it may be, is still a very valuable thing to have."

"True-true." Marva nodded. "I never liked living there. Too much bad memories. That place cursed. She still gonna be there haunting me long after she dead. I like being here best."

"Oh, my stomach is still so upset from too much food. I'm going to lay down again for a while. You take it easy today, Marv, and stay as long as you like." The Missus finished her tea and placed the cup in the sink, then headed gingerly to her room.

Although the Missus hadn't jumped on Marva's bait, she was sure she had planted yet another seed that would soon bear fruit.

Later that evening it was just the two of them again in the kitchen. Desi was finally resting from being up most of the day with violent stomach cramps. The Missus wanted him to go to the hospital, but he blamed the alcohol and promised it would subside in time. Carlton was out with his mother somewhere, Junior had snuck off with the girl who'd spent the night in his bed, and Ricky was upstairs with a neighborhood boy, playing video games so loudly that it sounded as if the whole block was up there.

The Missus, who was still not feeling like herself, snacked on a tuna sandwich while watching her comedies, which she had turned up loud to drain out Ricky's noise. Marva, now long since finished work, sat down with her at the table.

"Well, I guess I better head on down the road," she mumbled.

"It's getting late. Are you sure you don't want any more of this food? There's still a lot left over, and I doubt most of it will get eaten."

Marva knew this only too well and already had food for three days in her overnight bag. She would come claim the rest when she returned to work in a day's time. "Leave it for me," she said. "You sure you don't want me to stay on with Desi being sick? He don't look too good. He normally handle his liquor fine."

"I think he simply needs a proper rest, Marv. He's been working himself too hard. His body has finally had enough and is forcing him to be still. Junior should be able to finish off that restaurant now anyway."

Marva wasn't ready to give up yet. "Could be, could be. Seeing Carlotta nuff to make any man puke out his guts!"

"What the hell was that about? The way she was carrying on! And all over Desi. You know what she had the nerve to tell me?"

Knowing full well, Marva shook her head and leaned in.

"That I am lucky she left Desi for me. That I should be grateful to her for having all these things I do, as if she made this possible. She never worked for it. And what about how she was all about the place like a social butterfly, as if this was her home? Clearly trying to show everyone that Carlton is hers and Desi's and I had nothing to do with it. Have I ever claimed otherwise? Have I ever tried to take her place with Carlton? Since I organized everything for his party and he enjoyed it ..."

"True-true! She trying to ruin the party, carrying on like a fool," Marva interjected. "She never change! Always running her mouth too much. Carlton the only good thing in her life, and she didn't even have much to do with that. Now he looking to set himself up to earn good money and a share in the business, so she coming 'round to make her claim. She couldn't get her hooks in the father, so she not letting go a the son."

Marva had hit the nail on the head, as usual.

"It seemed to me she was trying to say I wasn't good enough for them. That I didn't deserve what I have," the Missus said thoughtfully.

"Yes, you had the place looking real-real nice. All the food you put out and everyone having a good time. She must be thinking she should'a been you. But she can't never be you! No matter how hard she try rubbing on Desi."

"And what was that about?" the Missus said. "She was so petty. Rubbing against him and kissing his neck. Bringing up how she gave it to him so good in bed that she would be soaking wet and he would lose his mind! I mean, how inappropriate and disrespectful."

"Talking loud-loud too. No one bothering with her though. Poor Carlton look shame and Desi push her off. He cuss her in private when he pull her aside. She get real quiet when he get cross with her."

"She looks so young to be Carlton's mother. Don't tell me she was a teenager when she had him?"

"No, not so young. She was round thirty, maybe thirty-one. She come here for schooling and didn't go back to Trinidad when it finished."

"Well, no sense worrying about it when she'll be out of our lives by the weekend. Right now, my only concern is looking after Desi and getting those two up there to be quiet. Is it too early to send the boy home, you think?"

"He good company for Ricky though," Marva said. "He need that, the others don't have much time for him now. I could stay, you know. I ain't in no hurry to get back."

"No, no. Go on, Marva. Your mother's a pain in the ass, but you still need to check in on her. Just medicate her and shut the door. I can handle things. Goodnight."

Marva, recognizing defeat, let it go and caught the van home. She climbed the four block steps up to the covered front porch of her mother's nine-hundred-square-foot ramshackle house and opened the door to the rank odour of urine. She took a deep breath and walked in, entering a room that contained two chairs to her right and a worn three-seater couch against the wall to her left. A small black-and-white television sat dark in the left corner, and a sitting stool piled with old newspapers was in the right one.

She drew the curtains closed across the slat windows on either side of the door and an even larger one on the left wall. Unlike the dilapidated house, the curtains were immaculate as that was Marva's weakness. Then she made her way past the door to her mother's room on the right, which was also at the front of the house so that her mother could see the daily goings on and gossip with those who passed by. The house was known for the big woman always peeping through that window.

"Yuh take long nuff!" Marva's mother snapped. She spoke with a drawl out of the right side of her mouth due to one of her strokes. Her lips didn't protrude much, but they were always in a scowl on her wrinkled, puffy face. Rose was nearly eighty-seven years old, but her long bushy hair was still jet black and she told everyone that she was twelve years younger. In passing, one could tell that she and her daughter were related as they had the same dark complexion and were similar in stature, although Rose was more than twice the width of

Marva. She was forever adjusting herself wherever she sat since her weight did not hang right on her body, and her extremities were so crusty that they already looked dead. Persistently musty and full of odours, Marva would leave her in a long white cotton robe all day since she could no longer fit into much else, and Marva refused to spend a cent on new clothes for her.

"Don't start with me, ol' lady," Marva said as she made her way through the passageway to the dining room. She set her bags down on an old mahogany table covered with a flimsy peach tablecloth protected under clear plastic, nearly knocking over the fake bouquet of flowers at its centre. To her right was a hutch with several mismatched glass and plate sets, as well as the door to her mother's second room, which connected to her front room. This second room was the largest in the house, and it's where Rose used to entertain men.

Marva took the party food out of the bags and carried it into the kitchen, which was actually the same room as the dining room, but divided by the back of a row of cluttered kitchen cabinets. Marva's room was right next to the fridge, as boxed in as a pantry, that was painted a bright yellow. She slept on a simple twin bed that she had covered with designer sheets. There was a lamp to the left of her bed and a large window on the right, where she could look out at their mango, golden apple, banana, and breadfruit trees. She could also see her kitchen garden, in which she grew many root vegetables and herbs that she would bring to the Franklyns or sell to neighbours. She had a decent thirty-two-inch television that Desi had passed down to her, and her closet ran all along her back wall. The only bathroom in the house was on the other side of that wall.

"Me sitting in here filthy, and you don't give a damn!"

"Why didn't you get Cicely to change you when she passed?" Marva said as she prepared a plate of food for her mother.

"You know I don't like no one in my business! That your job! I done tell everyone who could hear me how nasty you is. Leaving me like this."

"If you too lazy to wipe you own ass, that you business," Marva snapped as she carried the food to Rose's room. "You got strength nuff to wheel yourself to the toilet. You still got one good leg and I seen you do it. How come you can't do it now?" She put down the food on a tray in the corner, then rammed the wheelchair Rose was in and rolled her into the shower and stripped off her clothes.

"My eyes ain't good no more and you know it," Rose argued. "I can't barely see. How the hell I gonna get back here by muhself? All these medications you got me taking got muh head confused."

Marva turned on the warm water and let it run over her mother, who began soaping herself. Marva took cleaner out of the adjoining tray and wiped down the wheelchair, then went to tidy her mother's front bedroom. She pulled off the sheets, lifted out the mattress after treating it, and left it to air out. Once the room was otherwise organized, she made a place for the chair in front of the plate of food.

Once her mother was powdered and dressed again, she sat frowning at the meal in front of her. "What nonsense this is you bring muh to eat?"

"Shut you mouth! Ain't nothing wrong with the food."

Rose held up a large vegetable samosa. "How you expect me to eat these crunchy things when I ain't got but three teeth?"

"Then eat the lasagna and the garlic bread, or try a sandwich." Marva stamped her foot and went to her room to change her clothes.

"This sandwich got too much pepper! What meat this is?"

"It deviled egg with crab. You know you love crab."

"Don't love nothing so," her mother bickered. "I never cared for this fancy food. I an island girl. And look at this lasagna ya bring muh. Hard and dry as ever! You can't even—"

"Fine!" Marva interrupted as she re-entered the room, grabbing the plate away and slamming it down on the other side of the table. She stomped to the kitchen and said, "I'll eat it, then. You can finish off the stew I left for you."

While digging out a suitable pot, Marva visualized knocking her mother over the head with it and laughed to herself. She then went to the fridge to pull out the leftovers when she noticed her mother quickly cramming the food into her mouth with her hands before she could come take it from her. With that, Marva slammed the door shut.

Chapter 9

The next morning when Aya rose bright and early to begin her routine, she heard soft conversation coming from the family room. She was dismayed to see Carlotta, with her striking Spanish and Amerindian features, lying on the couch with her broad feet, which were stuffed into shoes two sizes too small, up on the arm and mumbling to herself.

"What the hell?"

"Oh!" Carlotta jumped up to greet Aya, her gaudy jewellery clanking. "Morning, darling!" she said, her thick accent spilling over her puckered, bright-pink painted lips. "I'm here waiting on my son." The plump, noisy woman was very light-skinned with short, thick, curly black hair. She wore the most unflattering skintight leggings, paired with an oversized blouse.

"Carlton's back?" Aya asked, since he had not been home since the party.

"He's gone to fetch something and then we go, darling." Carlotta smiled. "I didn't want to wake you, but I'm glad. We didn't really get a chance to talk last night."

Whatever could we have to talk about? Aya thought, giving Carlotta a confused look. It was much too early in the morning to deal with this, and Desi would be of no help whatsoever. Although he had managed to keep a little bit of food down the night before, he had slept fitfully and was only now getting a proper rest.

"You know, darling, Carlton won't be gone for too long. Time flies very fast. He'll be back to his home before you know it."

Aya, seeing nothing to respond to, did not reply.

"So, don't give his room away."

"What are you getting at?" Aya asked firmly.

"Oh, darling, this is his proper place. He was brought up here, and he's coming back for it," Carlotta concluded, plainly trying to get a reaction.

"Well, you've made it very clear you don't think I have any rights to the place, Carlotta. Tell me, where have you been these past twelve years while Carlton was being raised here?"

"Don't take that tone with me, lady! You know damn well I had to leave. I couldn't come back." Her eyes blazed.

"Why are you back now?"

"Well, I couldn't miss my only son's graduation."

"You've missed birthdays, most Christmases, and school breaks."

"You nasty bitch!" Carlotta snarled. "You think you're the shit now because you got my man and this big house? Well, that don't mean a damn! I had him first. I had it all first. You wouldn't have nothing if it weren't for me. Remember that!"

Aya wondered what the point of this weak, repeated argument was. What did any of this matter now? "I think you need to lower your voice so you don't wake my family," Aya said, looking down on Carlotta, who had seated herself back on the couch. "I won't put you out, but only out of respect for Carlton."

"I dare you to!" Carlotta said, rising again. "You couldn't even if you tried. Darling, I know all about women like you. You're only after Desi's money! Anyone can see you don't give a piss about him. You sure do love his things, though, don't you? Like that fancy car you're driving? I'm not having you take what rightfully belongs to my son."

Now Aya understood Carlotta's beef with her—beyond jealousy. Every dollar Desi spent on her was one less for her only child. If she had a new ride, then Carlton should have one too—and better. After all, Junior had his.

With Carlton going away and no one there to protect his interests, Aya realized Carlotta was afraid that his piece of the Franklyn pie wouldn't amount to much when or if he came back. Although not Mrs.

Franklyn, she felt entitled to all the benefits of being the mother of the brightest Franklyn son.

Perhaps it worried her that Carlton's homosexuality might jeopardize things in the future, so she wanted security now. She was adamant that he stay closer to home for his education, only he wasn't having it. He wanted to get as far away as possible from the island that he felt was beneath him.

"Unlike your reputation for snatching and grabbing anything you can from a man," Aya challenged, "I don't want anything from your son. I am incredibly proud of him. He's a wonderful young man. *Desi* did a great job with him."

"Darling, I'm putting you on notice. Desi's too blind to see it, but I can. We all can. I don't know what you're doing to him that he looks dreadful! He was never that way with me. You sucking him dry and making him miserable. Look how skinny he is! And all the veins. What? You got him on drugs?"

"Oh, that's enough." Aya turned to go back to her room, only Carlotta wasn't finished.

"I told Carlton that if he leaves this house he won't ever see his father again. I warned him. The eldest too busy with his women to care about anything else, and the youngest, with his empty head, is as simple as his mother—I've never known a more witless hussy. She thought she could take my man? Serves her right! I hope she died slow and painful."

Aya's eyes widened and her mouth fell open. She backed away, holding her nose as if she smelled something rotten. "You are nothing but trash," she said. "I can hardly believe Carlton came from you. Desi was never your man. You were an easy screw, that's all. He never cared for anything other than what was in between your legs, and you know it. You were the babysitter! He never took you anywhere or did anything else with you. He certainly never married you or asked you to move in with him. Even Lucinda lived here sometimes."

Aya walked away and was passing the front door when Carlotta caught up with her. Furious, she yanked Aya's arm and spun her around, shrieking so that her voice echoed. "You don't know nothing about me and Desi, so shut your mouth, lady! There are many things I could tell you. Darling, you think Desi loves you 'cause he married you? Ha! He's putting on a show, that's all. He's got you up front, on display. I'm the one always in his heart. Always! I've never gone anywhere because he never wanted anyone else. Never! It was me and Desi from the first, and it will be until the last. I gave him the only child he treasures, and you can't even give him none! Skinny as you are! Probably making him eat all that frilly food you had out the other night. Desi needs *man* food, darling!"

Aya could not believe any of the rantings of this madwoman and jerked her hand away. The front door opened and Carlton stuck his head in. "Ma! I told you to wait for me outside! Don't go waking everyone up. Oh, hey, Aya."

He took Carlotta's arm to usher her out. She tried arguing, only he handled her well. Aya could hear a sharp conversation on the other side of the door, so she locked it and went to do yoga to calm her nerves.

Halfway through her session, Aya realized she was only going through the motions of her postures. As much as she hated to admit it, Carlotta had gotten to her. What the hell did she mean, she had always been here? She didn't even live in the country, surely? It was a shame that she hadn't let Marva stay over as she would have put Carlotta in her place. Aya would be sure to fill her in on everything upon her return.

Later that evening, Desi cuddled up next to Aya on the couch while he watched one of his favourite army movies. Aya, still upset from earlier, found it hard to be pleasant with him. He was rubbing her in such a way that she knew he wanted to get on top of her.

She looked at his hands as he touched her belly and noticed the large veins that Carlotta had remarked on. She looked up at his gaunt face and realized his dark eyes lacked much of the joy they once had. Although he often pursued relations with her, it was not with the same vigour, and he no longer made the effort to get her worked up to a frenzy even though she no longer acted anywhere near satisfied. At the beginning of their marriage, he had worried immensely about whether she was getting some satisfaction from him, but that had now fallen to the wayside. When he was done, it was over. He would be rank with exhaustion and fall easily to sleep. When he began to snore, Aya couldn't help getting up to bathe and rid herself of the odours and wetness of their lovemaking.

She could feel that he loved her, while all she felt for him was a warmth that was far from matching his devotion. He kept buying her things that he felt she should want. Like an oversized designer handbag she had no use for, gold necklaces to match his even though she only ever wore silver, and stinky perfumes or makeup kits with shades horribly wrong for her. Most of these she would pass on to Marva without him knowing.

She performed her duties and kept herself looking good so that he felt lucky. None of the other guys in his industry had wives who were as fit as she was or as nicely put together—not even their outside women. Desi seemed pleased with her, yet something was wrong, and it pained her that Carlotta had pointed it out. Were people talking about her? Why did Desi look so haggard lately? Why hadn't she noticed?

He had been working very hard, and Aya was sure it had to do with that. Maybe finances were an issue and he didn't want her to know. She had noticed he always kept two drawers in their room locked, and that troubled her. She knew one was something of a safe; he would go there to take out his US cash or any large bills of local currency. He had never offered her the code, and she didn't push since he gave her money out of it easily enough when needed. She had seen that the other drawer had papers in it. Probably his important documents, which she was never much interested in. Nonetheless, something was troubling him, and she decided to broach the subject as the skies thundered above.

"Are you going in tomorrow?"

"I oughtta go in and check on things. Even though Junior's got it all under control, I still need to show my face to the customers," Desi said, focusing on the explosion on the television.

"Des, you need to take it easy. I don't want to interfere with your business, but even people at the party were talking about how tired you look."

"Oh, don't pay any attention to that." He patted her thigh. "I'm gonna take it easy these days. Don't worry 'bout me, I'm fine."

"No, you're not, Desi. I'm worried. You've lost a bit of weight, and you're so exhausted all the time now."

"That's because I had a little too much to drink the other night, Aya."

"No, it's been going on for some time before that. Talk to me. What's going on?" With dramatic effect, the torrential rains started and Desi jumped up to close the windows.

"There is nothing going on," he said, but she thought he was not able to muster much conviction.

"Is the business having problems? Is it money? You can talk to me you know," she said, turning off the movie as the noise of the storm took over.

Desi sighed. "There's no problem with the business. You been talking to Carlotta? Don't take no time thinking 'bout what she says. She's just miserable. Worse now than ever since she feels everyone is doing well but her. She's jealous, don't give her any notice." He returned to the couch.

"She thinks I'm keeping you from her, that she's who you really want."

"She said that?" Desi asked, looking stupefied. "You can't be serious? Now the woman done lost her mind. Believe me, Ay, it was you I wanted, and always will. She was a distraction."

"You say that convincingly when trying to avoid the topic of what is bothering you. Is it because your company is growing too fast? You can't manage?"

"How can you say something like that, Aya? The boys are grown and I need to put the business in order now that we are a corporation with shares. It makes sense to get an accounting firm to handle things from here, we discussed that. You're working so hard on your book, I thought you'd be pleased. I offered you shares in the company, too, remember?"

Aya had declined the offer. It was his hard work that had made the business, and her taking a few calls for them hardly seemed worthy, especially given that he made sure she had enough money every week to cover her limited expenses.

Aya remembered how offended she had felt when she had started receiving an allowance at her age; unfortunately, she had little recourse. Her savings were beginning to build now that all of her debts were paid. It was considerate of Desi to be so generous without her having to do too much for it, so she couldn't complain. She hoped her novel would get published so that she could silence the Carlottas who saw clearly what was going on. Aya was embarrassed to be a kept woman as she felt better than that.

"Well, what is it?" she asked. "Do you have debts or something? Are we spending too much money? I can cut back."

"I don't have debts anymore, those are long time settled. I told you, I'm working to get us fully secure, and we are getting to that now."

"You've been working like a maniac though, Des. Like you're desperate. There has to be more to this."

"Nothing's going on, I promise you. I love my work—not as much as you though. These big projects all come back to back. That happens maybe once every twelve years or so when we get so much construction and new developments going on. I can't ignore that. Besides, it gives the boys excellent training. Our business is strong now and we got a good reputation. It won't be like this much longer, Ay," he promised.

"You're not eating, Des. You fill your plate, then you pick and pick. I thought it was because of my cooking, yet when Marva makes your beloved tuna casserole, you still don't eat. You keep making it seem like you're too busy or tired, only I don't think you have much appetite. When was the last time you went to the doctor?"

"Not this again. I don't need a doctor." He looked frustrated and crossed his legs on the coffee table.

"You used to go every few months, but I don't think you've been in quite some time. I'm making an appointment."

"Oh, Jesus, Ay. I tell you, I am fine. Okay, I'm a little light, which happens when I got a lot going on. I get focused and food ain't a priority. Really, I hear you loud and clear, and I will take proper care of myself. I will make sure to eat three square meals a day, okay? You happy?"

"If you really want me to be happy, we'll both go to the doctor and get a proper checkup. You have diabetes and high blood pressure in your family, so you should be monitoring it anyway. Your body is clearly under stress and you might need medication."

"I do not need medication!" Desi yelled, startling Aya more than the thunder. He apologized and put his hands on her shoulders. "I know you love me and trying to take care of me. I didn't mean to shout, I'm just frustrated because you're not listening to me when I tell you that I am fine."

"Go to the doctor and prove it, then."

"Ain't my word enough?"

"I'm afraid not, Des," Aya said, immediately regretting sounding so childlike. "I'm looking at you and can see that something's wrong. You're worried. Have I done something?" Carlotta had succeeded in making her believe that this was somehow all her fault for receiving a lot for giving very little.

Desi whistled and looked resigned. "Aya, I will go to the doctor next week if you promise to stop worrying 'bout me. I can't stand to have you looking at me like that. I'm sorry, honey. I'll go, okay?"

"Are you happy with me, Desi? I mean truly?"

"How can you ask me something like that? I love you! I'd do anything for you, you don't know that? You can't tell?"

"I don't ever want you to feel that you're chained to me. I know I'm not working and that you give me everything, and—"

"Now you hold on just a minute. I know that Carlotta's bitching. You been nothing but a blessing to me and my boys and a pleasure to spend my life with. I'm happy to share, you do great things in the house and help me in many ways. I couldn't do so much if it weren't for you. You don't ask me for nothing! What man has to convince his wife to accept a diamond ring on their anniversary?

"I know when we married you weren't convinced, now I see you content and settled in our life, much like I knew you would be. People thought we were crazy and would break up within weeks, but here we are." He took her face in his hands. "I'm thrilled you my wife, Aya Franklyn, so don't you ever forget. I'll never let that woman back in this house! Don't let someone like her come between us. I couldn't stand to lose you."

"Yes, Des, though I feel I'm basically the same as Carlotta. Taking from you and not earning my own money. That's why she hates me so! You spurned her and then married a woman who's doing the same thing."

Desi's eyes widened and he was quiet for a moment. "I'm sorry, Aya, I never realized you felt that way. I didn't mean to make you feel like a minor in the relationship. To me, I was just taking care of my family. You never made any demands, and I know you could'a made big ones. I know you wanna be a writer, and I'm more than willing to support your dream."

"I mean, what if my book doesn't sell? I have to get other work since I won't feel comfortable any other way."

"Why don't we cross that bridge when we get to it, hon? Your book may sell well or it may need more time for you to polish. We don't need the money, trust me. I understand you wanting to be your own woman, even though you're that already. It will all work out, let's be patient." He held her in his arms as if she were his dearest child. "Don't think I ever regret marrying you. We can easily afford to cover your expenses, so why not? Take your time and develop your talent. Even if no one publishes it, you're not a failure. Keep working and never give up. One of these days you'll write a bestseller and buy me a boat."

"You never told me you wanted a boat," Aya said sullenly, knowing her position was secure.

"Well, I was saving that for retirement," he said and laughed.

Unfazed, Aya said, "So we'll go to the doctor on Monday and get a full checkup, right?"

"Yes, yes, I'll go," he answered. "Now stop worrying. I will say that I'm going to miss Carlton, bad. Maybe that's why I look so."

"Well, we can always visit, or maybe he'll come during breaks?" Aya offered, knowing that Carlton had no intention of returning to that tiny island any time soon. Perhaps Desi took it as a rejection.

"No, he says he will need to apprentice during his breaks. It's like he's not interested in the business anymore. I know he was meant for better things—working in an office, not with his hands like me. I hope he sees sense soon. He really doesn't wanna live here anymore."

"Hey, take it easy. He's young and wants the bright lights and big-city living. Everyone is different. I grew up that way and realized it wasn't for me, but maybe it is for him. Don't take it personally. You should be proud to have raised a man who wants to make his own way."

"I am proud of him, so proud. I just wish he could be closer," he said sadly. "I feel like I'm losing my son." He quickly wiped his eyes.

This touched Aya, and she gave him a deep, long kiss. Desi tried to take his time making love to her, and although most of the island got flooded, Aya would always remember it as the night she started to fall for her husband at last.

Chapter 10

"That clot!" said an irate Marva the next morning over tea. "She actually tell you that?"

"Uh huh," Aya said. "With so much malice too. She made me so angry I was trembling. She upset my whole day, worse than that tropical depression. I try to be a good wife for Desi."

"You is! Don't mind her. I gonna talk to him 'bout it again, serious this time. He losing too much weight. I'll make sure he eat, don't you worry," Marva promised.

"He's already agreed to go to the doctor, finally! He realizes how serious this is and I think he's going to do better this time, but do talk to him. I don't want to be nagging him all the time."

"All right, you put that heifer out you head. She ain't got no sense! She cuss and carry on the last time she leave Carlton with Desi. She was gonna get a better man and then come back for her child, and that never happen. She quick to set out for men with money, who soon drop her. Only ones who keep her 'round for a while is pretenders. She get burned time after time and won't never learn. She knows Desi don't want her so she using Carlton to stay near. She must be trying to get you to turn on him. Now I know Desi's bad ways when it comes to fornication, but he love you and not gonna pick her over you ever." Marva could tell Aya was relieved by that and grateful for her support.

"I do think Carlton's leaving has him a little down. I believe there's something else going on though."

Marva agreed. Perhaps he did know about Carlton's homosexuality after all. That could do it; he certainly wouldn't say anything to anybody about it. She also wondered if the sickness was coming back, as he was a functioning alcoholic for many years. It may be that he was not satisfying his wife's needs that had him down. Even if Marva could hardly believe that the Missus could be such a prude. She would get to the bottom of it, soon enough. She actually hoped that whatever it was would work in her favour so that she would get to stay on permanently.

"You never know with men," she answered. "That's how they is. Especially those 'bout here. Ricky getting to be a handful now too. He needs his father 'round more. I mean doing fatherly things, not hanging 'round wires on a job."

"You're probably right. I could help more too, I guess. I don't know much about boys. I'm more the solitary type, and Ricky seems satisfied up there with his games so I don't bother him."

"Well, right now he needs discipline and he ain't gonna take it from you."

"Speaking of which, how is your mother? Still a torment?" Aya laughed.

"Missus, that woman gonna put me in an early grave. She got some nasty ways! I dunno why the Lord don't hurry up and take her."

"What happened now?" Aya poured herself more tea.

"The same as always, nothing ever change. I don't get no day off, no break. She always complaining and making my life miserable. She start to throwing things at me now. What next?"

"I'm sorry to hear that, Marv. Like you said, don't let her get to you. Leave her to stay alone in her misery and not bring you down."

"Oh Lord, you sound just like Glenda. Always talking that, but you don't understand. It's easy for you to say. You not living it."

"I bet she would be a lot better if she didn't get a reaction from you every time she presses your buttons."

"You think so?" Marva said sarcastically. "She just be worse. Trust me. She never gonna change, only when she dead, and she don't even wanna do that." At that moment, Marva's cellphone went off and, sure enough, it was her mother. She set the phone back down.

"You're not going to answer her?"

"Naw!"

"What if it's an emergency? You'd hate to find out she was in trouble."

"She got Cicely to call if she in trouble. She right 'cross the street. She calling to give me more orders that she forget. 'Pick up this' or 'Do that.' Me? Not now. She knows better than to call my cell from a landline." Marva turned off her phone.

Marva frowned and pushed her glasses to the bridge of her nose. She had made it clear how desperate she was to move in, and couldn't understand why the Missus was so evasive. She was bringing it up more and more now, no matter how often Aya tried to change the subject. It's not as if they didn't have the room. The two other cabins on the expansive property each had a washroom and a kitchenette. Desi had set up one for guests and the other so that Junior could have his own place, if need be. She knew he would never give up Carlton's room, even though it seemed likely to be empty for the foreseeable future.

It appeared that Aya wanted things to stay as they were for now, at least until Marva's mother had passed.

"Another reason to be happy we don't have any children of our own," Aya said. "I'd hate to be a burden to anyone."

"Well, who gonna look after you when you get old?" Marva asked. "You Daniels live well to a hundred. Mm-hmm. You see, you gonna need someone to take care a you."

Aya tapped her fingers along the rim of her cup. "Well, hopefully Desi and I will be together until the end."

Marva considered this. "You should at least have one child a your own," she said slowly.

"You keep harping on that. Why is it necessary for me when it wasn't for you?"

"'Cause you married and have means. Desi love you and love children. You can't be shut up writing all the time. Then this girl will take care a you."

"Listen, there's no guarantee she'll take care of me. She could run off for many reasons, or we could end up like you and your mother. At my age, I don't want to be running around after a child. You even said yourself that Desi has his hands full with Ricky and that he's already stressed out," Aya said defiantly.

"Yes, but a baby in the house would change all that."

"A baby is to be born from love and not to solve problems, Marva. Des and I want to settle down in life and travel. We've talked about going on safari for ages, and he even used to bring me travel guides when we were living in Canada. Once my book gets published, I'm going to take him on one."

Marva had to admit defeat on the baby issue as the Missus would not budge. However, she finally had the opening that she had been waiting for. "So, you and Desi start up since then?"

"No," Aya said, rising from the table. "He was a friend of the family who kept up with what was going on in my life, it seems."

"So, you come together here, then?" Marva looked down at the floor she was sweeping, acting as if she wasn't much interested in the answer.

"What are you getting at?"

"Nothing, just you seem to marry kinda quick."

"I know it looks that way." That was all Aya would offer.

"People didn't think you'd last," Marva said, knowing that she was primary among them.

"We're doing okay, considering." Aya said, giving Marva a pinch as she walked away.

Marva let her pass and watched her leave. The Missus was still not in love with the man, but she made him glad and didn't start any trouble. If the Franklyns intended to begin travelling, then they would need her to keep an eye on the house for them, so she still had hope. Now was the time to talk to Desi.

"So, the Missus tell me you going to the doctor?" Marva said to Desi one evening at the end of the week after Carlton had gone off and Aya was visiting Bea.

"Not you too. I already went to see him." Desi washed his hands in the sink as Marva put a dinner of salt fish gravy and cassava with steamed vegetables on the table for him. Junior had not come home after the job, and Ricky had already eaten and gone upstairs to play.

"And what he say? Why you walking so funny?"

"Hush. It's nothing, I'm just a little sore," he said as he spread his legs apart farther and then opened a container of small white pills and swallowed two. "I gotta go lie down."

"Nuh-uh," Marva said, pulling out a chair from the table. "You promised to eat proper food, and you gonna eat all a this. What those pills for?"

"Those chairs too hard for me to sit on right now, I gotta lie down. I wanna be sleeping before Aya gets back."

Marva would not relent. "Not before you eat all," she said as she picked up the pills he'd left on the counter and read the label. "'To reduce swelling or inflammation'? 'To prevent infection'? What you been doing with your doggie now? You wanna lose the Missus?"

"I said *hush*!" Desi grabbed the prescription out of her hands. "I've not been stepping out on her. You read it wrong."

"The hell I didn't. I ain't the smartest but I ain't dumb. You gone and catch yourself one a them diseases and trying to hide it. You won't learn! Who the woman this time?"

"Look, I don't have nothing like that. I had a procedure done."

"On your balls? So quick? How foolish you think I is? What you get done?"

"That ain't none of you business, and you not saying a thing to anyone 'bout this either."

"You don't scare me!" Marva yelled. "You can't frighten me. I'll tell whoever I please. The Missus got a right to know! She could be infected all like now, like you give a damn. You wutless piece a—"

"All I'm trying to do is give her a child," Desi said finally. "I got the vasectomy reversed."

Marva smiled wildly at this. What an interesting turn of events! "Why you not say so before I start to cuss? I didn't know you all agreed to do that."

"Aya don't know 'bout it yet," he said flatly.

"Mm-hmm," Marva said, worried. She knew the Missus would not like this at all. "What you mean by this? You know she don't want no children."

"She'll get used to it. Once she holds our baby in her arms, she'll fall in love, I know it. You need to help me make her see that," he said calmly.

"I dunno, Des." Marva's mouth twisted. "She stand firm on that topic. She'll probably wanna get rid a it, if anything."

"Don't say that. Don't say that. It will work out. I was right all along 'bout us, wasn't I? She's happy here, ain't she? Even the boys have taken to her, haven't they? It will be the same with the baby. And you can live in and be the nanny and I'll get someone else to clean the house. Not a hell of a lot you do now anyways," he joked.

Marva thought hard about this. A lot would be gained if this worked out; hell to pay if it didn't. She could take Carlton's nice bright room and make a nursery out of it. Her things would go well, and there was a fantastic view of the not-too-distant sea. It would be a bigger come-up than she could have ever dreamed of. The child would secure her position in the family and certainly see to it that she was taken care of in her old age, especially if it was a girl. Only how to get around the Missus? Perhaps she didn't mean all those things she'd said. What if she wasn't able to get pregnant after all? But wait, Desi never had a problem planting his seed; she knew of several that had been torn from the soil.

"Marva! You listening to me?"

"Yes-yes," she answered slowly. "If this don't go right, I not taking the blame."

"It will go fine." He gave her a hug. "Now let me go lie down so I'll be healed by morning."

"Well, the bottle say to take pills with food, so you stand there and finish this and then you can go."

Chapter 11

On the other side of the country, Aya was making herself comfortable on her auntie's couch, watching comedies as she had done most nights over two years ago. She looked toward her old room and let out a loud sigh.

Bea was in the kitchen preparing a meal she knew Aya loved: fresh red snapper with grilled vegetables and a pickled salad. Although unhealed hurts remained between them, they had made peace and Aya had begun visiting once a month about six months prior.

"So how is Desi?" Bea asked as she brought the food out and laid it on the birch table of the sitting room. "He looked a little delicate at the party, something wrong?"

"He's been working too hard, but he's taking care of himself now. Marva made him a big plate of food and promised she wouldn't leave until he ate every bit of it."

Bea sat down as her niece pulled out her chair. "Oh? What's Marva doing there so late? She should've been done her work hours ago, Aya."

"Marva doesn't like to be home, and she's like one of the family. Just because you don't like her—"

"I don't know anything about that bitter woman except she treats me like trash. I keep telling you to talk to her about that. She needs to know her place."

Aya took her seat at the table in front of her plate. "Well, let's not argue about it. Marva is Marva, she can't be anything else. She takes very good care of the Franklyns and we are grateful to her. She knows that if you had your way, she'd be out the door. How do you expect her to like you?"

"Whether she likes me or not, she should show me proper respect, Aya."

"All right, I'll take care of it. She'll be on her best behaviour your next visit."

"At least you have someone to talk to as Desi is never there."

"Oh, Auntie, please. You don't know how often he's home or not. He works very hard so that he can retire in a couple of years. Not like you would have anything to say to him even if he was home. Talk about disrespectful! He is my husband, and not going anywhere. You should know that by now."

Bea swallowed hard. It was true that she had heard Desi was a big shot now with a lot of contracts for his father-and-sons operation. He was never seen with another woman. He worked and went home to his wife. The two of them actually appeared to be happily married, although she was certain there was more going on under that thin veneer. Except the more Bea tried to reach Aya, the more her niece pulled away from her and turned to Desi.

If only he would mess up so that Aya could see him for who he truly was. It couldn't be much longer. She had eyes all over him, as she knew people in most places. When he slipped up, she would know all about it.

It was not that she was resentful, as Aya accused. Bea had never married, despite being close enough on a few occasions to not feel slighted by this. She had everything she wanted out of life other than a true love connection, which she believed was still possible. It was that she didn't trust Desi's motives. He had masterminded this somehow, and Aya would be well entangled before too long. Bea had to keep the lines of communication open, so she had bit her tongue and apologized to Aya just before Christmas.

"You're right," Bea said as usual. "Let's not argue. How are the boys? Did Carlton get off okay?"

"Oh yeah. We just spoke to him this morning. He's getting settled in and complaining about the cold. He might end up coming home sooner than later after all." Aya laughed.

"What about his mother? That horribly wicked woman!"

"I couldn't agree with you more, and we're glad to see the back of her. She's not welcome in my house."

"What about the little one, Ricky? Still giving trouble?"

"I can't understand it. Desi feels sorry for the boy since his mother died on him, and I guess he makes allowances. He won't see reason no matter how hard I try. Mind you, he has raised children before, and maybe this is a phase."

"Maybe," Bea said, unconvinced. "We will soon see. So! How's the book coming? When can I read it?"

"Soon, Auntie, soon."

"Oh, you always say that. I should be able to see a draft or something by now. Don't worry. I can be objective."

"Ha! You won't lay eyes on it unless it gets published. Well, your friend Marley is going to help me get it ready. Thank you for setting that up, Auntie. He really knows his stuff."

"Oh, I knew you'd love him. He's a sweetheart, you two are well suited. He's written several books on the Caribbean, and they're all doing quite well. He'll be able to put you in touch with the best people, and look over your work too."

"Yes, I know, Auntie," Aya said, rolling her eyes. "I'm really pleased to finally be meeting with him. We're getting together next week."

"Where are you meeting him?"

"He's coming to my studio," Aya said simply.

Bea smiled. "Really? Does Desi know?"

Aya put her head down and began eating her food.

Chapter 12

Aya had asked Marley to come around to the back of the property to her rather than the front door, where Marva would be waiting to pounce on him. But he must have been so impressed with the sprawling layout of the property that he did not follow her instructions.

"Who you?" Marva inquired upon opening the door.

"My name's Marley Wright. I'm here to meet with Aya," he said with a smile.

Marva let him in and sucked in her breath. The Missus had said someone was coming to look over her book, except she hadn't mentioned he looked like this. The man had a deep bronze complexion and eyes that sparkled like crystals. He was about six feet tall, with narrow shoulders under his simple white T-shirt and thick muscles throughout his toned body. Thin dreadlocks fell below his shoulders, and a scraggly goatee surrounded his broad pink lips. He oozed sex appeal and smelled divine.

Marva watched him bend over to remove his tan leather sandals. Bangles tinkled on his right hand, a thick silver ring of skulls shone on his left index finger, and she noticed not only that his large feet and hands were smooth but also that his butt was rock solid under his ripped blue jeans! He also had a nice package that she couldn't take her eyes off of.

She had been worrying herself silly over Desi's actions, and now she would have to keep an eye on these two.

"You a writer?" she asked as she led him through the kitchen and out to the veranda, then pointed to were the Missus was waiting.

"Yes ma'am," he answered politely. "Working on book number nine now. You may have seen me in the Sunday paper. You can read all about me there."

Marva was going to do just that. She vaguely remembered seeing something about a Caribbean writer's event to be held later that month that had been of no interest to her at the time.

"You from here?"

"Yes and no, ma'am. I live in the States now, but I still have family here and visit at least twice a year."

Marva watched him make his way to the cabin and listened as the Missus welcomed him in. Then she ran to the garage to dig through the newspapers.

Marley stayed for four hours and did not pass back through the house. Marva observed him get into a small Mitsubishi. She could hear his loud reggae music as he eased himself out the driveway.

The Missus came into the kitchen, carrying bundles of paper covered in handwritten notes in red ink. She was smiling excitedly as she put them down on the counter and took an iced tea out of the fridge.

"So, you got a big shot to look over the book?" Marva asked. "What he say?"

"Oh, he's very nice and helpful," Aya said happily. "Gave me a lot of good advice. He's going to come by again tomorrow. I've got a lot of work to do."

"So fast?" Marva did not like this at all.

"He's a very busy man, Marv. He's only here a little while, and we have a lot of material to cover." Aya gulped down the entire bottle of tea.

"Well, you look happy nuff. He like the book, then?"

"Yes! He says I have a unique style and the story is complex yet universal in scope. He's sure the draft will be ready for publishing by summer. Oh, Marva! Can you believe it? Things are finally coming together."

"How you find him?"

"Questions, questions." Aya smiled and set two cupcakes on a plate. "He's legit, don't worry. He comes highly recommended. I've never read anything of his, but Auntie raves about him. He's taken one of my drafts to review tonight so he can give me a full analysis tomorrow."

"Big man like him making a lot a time for you," Marva said curtly. "You paying him?"

"Oh no, Marva. He loves finding and developing new Caribbean talent. I'm not the first, believe me. I'm sure he'll get a cut of the book sales, and that's fine by me. Now, I have to go back to work. I'll probably be up most of the night." Aya cheerfully took the papers and the plate with her back out to the cabin.

Things went on this way for the rest of the month. Aya and Marley would be together from morning to early evening. She knew nothing kinky was going on, but Marva still didn't like it. Marley only came around when Desi wasn't home, and when Desi was home, the Missus was too busy working to acknowledge him anyway.

Unable to resist Aya's excitement, Desi did not interfere. Marva could not imagine there was much sex going on between them and wondered how his pregnancy plan was going. But Desi had put on a good twelve pounds and could do with ten more, so she didn't want to push him. He had initially cut back his hours, but with the Missus so preoccupied, he had quickly gone back to his old ways.

In reality, the Franklyns were spending very little time together, which was concerning. Aya often fell asleep in her studio, and Desi would bring breakfast out to her in the morning before he left for the day. She even did her yoga in there now and rarely had time for chitchat with Marva anymore. When she did talk, it was all about her chapters and "Marley said this" or "Marley thinks that."

Marva kept silent as Marley was leaving the following weekend to continue his book tour. As hard as she tried, there was nothing not to like about the incredibly affable man, and she studied the article on him, looking for clues.

He was born Marlon Wright, and had adored the reggae superstar from so young an age that the name Marley stuck. His mother was a local and his father was an American. He had played football during his college years in California, travelling extensively throughout Europe and the Americas. A near-death experience from a car crash had ended his career by twenty-eight, and he had started writing while recovering on the isle.

His first three books had sold reasonably, and his fourth on the cycles of life and death had become a bestseller. He was now thirty-three years old, never married, had no children, and was doing very well for himself. Marva could not understand why he would still be single with his looks and success. He certainly didn't seem gay, although she hoped he was.

On the afternoon before he was to leave, Marva saw Marley walking down to the studio with a large bouquet of the Missus's favourite tropical flowers and a bottle of bubbly. She turned up the volume on her soap opera and followed after him. She watched as he gave the Missus a big hug that seemed way too familiar and a kiss entirely too close to her mouth.

"These are just lovely, Marl! And my favourite."

Marley put his deeply tanned arm around her shoulders as he guided her to sit down on the plush chair. Aya laid the flowers on the ottoman and took the bottle from him.

"I thought you deserved a toast for all the hard work you've been putting in. I am so proud of you, woman. Mentoring you is one of *the* best things to ever happen to me."

Aya blushed and brushed her cheek against his as they inched ever closer together. Marva put her hands on her hips and jutted out her lips as she carefully observed them through the window.

"Aren't you sweet. I feel so guilty, taking up so much of your time with this. Do you really think your publisher will buy it?"

Marley chuckled, flashing his dimples. He flipped the locks out of his face and then rested his hands on his protégé's lap.

"I've told them that I've found something special in you. This is a fresh concept that is right up their alley. Don't worry, my dear—you are a proper novelist now." He delicately took her hands in his and gazed deeply into her eyes.

Marva stomped her feet and clicked her tongue.

"I wish you didn't have to go so soon. It feels like we're just getting started."

"You're not getting rid of me so easily. You can have me *whenever* you want me, Aya. All you need do is say it."

There was a long silence as Marley continued to stroke Aya's hands. Marva was about to storm in under some false pretense when she heard her Missus clear her throat and mumble, "Maybe you should open the bottle."

Marva lingered in the bush for the duration of their awkward encounter, but she remained alarmed long after he had left since it was clear that she had just witnessed two people that were smitten.

Even after Marley left on his book tour, the household constantly felt his presence through his continual calls, texts, and emails. Desi let it go as the book release was just a few months away. Aya no longer had time for movie or date night, leaving Desi to his own devices. She was as much a workaholic as he was—maybe worse—and so Desi refocused on his business and started spotting Junior when in the garage in the evenings.

The months coasted by and life went on. Junior had a close call with one of his flings and was determined not to be the father. Ricky was sent straight into summer camp once school let out, and he spent the rest of his time on assignments with his father or playing video games until the early hours of the morning. Any attempts to get Aya to join him the way she used to on occasion were ignored, so he didn't bother her anymore.

Marva's bottom lip pushed out ever more as she saw the Missus moving further apart from her family. She wanted the book to fail so that things would go back to normal. At this rate, no baby would ever be conceived, and she was no closer to getting away from her mother. She thought she was going to have to get Desi to force the issue, only that happened on its own soon enough.

Chapter 13

That August, Marley arranged for Aya's book to be published under an assumed name. Marley and his team heavily promoted it and sales slowly came in. The mania of the past six months had left Aya, and she was acting more like her old self.

Desi had decided they needed to spend some time alone together. He came home early to beat that September long weekend's rush hour traffic. He had sent Marva home and arranged for Ricky to stay with his friend's family at a beach house, and Junior had already gone off with one of his girls.

Desi found Aya sitting upstairs on the balcony reading over some reviews with a glass of white wine.

"Well, here she is at last!" he said loudly as he enveloped her in his arms. "Can I have a minute of the great writer's time?"

"Not all that 'great,' if I listen to what these people are saying," she said, putting down the printouts and returning his embrace.

"Listen, I've arranged for us to go out tonight. Go and get dressed."

"Really? What about the boys?"

"We have the place to ourselves this weekend. They won't be back until Monday," Desi said, rising and guiding her out of her seat.

"All right. Where are we going?"

"It's a surprise! You gonna love it, go get dressed."

"Well, how long are we going to be? I have to let Marley know what time I'll be back so we can discuss these reviews."

Desi breathed in deeply. "You can leave the reviews for the weekend, or one night at least. We're getting date night going again, and I won't have any argument," he said dismissively, then headed down the stairs. He listened as Aya quickly tried to get Marley on the phone to explain, and decided to let it slide. He knew that after tonight he would play a much bigger part in the equation.

Desi had arranged a beautiful beachside table at one of the top restaurants on the North coast. Although he thought Aya initially looked unimpressed, he felt her relax as the evening wore on since she became bubbly and talkative.

He tried to catch her up on what had been going on in his life, and she listened in earnest. Whenever the conversation came around to her, it was nothing but the book and Marley. Desi decided to put a stop to that talk early.

"You know, it's our third anniversary in a couple of weeks?"

"Of course," she said, appearing to thoroughly enjoy her vanilla bean cheesecake. "I can't believe how quickly the time has gone. I was just telling Marley—"

"And I thought we should go away this time, just the two of us," he interjected. "I thought I'd check with you before I book."

"Well, Desi, I don't know. For how long?"

"I thought a two-week cruise of the Panama Canal would do it," he said happily, finishing off his coffee.

"Two weeks is a little long though. You've never cruised before, you may not like it. And what about Ricky?"

"What about Ricky? He's nearly twelve now, and Junior is there to pick him up after school and make sure he gets home. I'll have Marva stay over too, it'll be fine."

"Hmm." Aya frowned. "I guess that will be all right. I still have to check with Marley," she answered finally.

"You have to check with Marley?" Desi raised an eyebrow. "Am I no priority at all?"

"Oh, you misunderstand me, Desi. It's just that—"

"It's just that I am your husband, who's trying to spend a little time with you, and you can't even do that unless Marley says so? You shitting me?"

Aya sat straight up in the chair to compose herself.

"Any woman would be thrilled to have a husband wanna do this for them, and you make me feel like I have to beg. I mean, all you care about is that blasted book! What 'bout me?"

"I didn't mean that. Of course I care about you! I've worked so hard, and things are finally coming together. I need to promote my work so that Marley won't lose money and—"

"Why should I care 'bout Marley or his money?" Desi snapped. "I could'a funded the damn thing for you like I do everything else."

Aya's eyes narrowed and she was quiet for a moment. "That is exactly why this is so important to me. I want to make my own way, Desi. I need to be able to contribute! I need something of my own, and I thought you understood that."

"I do understand, and I allowed you to do as you pleased."

"Allowed me?"

"I let you live your dream," Desi continued. "I gave you that cabin to *work* in, not to live in. You don't spend any time with the family."

"Who are you to talk?" Aya said angrily. "You are always off on some job or another. You expect me to just sit around and wait on you? Can't I have a life of my own?"

The couple's server hovered nearby, twisting their bill in his hands and glancing at the other guests as their argument grew louder.

"You always on you own, that's the problem. We need you too, you know. *I* need you. When was the last time you spent any real time with me?"

"That's not my fault, Desi. You work late most evenings and have the boys with you. Then you go into bed and—"

"Ain't nothing much going on in that bed for months now," he said harshly. "Or didn't you notice?"

Aya took a deep breath. "We've both had a lot going on. It happens. Only now that you have to wait on me, there's suddenly a problem."

"That ain't true. Ain't true at all. I've given you months to—"

"You've *given* me?" Aya shouted. "You've *allowed* me? You've *let* me?"

The waiter finally approached their table. "Ma'am, I'm going to have to ask you to lower your voice, please." He slipped the bill in front of Desi.

Aya's gaze didn't leave Desi's face and she started huffing. "You think you own me," she said quietly. "I'm supposed to be home in bed with my legs open when you get home."

"I did not say that," Desi said through clenched teeth. "Never meant that. I give you all kinds of freedom."

"There you go again!" she cried. "You give me freedom? Why? I haven't earned it? Now that I'm making a little bit of money and trying to do better for myself, for both of us, you can't take it! I can't believe you are trying to control me. Why don't you focus on Ricky? He's the one who needs it."

"You've gone too far now." Desi raised his finger and pointed to her with a warning look.

"You don't really care about my dreams, do you? Marley believes in me, but my own husband wants to keep me in my place."

Desi's fingers curled into a fist. "If you say his name just one more time ..."

Aya inhaled deeply, let out all the air in her lungs, and looked squarely into the face of her husband. She snatched up the car keys and left him at the table.

Aya stormed to the car. She was planning to drive away and leave him, then decided to curse him all the way home instead. When Desi finally got into the vehicle nearly a half-hour later, he promptly told her not to start with him. So Aya sat fuming and ranting and raving in her head on the drive home. She jumped straight into bed and waited to bash him then, only he didn't come. It was almost midnight when she realized that he must be waiting for her to go to sleep before he would come in, so she sat up, undeterred. More than an hour later, she turned off the television and heard the loud, heavy breaths of his deep sleep coming from the family room.

The seasonal rains started so Aya laid down, feeling deflated and hopeless. Desi had never spoken to her like that before, he was usually so gentle. He never raised his voice—then again, neither did she. These past years of marriage had been fine, even if they had become routine. She could not understand why Desi would oppose her having her own money.

She knew from doing the accounts when they first married that he pulled in over two hundred thousand dollars a year. He had driven her around and shown her the small grocery store he owned in town as well as the rum shops and restaurant he had invested in. He owned an apartment complex that housed six units, which was completely free and clear. Many of these assets had been passed down to him from his grandfather, which made Levi despise him all the more. With all the projects Franklyn & Sons Air Conditioning and Refrigeration had completed, it was likely he had pulled in a substantial increase in income.

Aya was beginning to realize that she required more from her life. Desi knew this about her and had loved her for it, and was now turning against her. Yes, she leaned on Marley a lot because she wanted the book to be perfect. She didn't mean to isolate herself, it was just that she was finally fulfilling her ambition. She did not wish to hurt Desi, even if he had said some ugly things that she could not get over easily.

Sadder still, she had no one to talk to about marriage. Her mother and aunt were obviously out, and the colleague she would occasionally go out with was never invited to her house. Her married friend struggled just to make enough money to get by and Aya did not want her to see know how well she lived. Aya did not trust her with this type of gossip, and was sure she would probably agree with her cousin, whom she had given up confiding in.

Every time she had sought advice from Nicola when faced with one of Desi's issues, Nicola would caution her to stop complaining. She had a man who paid the bills and treated her properly and she should be satisfied. There were many women who would love to have her circumstances, she said, and if she didn't stop bitching, one of them might swoop in and take it all away from her, and where would she be then?

All of a sudden, a lump formed in Aya's throat and hot tears streamed down her face. If Desi put her out, she couldn't do anything about it. She couldn't be anyone other than who she was meant to be. Her cell started to ring, and when she saw that it was Marley, she immediately picked it up.

"Oh, Marley, it's very late to be calling," Aya said, wiping away her tears.

"I'm sorry, love, I knew you wouldn't be sleeping. You're usually up reworking a chapter, even though I keep telling you to leave it. You sound down, friend. What's wrong?"

"I'm just tired, so tired my head is dizzy."

"You're not editing, are you?"

"No, I'm in bed already. I was about to sleep." She sniffled.

"You sound like you've been crying. He there with you?"

"No," she said, then cleared her throat to harden her voice. "I'm alone."

"So wait, he didn't come home, then? Didn't you all go to dinner?"

"Yes, only I don't want to talk about it, Marley. I'm fine, really, and I'm leaving the book alone for now. I'll let you know about the festival soon," she said softly.

"You are not fine, Aya. I know you better than that! You can talk to me about anything, you know. What's bothering you?"

"You've never been married," Aya said flatly.

"Too damn right." He laughed. "I was waiting until I found the right woman. I am patient. Others are not, and jump into something that ends up drowning them."

"You're talking about me, I suppose?"

"Well, you don't say much regarding your husband, yet I can see you don't spend that much time together. I know he's significantly older than you, is busy with business, and you don't have much in common. Maybe the age gap is catching up with you."

Aya hadn't considered this. Although Desi was like family, he was from a different generation and shared many of the same limited beliefs that she couldn't stand in her father. In fact, Desi's behaviour reminded her a lot of how her father had acted while divorcing her mother. Making demands and trying to defeat her with silence.

"I don't know," Aya said finally. "He doesn't like this book business."

"Oh, it's probably me he doesn't like. I can't blame him, I would hate me too," he said jovially.

"What do you mean?"

"Well, the man was patting himself on the back when he thought he had given you everything you could ever want. Now he knows you don't really want any of that, and what you do want, you can get on your own. He doesn't know what his place is anymore," Marley explained. "He's looking over his shoulder now because you're becoming who you were made to be, and he doesn't know who that person is. I happen to know it very well, and I'm helping you with what he wishes he could. You get me?"

Aya could see things clearer now. "Yes, I do. There's no turning back now though, no matter what happens. I am an author and I want to be a great one. It takes time, patience, and focus. He has to understand that."

"If he is fighting you on it, you mustn't give in, love. You have to stand up for yourself or you'll be lost and won't forgive yourself later. I've seen this happen to so many women. Don't let him think that you owe him because it's not true. He's a very lucky man, if you ask me."

"Thank you, Marley. You always talk sensibly and make me feel so much better. I guess I need to get a good night's sleep and deal with the world later. I better go," she said, yawning.

"Wait a sec. You're coming to the Caymans, aren't you? You can't miss this one, Aya, it is important to your career, trust me. Potential buyers from all over the Diaspora will be there. You need to let me know so I can make arrangements soon."

"I'll let you know," she said solemnly. "Good night."

Chapter 14

Marva had never felt tension like this outside of her own home and wondered what had happened now. When she left on Friday, they were embarking on a romantic dinner and dirty weekend, and now they were barely speaking, having brief, blunt conversations but trying to act as if everything were normal when she or the boys were around. Aya had shut herself up out back and Desi was fiddling with anything to occupy his time, his jaw set and his eyes bloodshot.

"What happening here?" Marva asked when she caught him upstairs on the balcony, looking out toward the sea and Aya's cabin.

"Mind you business," he growled while rubbing his scruffy cheek. He hadn't shaved in days. "You don't have any work to do?"

"I'm doing it. Now I seeing to you," she said, putting down her garbage bag. "You ain't gonna get no baby this way."

Desi gave her a murderous glance.

"Unless you splitting up, you gotta fix this," she said, holding her ground.

"I've done everything I can do." Desi pursed his lips and looked back toward the cabin. "I can't get through to her."

"There always something to be done. Go talk to her, fool! What you sitting 'round here for?"

"Keeping my eye on you, among other things." He turned around to go in. "She's angry with me. I guess I should'a handled her better."

"What you say?"

"Never you mind. She don't wanna talk to me right now, is all."

"Well, you want her talking to him?"

Desi turned away from her and walked back over to the balcony, placing both arms on the railing. "She's gonna do that anyways."

"Seems like you should go down to her instead a hoping she gonna come to you. Be the man! I know you mad 'bout that Marley, but they ain't done nothing—yet," she added. "I been watching them real close. I know he want her and trying to get her in his web. She too busy with her work to notice. But she leaning on him too much, and that ain't good."

"Don't put that on me, Marva. I've tried and tried. I planned the dinner and weekend, didn't I?"

"Then what happen to make you all so miserable?"

"She didn't really wanna be there. I could tell she preferred to be working ... and with him, I think," Desi said, staring off into the horizon.

"Well, that you fault," Marva said harshly. "I warned you 'bout that long ago. I told you stop working so much and take an interest in what she doing in there. You think since she sleep with you when you come home that nuff? You think her catching a child will change her? Not so. The Missus love what she doing. That as clear as day."

"I wanted her to be happy, didn't I? I gave her that place to write the damn thing. I didn't wanna get in the way. I made a lot of allowances ..."

"Well, get in there to her before it too late. The book done finish so he don't need to be calling her so. I thought you was taking her away on vacation?"

Desi flushed with embarrassment and Marva realized that she was kicking him when he was down. She only wanted to help, but he was too set in his ways. She was surprised that this was only now rearing its ugly head after almost three years.

"Look, the Missus reasonable, not like the others," she told him gently. "She'll listen to you, but don't command her. She won't take no orders from nobody. Why you think she stop speaking to her family? She don't wanna hear it. Now not the time to lay down the law."

Desi sat back down and was actually listening.

"I dunno no one like you when it come to women, although Junior getting there. Go work you Franklyn magic, say sorry though you not.

Get back in her good books again. And make it quick! She married to you, ain't she?"

Desi shrugged his shoulders. Not that he would thank Marva or act as if he hadn't come to the decision on his own. He jumped to his feet and ran down the stairs. Marva was full of hope until she heard them yelling and then the cabin door slam nearly off its hinges. When she reached the railing to see what was going on, she saw Desi storming away with his arms flailing. He got into his truck and drove away, nearly taking out the bushes.

Marva sighed. He'd probably gone back to his usual ways and the Missus wasn't having it. Why couldn't he listen? Did he really want another divorce? Marva sure as hell could not allow that to happen and decided to go down and have it out with the Missus herself. The book had created a distance between them and she needed to recover ground. She walked the narrow pebble trail down to the wooden abode that utilized the old frame of Desi's grandfather's house. She passed the garden lights that lined the last steps to the orange chattel house, opened its deep-red door, and went in.

Aya kept the eight-hundred-square-foot workspace immaculate. It had a high-vaulted interior with a large brown ceiling fan in the centre, which was rarely used since it was consistently breezy. The floor was covered in warm brown tiles and the walls were painted dark mustard. Bright orange curtains were thrown over the rod above each window.

The back wall consisted of a kitchenette while a small modern full bathroom decorated entirely in cream was in the back corner. To the left, under the window facing the sea, was Aya's desk and her computer with its many attachments. To the right, beneath a window facing the main house, a double bed was flanked by side tables holding lamps. A plush beige sofa was in the room's centre, along with a large ottoman that Aya often used as a table. A simple wooden chair rested by the door, and Marva took a seat while waiting for Aya, who was washing a dish in the sink.

"You ready to talk to me properly now?"

"I talk to you good nuff," Marva mumbled.

Aya spun around. "Marv? Oh! I thought you were ... well, I'm glad it wasn't him anyway. He makes me sick!"

"You two need to stop all this foolishness," Marva said, pushing out her lips. "It ain't good. Ain't good at all."

"Marv, the man won't take my feelings into consideration at all. That is not fair. I never asked him for anything, ever. He gave it to me. I'm not ungrateful or spoiled like he says. I'm a grown woman trying to do something with her life. He thinks being Mrs. Franklyn should be enough." She sat down on the sofa and crossed her arms and feet.

Marva agreed with Desi that Aya had it pretty good being his wife. On the other hand, she had seen the Missus all these months working so fervently, and she knew how important a career was to her too. There had to be some place in between where they could meet.

"I thought he'd seen sense! He said he was coming to make peace."

"At first, maybe." Aya rested her hands on her knees and leaned in. "It was all good until I told him about the writer's convention I need to go to in the Caymans to promote my novel. It's right before our anniversary."

"Can't he go with you?"

"Of course he could," Aya said angrily. "He didn't even let me finish. He went off about me running away instead of being with him and dealing with our issues. If you heard how he spoke to me! I can't stand him when he acts like that. He's worse than my father, and I'm no bloody child."

Marva sucked her breath in hard and took off her glasses. It was worse than she thought. It was clear the Missus didn't have much at all to do with her father, and Desi was going to wind up the same way if he wasn't careful.

"I didn't respond to his caveman antics, and he got pissed and marched away like a brat. I simply told him that we could go on our anniversary holiday after, and he started. There was no reasoning with him."

"Pay him no mind when he get like that. It just you first lover's quarrel," Marva tried to explain. "He upset that you put you work first, is all."

"I do not!" said a flustered Aya. "I'm tired of hearing that accusation. Only lately have I been fully tied up with this, and I reassured him it wouldn't last long. He was working anyway and said he wouldn't mind my absence to do this."

"Yes-yes, I know. But he didn't like it all the same, Missus. He a man and a man gotta be made to feel a man. You always on Marley. That hurt his pride. Now the book done and finish, he want his wife back. That ain't wrong. You gotta give him that. What? You prefer him to not give a damn what you do?"

Aya shrugged her shoulders and pursed her lips.

Marva ignored her agitation and continued, "You gotta know how much that man love you. More than anything. You so lucky, he don't even look at other women now or put himself anywhere one could find him. Yes, he work long, but he do it for his family—you, mostly. He don't wanna lose you and that make him act a fool."

"So you're taking his side now?"

"I ain't on nobody's side," Marva said firmly, stamping her feet. "I trying to make you see where he coming from. Letting you know how much he love you so you forget 'bout the nonsense he saying. I don't agree with how he acting, but I don't think you should be putting yourself with Marley like you do neither. Don't look at me like that! This my business too. I trying to help you all work this out."

Aya took a deep breath and looked down at the floor. "I apologized to him for all of that. And I apologize to you too, Marva. I'm sorry I've had no time for you, I didn't mean for it to go on as long as it did. I really didn't. I simply wanted to get my book done, and done right. Desi says he forgives and wants to move forward. Somehow, I'm not so certain."

"You could'a given me a copy," Marva mumbled.

"You told me you weren't interested in my story of how slavery, racism, sexism, and colonialism with classism has burdened this land. You said it was too many *isms*. You remember that?"

"Yes, but then you make it a love story, and I wanna see how it all turn out. I'll just go to the sexy pages."

They both laughed for a time at that.

"Well, you need to be sleeping in you own bed," Marva muttered. "He rub up on you a little bit, you like it and rub up on him. Then you start loving and forget all this. It break the tension. That the best part a fighting, they say. In the morning you wake up and can't figure why you was so angry."

Aya rolled her eyes. "I don't know about that."

That got Marva's ire up. "Yes-yes. It true nuff. Stop looking at me like that! Can't I know 'bout marriage? And you gotta struggle to make it work sometimes, even when you don't feel like it. Love worth fighting for, and you do love Desi, don't you?"

Aya looked down at the floor again. "Yes," she said quietly. "I do. Of course I want our marriage to work. It's just—"

"Then go back to you bed and sleep there tonight. Even if he don't say much, you body there, and he need that. He want that more than anything."

"I cannot possibly have sex with him tonight. I don't see that happening again anytime soon, either."

"I didn't say you got to do nothing but be there with him. He don't like you sleeping out here. It make him feel bad."

"Well, how do you think it makes me feel?"

"I know-I know. But he feel it worse. Trust me. Don't say nothing so you won't argue, just lay with him and see how things look 'pon the morning," Marva said. "I dunno 'bout Ricky, but Junior know you ain't agreeing and he starting to ask questions. That make Desi feel even worse."

"Oh, all right, Marv," Aya groaned. "If he rejects me, it will be your ass tomorrow."

"He ain't gonna do no such thing. I tell you he love you! He want you there with him no matter what. Ask him to come with you to the convention. Tell him you'll rock his dicky into a bend if he come." Marva laughed.

Aya smiled. "I'm glad to have you back, my friend. I've missed your counsel more than I realized. Can I get you a drink?"

"No-no, I gotta finish dinner before it get too late. Glenda coming to pick me up so I can spend the night."

Marva felt a lot better now that the Missus had confided in her. There really were two sides to every story. All the Missus had to do was give Desi more favour with her time and this would all blow over. Except the Missus loved her work so much more than she loved her husband, if she loved him at all. She couldn't wait to tell Glenda all about it.

That night Aya crawled into bed beside Desi, and he turned to face her. They lay like that for an era, staring into each other's eyes, hoping the other would not start an argument. When neither did, Desi finally smiled at her and closed his eyes to rest. Aya was relieved that Marva had been right after all. They both slept deeply and long into the morning.

They continued in truce mode in the days that followed, Desi pleased to be getting it regularly again, and Aya eventually went to the writer's convention without much argument. Although she encouraged him to join her, he wanted to stick around to finish off a job, and so they agreed to meet at the airport in Miami so they could go directly on their anniversary cruise as planned. The night before her departure, Aya sent Desi into rapture by giving him some of the best he'd ever had.

Aya was excited to get away. Marley gave her a warm embrace when he met her at the airport, and he did not leave her side for three wonderful days as he introduced her to everyone, his arm draped comfortably around her. She thought it felt especially nice, and she was proud to be with him, noting the curious looks she was getting from some of the single ladies at the convention. They must have thought they were a couple! She had to admit, they did go very well together.

She prized being around Marley. He had an infectious laugh and she could talk to him endlessly about most anything. She loved hearing about his adventures in the many places he had travelled. There was naturalness to their rapport, a comfort she had never felt with a man. Perhaps that was because they were only friends and intimacy didn't get in the way.

Aya had expected Marley to be too busy promoting his own work and giving interviews or talks to have much time for her; however, that was not the case. They ate all of their meals together and went for long walks on the beach. When he did have to go off for a meeting, he would run right back to her. He would act guilty if she had to spend a moment alone; naturally, Aya basked in his attention.

She did not get much of a crowd for her book discussion even though it was a welcoming group. They really appreciated her art and it made her feel proud.

Desi checked in with her every morning and evening and was pleasant enough. He was very excited about the cruise, but Aya would have loved more time in the Caymans.

On their last day, Marley was catching the morning flight out, while Aya was catching one in the afternoon. She decided to go with him to the airport to see him off and then wait for her own flight. She honestly didn't want it to end. She gave him a tight hug goodbye, and he held her so long that she peeked up at him curiously. He looked longingly into her eyes, brushed her nose with his, and flashed his pearly whites. Aya smiled back, breathing in his scent and loving the feeling of his powerful chest against hers. Effortlessly, he gave her the most tender and generous kiss she'd ever experienced while gently guiding the locs that were dangling in her face to one side.

Marley pulled away before Aya was ready and looked into her eyes once again as her frenzied mind suddenly went still. He chuckled, turned abruptly and headed toward the gate. Aya stood there speechless, her mouth hanging open. *Say whaaaaat?!*

Chapter 15

Desi greeted Aya at the airport with uneasy eyes. When he didn't find anything to question, he rubbed his wife's behind and kissed the top of her head. They walked arm in arm to catch a taxi to the port.

Desi did everything to make the cruise incredibly memorable. He bought Aya flowers, wine, and sweets. They ate romantic dinners and strolled on deck. He took her on exciting excursions even though he would have preferred a nap. He was charming to Aya, and basically at her beck and call. He was very engaging, although Aya had little interest in his conversation. In fact, she felt boxed in with him on that ship. He was on her at all times, asking if she was all right, wondering what he could do—and grating on her very last nerve. Even their lovemaking bored her to an extent that was progressively harder to disguise.

Aya booked herself a spa day to get some time alone and left Desi reading on their private balcony. She lay down on the massage table to relax but could not get Marley out of her mind. She had not spoken to him since the kiss, and wanted to desperately. Only what could she possibly say? That she loved how he made her feel and that he had ruined what little tolerance she had for her husband?

She wondered if Desi noticed as he was desperately trying to get and keep her interest. She couldn't go on this way, with either of them. She was tempted to keep her cellphone with her in case Marley called, even knowing that Desi was watching and it would cause trouble. Marley had not called, however. She checked her messages and emails constantly, but there was no word from him. Aya knew that he was aware of her cruise plans and would probably wait for her to be back on the island before reestablishing contact. Or was he kissing her off?

She desperately wanted to know. Only he had to be the first one to call, or Aya would look bad. She had to tell him she was offended that he had kissed her like that, even though she wasn't. What if he didn't call?

All these thoughts whirling in her head were making her tense, and when the massage ended, she realized it had done little to alleviate it. Her mind was still full of Marley. When she returned to the suite, Desi was waiting for her.

"Something wrong?"

"Why do you ask?"

"Well, you don't seem like yourself, hon," he said. "I thought the spa would do you good, but you seem just the same. Something troubling you?"

"Oh, I'm fine. I'm having a great time, aren't you? What time is supper?"

"We're booked for eight, and don't change the subject." Desi turned her to face him. "Is there a problem with you book?"

"I thought that topic was not allowed," Aya said, quietly sitting at the table. Desi pulled out a chair and sat next to her, taking her hand.

"Anything that upsets you upsets me, Ay. Don't worry that it's not a bestseller, maybe the next one will be," he said, smiling.

"That's the thing," Aya said slowly. "We started having problems because of my writing and the time that I need to put into it. I'm not sure what to do now. I'd like to keep going, except I don't want all that arguing again, Des."

Desi nodded.

"I know I could've handled things differently," she continued, "and I'll do my best to not allow that to happen again, yet when crunch time comes, there really isn't any other way."

Desi looked down and thought for a moment before replying. "So this one's finished, then? You not doing any more promotion for it?"

"Here and there maybe," Aya said. "I might turn it into an audiobook at the end of the year, depending on sales. We really don't have anything else planned."

"So, Marley wants you to write another one?"

"He thinks I should keep writing. I wanted to do that already, you know that. The writing phase is my own, really. Marley comes in once I have a draft and reworks it if time allows. He has a screenplay that's being made, so I doubt he'll have much time like he did before," she said, trying to convince him.

By the look on his face, she thought Desi liked the sound of that. "Ain't there anyone else who can work with you if he's busy? It doesn't have to be him, does it?"

"Well, no," Aya said slowly. "I suppose not. That is, if he even wants to publish it. I don't know what I would've done without his help though. He's taught me so much."

"Then you go to another publisher. There are a few on the island. I could ask a question. You don't have to be tied to him, you know."

"True," Aya said, thinking rapidly. She owed everything to Marley's support and was not willing to sever ties with him just yet. After all, she owed Desi too. She couldn't make his life miserable, especially since he'd set hers up so nicely. "The main thing for me is to learn from my mistakes and do better next time. I don't even know how long it will take to complete. I hardly have a whiff of an idea to see where it takes me."

"Well, take your time. I hate to see you so stressed and under pressure. Let the words come through naturally. Listen to yourself this time and not what anyone else says. I have to say, there were wonderful flashes in the book even if it was heavy with too much structure," Desi said.

"You actually read it? Oh, Desi, you never told me. You really think so?"

"Of course I read it!" he said. "You my wife. I'll always support you no matter what, and you had some good things in there. I liked the idea that limited beliefs, more than our history, is what's keeping us back. You presented it in an interesting way, only I didn't feel your voice all through, only now and then. Next time make it all you—it's your book, ain't it?"

Desi's astute observation warmed Aya's heart. It was true that she had let Marley override her on too many occasions. So she let him make changes even when she questioned the logic of many of them. Aya made a mental note to talk to Marley about it and not let that happen with her next project, which was about how a single woman discovers the North American dream is a trap and that her island heritage is where she belongs. That is, if she ever heard from Marley again.

"Don't take offense. I don't mean to criticize your first effort, only I have to be honest. Ain't that the feedback you been getting?"

"Oh, don't worry, you haven't hurt my feelings. But no, that's not exactly the feedback I've been getting. At least not the way you've said it, although they probably mean the same thing. I'm not angry. Really. I appreciate you telling me the truth and will take it into consideration," Aya said quietly.

"Good. That's all settled, then. I think we should go to the show tonight, we could do with a good laugh, huh?"

Aya sighed heavily. "Of course."

Chapter 16

The upcoming November holiday excitement was looming large when the Franklyns returned from their cruise. Marva could see the difference in them right off. They were relaxed and comfortable with each other again, and Marva was well pleased. She was as rested as if she had just come back from vacation herself. The boys had been no trouble to her, with Junior keeping himself busy in Aya's cabin and Ricky occupied with snacks and pop on the couch. She rarely had to cook since the boys often ate out or ordered in with the extra money that their father had left with them. There was only Ricky to clean up after, and that was easy enough.

Before leaving to stay at Frankly Fine while Desi and Aya were away, Marva had filled her fridge at home with groceries and made sure her mother's prescriptions were topped up. She checked in with Cicely every day to make sure that things in the house were okay. Since Marva could afford to pay her a little something for her trouble, the middle-aged woman was even helping with the cooking and cleaning. Marva couldn't wait to have this set up full time.

Now that the Franklyns were back, she would have to return to 17 Calabash Road. The Missus just had to hurry up and get pregnant. They'd been at it like bunnies before they'd left and she could sense the pattern had continued, so what was the hold up? Marva decided to check with Desi to find out how his plan was going.

"You sure look happy nuff," she said as he drove her home later that day. "You making nuff babies, I expect."

"It shouldn't be too long now," he said, smiling. "Not the way we been at it."

"That don't matter if the Missus on the pill."

"That ain't fail-safe," Desi said dismissively.

"Safe nuff. Could take you a long time that way. You sure you don't wanna ask her and see what she say? She may go along now you getting on so good and the book done finish."

"She intends to write another one now, Marva, so I'm hoping she gets pregnant before it comes out. How you know she's on the pill?"

"I know, is all," Marva mumbled. "I still think it best you talk it over first."

"I think the opposite," Desi said sternly. "It has to seem like an accident. That way it will be as if it was meant to be. You make a good point 'bout her pills though. She has to come off them somehow. Maybe I could take them and act like they're lost, and do it a time when the pharmacy is closed, like a Sunday or the holiday, so she couldn't replace them right away. That could work."

"Dunno 'bout that," Marva said, pushing out her bottom lip. "That cutting it too short. You need to get rid a them pills for a good long time."

Desi had to agree with her and thought hard. "Well, it's a start for now. Trust me, she's gonna be pregnant before the new year. I'm even taking pills to make me more potent."

Marva burst out laughing. "You on Viagra now?"

"No, no," Desi said, laughing back. "I don't need help getting or keeping it up, you know that. I mean meds to make me more productive."

"I didn't know they had that for men," Marva said suspiciously. "You trust them things?"

"It can only help, and my doctor recommended it. I need to get my boys swimming again after being inactive for so long, you see."

Marva asked Desi to stop the car and got out. She never let Desi drop her off in front of the house; she didn't want him knowing how she lived. As she walked up her block, she worried about how much time Desi's plan could take. Long before she could see her residence, Marva heard the evening news blaring out into the warm, dark night. Her mother was refusing to use her hearing aid again.

As Desi watched Marva walk up the road, the idea came to him.

Chapter 17

Christmas was a week away and Aya had still had no word from Marley. She could not believe it had come to this. She was now certain that he was leaving it up to her to reach out to him and wanted to kick herself for not realizing it before. Of course he wouldn't call her! He had kissed her and was letting her decide whether she wanted to hear from him again. And she hadn't made contact. What must he think?

Every morning Aya would wake wondering if she should make up some excuse to call him and then would debate it in her mind the rest of the day. By evening, still undecided, she would leave things how they were, hoping to receive a sign.

Aya had lost her motivation to write. Upon returning to her studio, she could sense what must have been going on in her absence; the place felt violated. And then there were all of those memories from the hours she'd spent with Marley.

Junior decided that he was grown and wanted to move out back to have his own space, and Aya suggested he take her cabin, which pleased him immensely. Desi and Marva were stunned to hear her give up her sanctuary and knew that something had to be up. Desi offered to give the other cottage to Junior; however, Aya was adamant that she wanted a fresh start for the new year and that the move would suit her fine.

Marva was pleased that another piece of the puzzle was coming into place. With Junior's large room empty, it would be designated as the guest room, and she could have Carlton's room as hoped.

Marva knew that it was make or break time now as Desi had cut back his workload to four and a half days a week and the Missus was back in the house. She was spending significant time with Ricky as well, and he delighted in having something of a mother.

Yet Marva knew Aya was distracted, her mind racing about something or other that Marva could not get her to talk about. Marva felt it had everything to do with Marley. Typically, those two were always talking, but now all of a sudden, they had stopped. It was all very suspicious. Especially after they had spent that time alone together in the Caymans since Desi would not swallow his pride and go along. Perhaps he did not want to be confronted with the obvious fact that he did not make nearly as good a partner for his wife as Marley did.

Marva did not get the opportunity to see the Missus before she went on her anniversary cruise in order to sniff out whether anything had gone on while she was in the Caymans. However, the Franklyns were the picture of happiness upon their return and Marley was not mentioned anymore, so she had dismissed it.

But nowadays the Missus was acting strange and trying to hide it.

Chapter 18

It was the twenty-second of December, the house was fully decorated, and Desi had taken the boys out shopping. He still paid Junior's expenses even though the boy was making more than enough money of his own. Aya nibbled throughout the day on the boxes of chocolates she had set out on the kitchen island. She was ceaselessly in the kitchen, making special punches or roasting meats to make sandwiches. She baked cookies, cupcakes, and cheesecakes. Marva had never seen her so domestic or eat so much and wondered if she was expecting already. When Aya reached for another chocolate, Marva could hold her curiosity in no longer.

"You eating those things like you gonna dead without them. That not like you." She poured herself a tall glass of coconut water.

"Oh, I love these!" Aya said, mouth full. "I allow myself to eat them at this time of the year, and you usually can't find them here. I was shocked when I saw them in the grocery store! I bought, like, six boxes. Would you like one?"

"Naw, I don't like sweets. Don't wanna get addicted to them like you neither. You no health nut no more?" Marva laughed.

Aya closed the nearly empty box. "It's probably hormonal."

That remark got Marva's full attention.

"I'm about due for my time of the month. I hope it's over and done with before New Year's Eve."

"Why? You got sexy plans then?"

"You know that big party they're having at the Old Village? Well, Desi went and bought tickets. At those ridiculous prices they give you dollops of food and even less to drink, and we're supposed to be happy because of the prestigious location? I would've been happier curling up at home. Now I have to find a dress and shoes to spend a night with phonies! Desi says it's good for business, but Jesus." Aya shook her head.

"Well, it good that you get out. You stand home too much. You too young for that. Go show you face, you won't have to stay long. Desi gonna tucker out before midnight."

"He keeps thinking he has to make these big gestures, but he should know by now that he doesn't need to put out that kind of money to please me."

"You lucky nuff to have a man that let it go so easy. I know nuff men that hold their wallets tight-tight."

"I don't mean to sound ungrateful, Marva. I'm just saying those things are not me. I appreciate what he does for me, I do. He needs to take it easy, that's all."

"What happen with Marley?" Marva had not meant to shoot the question out in that manner but could hold herself back no longer. The pained look that came over Aya's face at the question aroused her suspicions all the more.

"Nothing. Why?"

"Well, you don't say boo 'bout him no more, and you used to always be calling his name. You not writing and you give up you office. Something gotta be wrong."

"I'm taking a break, and he's busy working on other projects. Once the holidays are over and everything's ready for me, I'll start back again. I'm still mulling over ideas," Aya said cautiously.

"So you not working with him no more?"

"Not yet. I don't have the book done now, do I? He'll let me know if there's anything more for me to do on *Sign of New Times*," Aya said about her debut novel.

Marva had more to ask only didn't want to push. She could sense by Aya's body language that there was an issue. Maybe the book hadn't done well enough for the big man, or maybe the Missus had turned down his advances. She would get the details in time. At least he was out of the picture for now and the Franklyns were back on track.

Marva's thoughts were interrupted by the Missus taking out her afternoon vitamin from a large silver-plated container.

"What you got now?"

"Oh, another of Desi's surprises," Aya said, fighting to reopen the clasp so she could show Marva. "He organized all my vitamins, herbs, and pills. Look. See? He took the time to set them up, daily, for the next month."

Marva went over and looked at the container. Although she thought it a wonderful idea for her mother, she was suspicious of Desi's intentions. Wasn't he supposed to get rid of the Missus's pills? What was he up to now?

"You got all you pills in there?" Marva asked.

"Uh huh. Even my birth control! I know he has cut back on his hours and it was a nice thing for him to do, but damn, he has too much time on his hands."

Marva picked up the container and looked it over. This didn't make any sense. Desi must have done something with her pills. Marva didn't like the escalating level of betrayal that was going on. The Missus simply had to get pregnant quick.

"You going by Glenda's again for Christmas?"

Marva still wasn't sure. Things had been getting very tense in that household as the couple was barely speaking. It was looking more likely that there would be a divorce. Glenda was whining and complaining over the same issues or crying all the time, which was a real drain on Marva's nerves. She wanted to be there for her friend, but it was exhausting. Not like her mother's constant bickering would be any better though.

"Not sure," Marva said cryptically. "Don't really wanna be no place this year. I wish I could go away like you."

"Really? Go and do what?"

"Go and get some peace and quiet. Just sit in a hotel bed and get room service. Let someone cook for and clean up after me for once. Always wanted that."

"That does sound like heaven," Aya agreed. "You sure you won't get lonely all by yourself? Don't you want company?"

"Not this time. I good all by myself. One day I'll do it for sure," Marva said and then took her leave to collect the garbage before the truck came around.

Aya called Desi right away. She wanted to give Marva a white Christmas in New York, but Desi argued against the expense. He finally relented when his wife informed him that Marva was due a bonus and that this trip would silence all her hinting for a raise in the new year. They came to a compromise, and Aya arranged for Marva to go to Miami for four days at a hotel and spa where she could have a hearty holiday breakfast and dinner delivered to her room.

Marva cried when, instead of being dropped home the next afternoon, she was taken to Gate B at the international airport. She hugged Desi and Aya, thanking them dearly after receiving five hundred US dollars in pocket money, then quickly ran to check in. Desi hoped this distraction would stop Marva from questioning him about switching pills.

Chapter 19

That Christmas was a good one. The Franklyns went all out with food, drink, and presents. Carlton called bright and early, waking up the family, and then Desi and Aya turned on the radio for carols and prepared a large fry-up for breakfast. They all sat together to eat and then opened their gifts. Desi put the turkey in the oven while Aya and Ricky watched seasonal cartoons on TV, and Junior sat at the table talking to his mother, among other females, on the phone.

Afternoon came fast and the turkey was browning when the doorbell rang. Ricky ran to answer it, leaving Desi and Aya lying together on the couch. Aya shot up when she heard her mother's brusque accent. Ricky brought Pearl and Bea through, the reek of Pearl's perfume trailing behind them.

"Mother? Auntie? What are you doing here?" Aya asked, shocked. Desi stood up beside her with his eyes and mouth wide open.

"Well, it is Christmas, isn't it?" Pearl answered, giving her only child a hug and waving in Desi's direction. She quickly glanced throughout the house and greeted Junior and Ricky.

Pearl was a few pounds heavier than her daughter and had reddish undertones in her complexion. Whereas her nose was larger, her lips were fine, her forehead broad, and her cheeks puffy. She loved vibrant colours and was wearing a clashing mishmash that Aya found confusing. Nonetheless her makeup, bob-cut wig, and nails were flawless.

"You didn't tell me that you were even on the island," Aya said, looking to Desi for guidance.

"We wanted to surprise you!" Bea said happily. "We brought presents. Don't worry, we're just popping in. It's not like we're staying for dinner."

"Well, we have plenty of food, so you more than welcome to stay," Desi said.

Aya whipped her head around and gave Desi a sharp look. "I'm sure Auntie has a big meal at home, ready since this morning."

"Actually, I made reservations this year. The Blue Wave restaurant is having a special that looks interesting."

"Well, they better have good proper ham like what I see on that table," Pearl said. "And lots of stuffing with no berries in it. Right, Ay? You know how we like to eat at Christmas. Oh, look, she found her chocolates. I brought some for you too, I didn't think you could get those here."

As the boys returned to the couch, Desi guided the women to the kitchen table and pulled out chairs for them. Aya slowly made her way to join them.

"So when did you get in, Mother?"

"Only the other night," Pearl answered as Desi pulled dishes out of the cupboard and proceeded to fix a plate for them. "It was an expensive last-minute decision, though worth it. Life is too short to be away from your family, especially at Christmastime. And then your father called me."

Aya swallowed hard. She had not heard anything from him since her nuptials.

Desi sat down to join them. "And how is Herb doing?"

"As angry as ever," Pearl said in Desi's direction, not looking at him. "He blames me for your marriage. Then again, he blames me for everything."

"It's been over three years now, you'd think he'd accept it," Aya said. "He's so stubborn."

"No matter." Desi smiled and took Aya's hand to kiss her palm.

Pearl put down her fork with a thick, juicy ham slice on it. "It should matter," she said sternly, stopping Desi mid-gesture. "He's her father! He was practically your brother! You can't cut people out of your life when they don't do what you want."

"He's entitled to his opinion," Desi said, forcing Pearl's eye contact. "He'll come 'round one day, hopefully not too late. All that matters is Aya's happiness, and you're looking at a very happy woman. Wouldn't you agree?"

"Yes, my daughter's happiness is the most important thing." Pearl put her arm on Aya's shoulder to pull her near and away from Desi. "Besides, it's Christmas. We don't need to get into all that. This is such a lovely house, isn't it, Bea? Will you give me a tour, Aya?"

"Sure, I guess. Once you finish up your snack. You coming too, Auntie?"

"No," Bea said. "I'm more interested in out back. Such lovely grounds. I'll have Desi show me."

The women made small talk with the boys while they finished eating. Desi and Aya gave each other looks that said to be on guard for whatever it was they were up to. As soon as Aya and her mother were out of the room, Desi ushered Bea outside.

"So, what's the real meaning of this visit, Bea? You not trying to cause problems, now, are you?"

"As much as you would like to keep her away from her family—" Bea began to say.

"We her family, too, you know," he said as they made their way to a bearing fruit tree. "Remember that."

"You don't own her! Remember *that*," Bea snapped back. "We loved her first. I changed that girl's diaper and watched her earliest steps. She's like my own daughter, and I won't let you take her from my life. Or from her mother like you've succeeded with her father."

"I never wanted that, nor was it ever my intention. There's no reason to hate me so," Desi said, trying to reason with her.

"I can't stand how you sleep with anything that breathes. Even her own mother."

Desi took her flailing arm and pulled her in close. He spoke in a hushed tone. "So that's it, ain't it? You feeling left out?"

Bea squirmed and pulled her arm away. "You have no decency. How could you marry her after carrying on with her mother? Soon enough you'll be fooling around with some younger piece of thing and hurt Aya like you've done all the others. Why couldn't you let her be with someone decent? You destroy everything you touch."

"That's enough now," Desi yelled. "You can't talk to me like that. Not in my own yard. You got no right." He pointed his finger right in her face. "You oughtta know me better than that, Bea. I ain't the only one to blame for what went wrong with those women. I love Aya, have always loved her. And I make her happy, can't you see that? I'm treating her right, I wouldn't have married her otherwise. She has the run of this house, we travel, she has security, and she even wrote a book."

"And you don't even approve of that," Bea said. "Now that she's making a life for herself, you've been acting an ass! I know all about it, and no, she didn't tell me. You are nothing but a distraction, Desmond Archibald Franklyn, and you know it. She felt like she was missing out, and you probably made her promises. Mind you, you've kept those promises—for now, anyway. I've known you twenty-seven years and you haven't changed. Even though things look good on the surface, something sleazy is going on underneath."

"You need killing for talking that nonsense," Desi growled. By this point, they had made their way to the far west of the property and were arguing under a tamarind tree. Although quite a distance from the house, their angry voices were carrying.

Upstairs on the balcony, Aya was concerned about what was going on down below, wanting to go to her husband and defend him.

"Don't you worry about them, Aya," Pearl said. "They've known each other for years and carry on like that from time to time. I'm more interested in you. Are you okay?"

"Yes, Mother, I'm fine. Desi takes good care of me, and the boys and I get on well. I live in this beautiful place and even have a helper. What is there to worry about?" Aya returned her attention to the action outside.

"Something's troubling you, I can feel it. In spite of what you say."

"It's nothing like you think. My marriage is in good shape—better than ever, really. We had a wonderful anniversary cruise. Even though we've been through some things, we've made it. He truly loves me."

"Yeah, you still don't love him though, do you? And don't even try to deny it 'cause I know better than that. You're settling for him 'cause you think it's better than nothing. And, yes, this is a nice house, only is it yours? All you have is what he gives you, and what happens if that stops? What will become of you then?"

Aya rolled her eyes and braced herself.

"I'm sure you care for him as he is taking care of you," Pearl continued. "Hell, you may even love him, but you're not *in love* with him, thank God. And don't ever let that happen. Trust me, you don't really know that man. There are so many things I could tell you, and he knew that. He only looks out for himself. He's betrayed everyone who's ever loved him."

Aya glared at her mother. "Oh, that's enough," she said. "I know you don't care for him anymore, but you two seemed close enough back in the day."

Pearl took in Aya's glare and kept going. "Yes, we were. We were there for each other when we were having difficult times. Your father warned me then and I didn't listen either. Desi was so kind and generous; I couldn't believe he could be so cruel." She turned away to wipe the tears from her left eye.

Aya was beginning to feel queasy. Was her mother seriously trying to tell her that she and Desi had a relationship all those years ago? "What did he do? How did he betray you?"

Pearl could not answer. She tried, but no sound would come, she was so ashamed.

Aya became defensive. "Dad felt betrayed by Desi's support of you, remember? Desi wouldn't ostracize you, and that cost him his lifelong friendship, only that is of no matter, right? Any time we had a problem, we could count on him to be there in no time and not even take any money for his help. He was consistently there for us, and I can't stand to see how you've turned on him because he chose me.

"And it's not like I'm suffering," Aya hammered on. "We were having a perfectly pleasant afternoon until you showed up out of nowhere. I will not let you ruin our day."

"How's Marley?" Pearl asked quietly. "Heard anything from him lately?"

Aya's jaw dropped. "What are you playing at?"

"I met him recently, a very fine young man. He talked about you endlessly and it's obvious he's fallen for you. When I told him I was coming to see you, he asked me to give you this." Pearl handed a card to her daughter and waited for her to open it.

Aya touched it as gently as if it were a newborn baby. The mix of emotions expressed themselves plainly on her face.

Pearl grinned. "He told me he hadn't heard anything from you for a while and knew that Desi had to be behind it. He said the two of you had a lovely time in the Caymans, and he cherished everything about working with you and hopes to do it again. I promised him you would never let Desi control you like that and would be in touch with him soon."

This time it was Aya who couldn't talk. She sat down, reeling from this development and fearful she would pass out.

"So now you're showing your true self," Bea chastised. "I never wanted you. Sherrie was my friend, remember? I couldn't be with any man who would creep with the babysitter. You don't give your cock a rest!"

"And yet anytime you needed anything done 'round the house, you'd call me," Desi said. "The scum of the earth was welcome as long as he came free. Ain't it? You thought I was foolish, but I didn't do it for you. I did it to be near Aya. I would put up with anything for that, even you."

"You slept with her mother, you bastard!" Bea yelled. "You don't see the wrong in that?"

"You never had a problem with me all these years knowing that, so why is it a big deal now? So we had a weak moment, you never had one? You don't think I know 'bout them that used to be coming out your back door in the early morning? That pimply one who bagged groceries, for Christ's sake! You can't judge me," Desi snarled.

"I was never married!"

"Several of your men were, and you didn't give a damn! This me you talking to, Bea. Stop putting on airs."

Bea did not like the turn the conversation was taking. She had no idea that Desi was so aware of her personal affairs. Her young lover from long ago to boot! She needed a moment to regroup and turn things around.

"I know I ain't the man you expect for Aya, but we happy," Desi said calmly. "We have a very nice life here, even with your sabotage of sending that Wright Rasta."

"I don't know what you're talking about."

"You know too well," Desi said and got right up to her face. "This a small island, and people love to be malicious. You don't think you friends could be friends of mine? You ain't the only one who loves to talk. I'll overlook it this time, but don't you ever pull that mess on me again. You got Aya thinking he cares 'bout her when he really don't give a damn."

"That's not true, he cares for her very much. He wouldn't waste his time if she didn't have any real talent. The book is selling, isn't it? I put him on to her because he is so gifted. How would I know how well they'd get on? You're jealous because she might start making her own life soon and won't want you anymore. Why don't you let her go and live, if you love her so much? Why are you trying to manipulate her?"

"The only one trying to manipulate things is you and that harpy up there," Desi said, pointing up to the balcony where Pearl stood with Aya. "So, what? Is she telling my wife we used to sleep together? Is that my Christmas present?"

"Do you really think you'd lose her if Pearl told her? Besides, she would've done so ages ago if she was going to. She's simply trying to spend some time with her daughter. Can't they rebuild their relationship?"

Desi started walking away from her and toward the house.

"Desi, wait!" Bea shouted, running to catch up with him. "Leave them a little longer. I promise she doesn't want to make trouble. Pearl loved you so and this marriage hurt her deeply. You let her think she had a future with you, and as soon as Aya showed up you cut her off and ignored her. That's not right, Des, not right. You can't blame me for being angry."

"You never asked my side of the story," Desi said. "Only what Pearl got made up in her mind. She thinks that if Aya gets rid of me then she and I will be together. She doesn't believe in my feelings for Aya. Which are real enough. I waited a long time to love her properly, and I ain't gonna let anything come between us. I never forced her to do anything, she came to me willing. She may not have known what she wanted then, but she do now, and that is to stay Mrs. Franklyn."

"Her supposed happiness is not genuine and you know it. She is satisfied because you're not beating her and you give her ridiculous material things. She feels obliged to you and that's how you want it. You're threatened by her independence, but even you can't delay that indefinitely. Sooner or later she will have to get away from you. In your heart you know that, so you keep paying and buying. She's already bored with you. There's no amount of money—"

"I'm done talking to you. Don't ever come back here, you are not welcome on this property. Get you things!" Desi stormed off.

Bea hoped she had given Pearl enough time.

Aya stroked the envelope gently.

"Why don't you open it?" Pearl asked as she watched Desi and Bea make their way back.

"Later, maybe. It's probably a note to encourage me to keep writing, and maybe a cheque."

"You're not fooling me, girl. I know you can't wait to read it. I'm sure he's written about his undying love for you and your resistance because you're married. That is no reason to deny yourself the true love that you wouldn't wait for. Don't settle like I did. Yes, I settled. I think we both did, your father and I. We did what everyone else was doing at the time. I think we only had, at most, a crush on each other. I married a guy I didn't even really know, and now you've deliberately done the same thing."

"How long are you on the island for?" Aya asked.

"I'm retired, and sick of winter. I might stay until spring, I haven't decided. My daughter needs me, whether she knows it or not, and I'm not going anywhere."

"Stay out of my relationship and we'll be fine. I don't want to be like Dad, but I won't speak to you if it's always going to be like this," Aya said. "You're welcome to stay for dinner, only I won't have you disrespecting Desi. He doesn't deserve that. He's been very good to me, and to you and Auntie. If you can't handle that, you might as well leave and I'll come visit some other time."

Pearl frowned and crossed her arms, but before she could respond, Desi came into the house and shouted up the stairs for his wife, who went over to the landing.

"What's happened?" Aya asked. "What was all the yelling about?"

"Don't bother 'bout her, she's leaving now anyway," Desi said as he came up the stairs.

"Well, you won't get rid of us yet." Pearl smirked, talking to Desi but looking at her daughter. "We're staying for dinner as we are family, aren't we?"

"Bea's already at the door. You gotta get to you reservation," Desi said firmly.

"My daughter insisted that we stay and enjoy the holiday together as a family, and I agree. We all need to learn to get along, and there is no time like the present." Pearl smiled as she made her way down the stairs to her sister.

"I thought you wanted them to leave?" Desi asked Aya harshly.

"You'd already invited them, and I want you to get along with everyone. A new year is coming and is a perfect time for changes." Aya said, watching her husband try to mask his irritation. She did not tell him that she wanted him punished as she was now certain that he and her mother had been lovers, and an evening with her mother would do just that. As it was they could barely look at each other, and Aya wanted to revel in their discomfort.

"What'd she say to you?"

"What are you so worried about?" Aya asked innocently. "I want to know what all the ruckus out back was."

"Your auntie bringing up her view of the past again. Like she was involved to know what really happened. I'm so tired of them judging me, Aya. Neither of them are saints, you know? I don't want them turning you against me. They don't know me like you do. They don't understand what we have." He put his arms around his rigid wife, who could only envision her husband in the throes of passion with her mother.

"You sure we should stay?" Bea whispered. "Desi's fit to be tied. He's about ready to kill me."

"Don't you worry about him," Pearl said with a smile. "Aya said it's okay as long as we play nice, and we're going to do just that."

"Why P, what are you up to? You seem very pleased with yourself."

"Quiet! They're coming back down. Come, let's fix the table."

Dinner was pleasant enough. Desi had his face set and glared at the intruders, although Pearl and Bea did not let on they noticed. They kept chatting and involved everyone else in the conversation. They ate heartily while Desi drank hard.

When Bea went to start the coffee, he made his way next to her and said under his breath, "I thought I told you to get gone, you don't drink coffee. Enough is enough."

"Be nice, Desi," Bea gloated. "You don't want Aya to see the real you, now, do you? I can keep up my act just as long as you can."

Once back at the table, Desi cleared all the dishes and excused himself to go out to the garage to fiddle around with his Aventura Navara. Less than thirty minutes later, Aya was ushering her relatives out the door.

"Did you see how miserable he got?" said a resplendent Pearl on the drive home. "He couldn't even hide it. So glad we decided to do this."

"Yes, but he'll make it up to her with some bauble or other. You see the size of that ring he gave her for Christmas? She doesn't wear those things, what's he thinking?"

"He's desperate, that's what. I'm so glad you convinced me to move back. I'm going to make him pay for what he's done to me and what he's about to do with my daughter."

"Did you let Aya know?"

"No, not yet. It's him I don't want knowing. You know what I realized today? I need to be around all the time and get under his skin. It's too easy on him if I stay away, that was our mistake. I'm gonna start coming around often, and he can't do a thing about it. He'll get vicious, of course, and hopefully Aya will see his true nature at last. And with Marley back in the picture ..."

"You really think she's attracted to him?" Bea asked.

"I certainly know it now. You should've seen her reaction when I mentioned his name. Something has happened between them already, I don't even have to push. Marley is exactly her type. If only you'd thought of him earlier."

"She wasn't writing a book when living with me, P. And I didn't know if she would be any good either. Besides, why doesn't he have a woman, as fine as he is?"

"Aya didn't have a man either, as beautiful as she is. Stop judging. We need to get her away from Desi a while so she will see sense and leave him alone in his big house."

Later that night in bed, Aya used chilly behaviour to make it clear to Desi that sex would not be on offer.

"You all right?" he asked as he climbed in next to her, clearly trying to assess the damage. "You been very cool since you family left."

"It's been a long day, I've eaten too much, and I'm very uncomfortable. I've got meat on top of meat up to my throat. I'm going to have to sit up awhile."

"You still didn't tell me what you mother said to upset you."

"I'm not upset. I invited her to stay, didn't I? You weren't friendly in the least. Not to mention the screaming match you had with Auntie," Aya replied crisply as she got out of the bed to lie on the lounger and read a magazine.

"I'm sorry 'bout that, she got to me. All those old accusations. I didn't mean to upset you or ruin Christmas."

"You didn't ruin it. It is what it is. My mother's going to be staying for a while, so I need you to make an effort to get along."

"I'll try," Desi said, bowing his head. "You sure you don't wanna come to bed now?"

"I told you, I need to let this food settle. I want to do some reading." She lifted the magazine she was pretending to study. She'd slipped Marley's card inside so she could review it as soon as she could get away from her husband.

"My belly's full too," Desi said, "but I'd still like to end the evening snuggling with my woman. That too much to ask?"

"You really going to pressure me to hit it tonight, Desi?"

"Hey, I'm asking to lay with you. As soon as I come, you get up and go to the chair. You say you ain't angry, when I can see you uptight 'bout something. I'm trying to relax us both. Don't insult me, I don't need to beg for some," he said, his pride clearly hurt.

Aya was not moved. She wondered how much loving he didn't have to beg for with her mother. Although it was ancient history, she was still repulsed. Desi must feel like some man, bedding them both. It made Aya's skin crawl, and she couldn't stand the sight of him.

Aya closed the magazine and held it tight to her body as she stood. "I'm going to make a cup of tea," she said as she left him alone in the room.

Once in the kitchen, she took out a plate of cold ham to nibble on while the kettle boiled as she was not the slightest bit full. She turned on the television and left it on an old black-and-white movie, then she sat down at the island with her back to the cupboards so that no one could sneak up on her. She opened the envelope from Marley.

It was a lovely card displaying a print by the Cuban artist he had introduced her to in the Caymans. Inside was a lined loose-leaf sheet of paper containing his handwritten note. Aya held her breath and devoured the words.

My Dear Friend,

How are you? I've been wishing that you would reach out to me after our loving farewell. I hope I have not offended you; I simply could not help myself. Even if it didn't seem to come as a surprise to you, and that warms my heart.

Since the moment I met you I have been intrigued. You are one giant puzzle, and I could not wait to put the pieces together. I love your smile, your laugh, your sense of humour, your style, and especially you. Yes, you, Aya.

I am well aware that you have a husband and can understand why you married him. As you are now coming into your own, I feel there are several changes you may want to make in your life, and perhaps he is one of them.

I am not sure why I haven't heard from you. I wanted you to know how I feel so that you would not be afraid. I am willing to give you all the time and space you need to consider what is nothing other than divine design that brought our two remote souls together.

I will always be here for you and you can contact me at any time. I am returning to the island on New Year's Eve to stay by my mother and would love to see you again. We have so much to talk about.

Please be strong, sweets. Life offers only few chances for our rare connection.

All My Love,
MW

Aya's heart rejoiced. It was everything she wanted to hear, only what now? Then she heard the muffled screams of Junior's young woman of the evening coming from her old cabin. She could not believe his sex drive and wondered if Desi had been the same way. Even if there wasn't much to do on the island, surely he could take a night off? Desi could not honestly believe this type of behaviour was the acceptable practice of becoming a man, could he?

If Aya was truthful, she would have to admit that she was jealous as Desi had never made her squeal like that. She was turning forty the following year and had never known anything close to ecstasy. She had tried suggesting that Desi be gentler, that he take his time and explore more, but sooner rather than later he would become a ramrod. Alas, she didn't have the experience to know what worked for her, nor the desire to explore herself. Now the universe was offering an interesting opportunity.

She had to pause at the thought. Did she really want to end her marriage? Or would she keep Desi for the benefits and let Marley fulfill her erotic desires? Could she seriously commit adultery? She simply could not imagine it. Although the prospect was exciting, it was fraught with danger. Someone was bound to find out on this gossipy island and Desi could put her out. Then what? Take up with Marley? She had no idea how they would function in a relationship. Yes, he aroused feelings in her that she was desperate to explore; on the other hand, was it worth wrecking her life and feeding into her mother's plan?

The back door swung open as a shirtless Junior came in with his boxers hung low and the tip of his penis exposed. He saw Aya notice his body and smiled proudly. He had been working out aggressively the past few months, and the results were remarkable. His upper body was buff and he even had a six-pack. Unfortunately, he had not paid as much attention to his lower half, which was entirely too scrawny to balance out his physique. Aya looked away and hid her card.

"You still up? I thought y'all would be counting sheep," he asked.

"I got an idea and couldn't sleep. I'm not as worn out as your lady friend."

Junior burst out laughing and sat next to her at the island. "Yeah, she make nuff noise. She pass out now so you won't be hearing any more from her. It bother you?"

Aya tried to mask her discomfort. "You're a grown man and it's your own place back there. That's your business. As long as you stay safe because there are some dangerous diseases out there and babies could ruin your good time."

"Well, you and Daddy ain't got no babies, and I never heard you making noise like that. Maybe I could show you something," he said, baring his very white, large square teeth.

"What?" Aya whispered, alarmed. "Did you say ... ?"

"I'm just joking with ya. Take it easy." Junior laughed. "I must've struck a nerve."

"Excuse me, do not talk to me like that. What goes on between your father and I has nothing to do with you," she said, trying to reclaim her dignity.

"I said I was joking. Calm down. I know you make Daddy happy since he don't look at other women no more. You, on the other hand ..."

"Me, what?" Aya asked. "I don't go with other men."

"Who dat Rasta that was 'round here so much, then?"

"Marley? Wearing dreadlocks doesn't make you a Rasta. Why'd you think I was involved with him?"

"I don't know what go on in that back house. I see how he be with you, and my father ain't 'round much."

Aya could smell the weed on his breath and rose, holding the magazine to her chest. "You are clearly high, so I won't mention this disrespect to your father. I know you love him and want to protect him, so I won't fault you for that.

"Marley and I are strictly professional. You don't see him around here anymore, do you? He is a very good friend, and I don't have many, so what's wrong with that? Pull up your damn pants!" she snapped.

Junior smiled as he pulled them up, which immediately slipped down lower and exposed even more of himself.

Aya fled to her bedroom, where Desi was still awake, lying on his back with a lamp on. He caught her flustered expression and asked what was wrong.

"Nothing, Junior just startled me in the kitchen. Good night," she said crisply and put her magazine in her bedside table, then turned her back to him and pretended to sleep.

Desi was not there when she woke, feeling unrested, the following morning. She'd had a nightmare about being on a bus full of strangers who were speaking a funny language. They kept talking, and she had no idea what they were saying or why she was with them or where they were going. She woke reliving the deep despair of her situation.

She heard Desi and the boys laughing in the kitchen and decided not to join them. Had Junior told his father about their late-night conversation? Had Desi been confiding in his son about their marriage? What were they saying about her? Although curious, she didn't really want to know. Some Christmas this had turned out to be.

She decided to take a long bath and soak in the salts that Ricky was considerate enough to give her as a present. Aya felt very alone and wanted someone to talk to, only, as usual, there was no one. This depth of loneliness was what she had hoped her marriage would take her away from.

As if on cue, Desi came in with a breakfast tray. He removed his clothes and joined her in the tub. Aya was somewhat relieved to see that he was beginning to fill out nicely, although his abdomen seemed oddly distended.

"I thought we should start this day on a good note. I've got fish cakes and a full plate of leftovers. No fruit or yogurt for my woman today."

"It does smell lovely," Aya said, although the idea of eating in a soaker tub seemed unhygienic. "You put a lot on here, are you having some?"

"I'll eat some," Desi said, forking a lean piece of turkey breast into Aya's mouth. "It tastes even better the next day. Do you have any plans for later?"

"No, just relaxing. Why?"

"Well, I thought we could take a drive. It's a beautiful day to get out the house. We can pack a picnic lunch and go to the beach for a bit. Ricky's real eager. What you think?"

Aya wanted to know if Junior would be going because she wasn't up to facing him yet. She also wanted to be home alone for a while with her thoughts. She noticed Desi was watching her closely.

"We won't be gone for long," he said. "It's near noon already. Come on, let's do it. Junior's too busy with his girlfriend out back and Ricky wants to try out his surfboard."

"You're right," Aya said. "That is a nice way to spend the day. I'll go get ready." She could do with the distraction. A day by the sea might be just the thing she needed.

"Wait a minute," he said, rubbing her leg. "There's still time. Let's enjoy our bath."

Aya rushed to finish eating before he could get any ideas and was out in record time.

By that afternoon, she had thawed to Desi and was laughing with him genuinely. The sea was bright turquoise all the way out to the breakers where the Atlantic waves were crashing in. The smell of salt in the cooling wind was delightful, and the colourful bougainvillea was so enticing that all Aya wanted was to take it in. Desi embarrassed himself by trying to guide Ricky on his board, but he said the smile on his wife's face was worth it. Aya laid back under her umbrella and relaxed on her beach towel while watching the clouds go by. When she couldn't have more to think about, she couldn't be bothered to think about anything at all. She decided to remain in the moment.

After a while Desi and Ricky called for her, and she ran to join them. They splashed and dunked each other in the surf. They floated on their backs. They played. They ate sandwiches, fruit, cake, nuts, and even drank beer. Desi bought roasted corn and coconut water from a beach vendor. It was a perfect day, and Aya forgot about her troubles and slept most of the ride home.

That evening, the Franklyns had a family dinner, and Junior made no mention of the previous night's conversation. Aya watched him closely nonetheless. Afterward, Ricky went up to bed exhausted after an hour of Wii and Junior went to hit the clubs, so Aya was left with Desi's amorous intentions.

He snuggled up to her on the couch, laid his head on her stomach, and rubbed her thighs. Aya focused on the television and waited for him to make his move. In the meantime, she thought about how bloated her tummy had become lately. She had been eating a lot of chocolate and heavy foods as it was the season; somehow, though, it seemed to her like more than food. It could have something to do with her cycle, yet there was a tenderness lately that she had not had before. She made a mental note to monitor it when Desi started kissing her.

Chapter 20

Marva returned from her vacation glowing radiantly. Her smile was so enormous as she handed out presents to the family that they saw teeth they had never seen before. She had so much pep in her step that Aya had to ask if she got "some" while she was away, to which Marva laughed so hard she fogged up her glasses. She spent most of her shift reliving those four days to anyone who would listen and helping herself to the last of the leftovers.

"You need to cool it, Missus," she warned after seeing Aya open the last box of chocolates. "You belly getting big."

"Yes, I know," Aya said gently. "I wish I knew what was going on. It's a little sore too. I wonder if it's hormonal? I'll take care of it in the new year, there's no point in me cutting back now."

"Maybe you catch a child," Marva said carefully.

"What? You crazy?" Aya laughed. "That's not possible."

"Never know." Marva grinned. "Nothing foolproof. You been married long nuff now, maybe you get an extra Christmas present."

Aya swallowed hard. Her eyes froze and her breathing stopped entirely.

"Somebody gonna be a mummy," Marva sang. "I glad nuff. Desi gonna be thrilled, he always wanted a girl."

"Shut it, you," Aya said, grabbing Marva and pulling her to sit down at the table. "Not another word, and don't you dare say anything to anyone, you hear me?"

"What you worried 'bout? This wonderful news!"

"Stop that! I am not pregnant. It's not possible."

"Why not? You can't have them?" Marva asked.

"What? No. I don't know. Desi had a vasectomy, remember?"

Marva's face twinged at that remark and she looked away, her bottom lip pushed out.

"Wait. What is it?" Aya said, picking up on her nervousness. "What did I say?"

"Nutting, Missus," Marva said sharply. "This you business. But what you gonna do if you pregnant?"

"That could only happen if his vasectomy didn't take *and* my birth control pills didn't work. What's with you?"

"But what you gonna do if you pregnant?" Marva persisted. "You gonna keep it, right? I just letting you know that I'll help you. I'll do it all, if that what it take. You don't got to worry 'bout nothing but staying healthy and birthing it."

"Look at you. You've got everything figured out already. I'm not pregnant, Marva, so just forget that."

"But if you was, you'd have it, right?"

"I don't know what I'd do, only I'm not bothered because I'm not. Let's change the subject," Aya said firmly.

"You gonna take the test?" Marva asked, knowing from the Missus's locked jaws that she was on thin ice.

"That is not changing the subject!" Aya snapped. "My period will be here any day now, and that will put an end to all this."

She got up and went out to Desi, who was putting the finishing touches on a coat of paint for her new workspace. Marva grinned deliciously. Everything was going as planned. Over her break, she worked out that it would cost her another five hundred dollars a month to put her mother in an old age home. She could manage if she moved in with the Franklyns and rented out the hovel to the migrant workers from South America, who wouldn't be bothered by the ramshackle dwelling.

Aya was not paying any attention to the conversation Desi was trying to have as her mind was a million miles away. She sat on a chair outside the cabin's front door, where the paint fumes were less intense, and stared out to the sea. *Pregnant? How could it be?* Marva was so sure about it even though Desi was fixed. She had never heard of such a thing happening after the procedure.

Aya simply had to know. She would get up first thing and go to the clinic to take the test, in addition to a complete physical, even if she had to wait all day. That way she would have all of the results by New Year's Eve and know what to do. Aya actually knew what she would do already; she would get the procedure before anyone was the wiser. She would have to come up with something to appease Marva's conscience and would deal with her later.

Marva wouldn't dare mention anything to Desi since she had no proof and it would be foolish to get his hopes up like that. Aya had no qualms about removing her unborn child or not letting the father know anything about it. She wasn't sure what the future held, or whether her husband would even be a factor.

Desi interrupted her thoughts by shaking her shoulder and asking her if she was okay. She assured him she was fine and that she was just putting together a story in her mind.

She looked back out at the sea and the dark clouds forming. The real issue was how to go about contacting Marley. She definitely had to talk to him in order to put things into perspective, then she would let nature take its course.

There was also unfinished business with her mother to deal with.

After staying out of Aya's sight most of the afternoon, Marva was finally able to get Desi alone while the Missus arranged her new workspace.

"Things looking good for you, Desi. How you get it done?"

"What you on 'bout now?"

"The Missus belly looking swollen, is all. She may be carrying a little Franklyn all like now. You didn't notice?"

"You think so?" he asked, looking just as pleased as Marva felt. "I figured it was from all the food, and she been complaining 'bout feeling sore. She's eating a lot like she does when she's stressed out, come to think of it. Your eyes don't miss a thing!"

"I said 'may be.' It may be something else, though I doubt it. She not convinced at all."

"You talked to her 'bout it? What she say?"

"She not believing 'cause a you surgery. What you do with her pills?"

"Never you mind, just tell me what she said."

Marva wasn't sure whether to sugarcoat the answer. "Like I say, she not believing. She don't even wanna hear it. She say her lady day's coming and that it."

"She wasn't excited? Not at all?"

"Not at all," Marva said slowly. "But don't take no mind to that. She'll come 'round sure nuff when it born."

Desi did not reply.

"You gonna ask her 'bout it? Tell her you notice she put on size like she expecting."

"I can't do that." Desi frowned. "I told you, it has to seem like a surprise. I might offend her or make her self-conscious. She'll know we discussed it since you talked to her 'bout it earlier and now I'm asking 'bout it. No, I'll leave it alone for now. You keep to you end of the deal and I'll take care of mine."

Desi went in to wash off the paint, and as Marva watched, a smile spread across his face.

The next morning as Aya was leaving to get tested, Pearl showed up at the door. "Mother, what are you doing here?"

"I was in the area and thought I'd drop by. You don't have a problem with that, do you?"

"Well, I'm on my way to an appointment and don't know how long I'll be."

"I could go with you," Pearl volunteered.

"No, no," Aya said firmly. "This is business, and like I said, I don't know when we will finish."

"You're not meeting Marley, are you, naughty girl?"

"You need to hush up about him," Aya said sternly. "I told you I'd come visit soon."

"Oh, I hate sitting around the house all day. I wanted to spend some time with you," Pearl said, feigning hurt.

"Mother, I have to go now. If I get through quickly I'll let you know and we can do something then." Aya put on her shoes and grabbed her car keys.

"Well, I can wait here for you, then. I'll make dinner. I'm sure you've missed my stuffed roast chicken and the boys will love it."

"You wanna stay here with Desi?"

"We'll get along fine, don't you worry. I'll keep in the kitchen until you get home. It'll be okay, I promise you. Go on to your appointment."

Aya did not trust her mother's motives, but she had to get going. If her mother wanted to make Desi miserable, so be it. Marva would be there soon, and neither one of them would want to make a scene in front of that mouth. "Okay, then, knock yourself out," she said and headed to her car.

Desi watched Pearl carefully as she waved goodbye to her daughter and closed the door gently, grinning like the Cheshire cat.

"Pearl? What you doing here? Didn't you just see Aya leave?"

"Yes, I did. I'm cooking dinner for you all, and it'll be ready by the time she gets back. You have a problem with that?"

"We don't need you to do that," Desi said shortly. "We have a helper on her way for that. You don't need to stay."

"I'm making Aya's favourite stuffed chicken, you remember that, don't you? You used to be rather fond of it."

"We don't need any heavy food right now," Desi reasoned. "Our guts have been stuffed for days, so we wanna give them a rest. Marva's making soup of the scraps."

"She can still make that, it'll make a nice starter. I haven't seen Marva in ages. It'll be nice to meet with her properly."

Desi gave up trying to convince her and decided he would simply go out and do a few small jobs that would keep him away until she had left.

"Well, none for me," he said finally. "The soup is plenty, and I'll be gone most of the day anyhow."

"Really?" Pearl asked. "Surely you have questions you want to ask me? Why not take advantage of an empty house?"

"My youngest is right upstairs and the other is 'round back. Both will be coming for breakfast soon, and I don't have time to get into anything with you," he said, turning his back to her and heading toward the kitchen.

"I'm sure you're dying to know if I've told Aya about us. And what she thinks about that," Pearl said craftily, stopping Desi in his tracks.

"You won't quit, will you? You a sad, desperate woman."

"What's wrong, Des? Have I touched a nerve?"

"Listen, don't think I won't put you outta my house."

"I know full well whose house this is," Pearl said, following him into the kitchen. "I helped with some of the planning, remember? That was when you promised it was for the two of us."

"That was all in you head. I invited you to visit, not move in. Why would you expect to live here? We were never in a relationship. I wasn't your man and you weren't my woman for certain. We slept together when the occasion called for it, and you had no complaints. I did what I could to help you out."

"You know what has me confused?" Pearl asked, ignoring his comments. "I don't understand when you and Aya got started. Were you screwing her under my roof the whole time? Was I merely filling in for when she wasn't available?"

Desi proceeded to empty an entire glass of orange juice before sizing her up. "What difference does it make? All that is ancient history, and why you try to keep reliving it is beyond me."

"It makes a hell of a difference to me. I need to know when you began messing with my daughter."

"I see that you think I used you, but that ain't true, P. It was mutual. You got from me more than I took from you. I was very clear that I wasn't interested in any relationship after that whole mess of a divorce. We talked 'bout it all the time. I told you to come by whenever you were on the island—"

"And here I am," Pearl interrupted. "So, you're not going to answer me, then?"

"What happened between me and my wife ain't none of you business. You need to keep out of things or, I promise you, Aya'll cut you off," he threatened.

"I know that's what you're hoping for, but it's not going to happen, Desi. I won't lose my daughter to you. How come you don't want to know what she said when I told her?"

Desi finished off a slice of rum cake, then took a hard-boiled egg out of the fridge. "I know you didn't tell her, so why bother? You trying to blackmail me or something? Threaten to tell her if I don't do whatever it is you want? Go 'head and try it." Desi beamed as he cracked the egg.

Pearl steadied herself. "She's gonna leave you. She's just waiting for the right time. As soon as she has herself together, she'll be out the door. She told me that! I'm here to help her get through quicker, and it is a great pleasure for me to tell you."

Desi ignored her and peeled the egg. Out of the corner of his eye, he watched Pearl huff and puff, waiting for his response, which was not coming. She took two chickens out of the freezer and soaked them in lime and salt. She went through the fridge, pulling out vegetables and bread, then went through the cupboard looking for seasonings. Every now and then she would look back at Desi, who was trying to act carefree as he ate even though he was bothered by her last comment.

Suddenly, Ricky came into the kitchen, and he gave his son a warm hug and kissed his forehead. Ricky was surprised to see Pearl and greeted her warmly. She informed him of the delicious dinner she was preparing, and he became very excited. He grabbed several sourdough rolls and a juice box and went to turn on the TV.

Desi finished eating and prepared to leave. "You know, I think Aya needs to know what kind of woman you really are. I ain't the one trying to control and ruin her life. You need to take a look in the mirror."

He asked Ricky to hurry and get his brother so they could get off to work. He had gone out to his vehicle to wait for them when Marva came walking up the driveway.

"Whose car that is?"

"The mother," Desi answered with a scowl.

"Oh Lord, what she want now?"

"The usual. Aya's gone out for a while, so she in there alone. Keep an eye on her and don't let her go poking 'round unsupervised. She's supposed to be making dinner, except I don't want any of it. Go 'head with the soup you making, I'll eat that when I get back. Hopefully Aya's not gone too long."

Marva practically ran into the house to see for herself what Pearl was up to. She found her sitting at the counter, cutting up fixings for her stuffing.

"Why, Marva! It's been a long time. How are you?"

"I good," Marva mumbled, setting down her things in the pantry. "What all this?"

"I'm not in your way, am I?" Pearl asked. "I'm making Aya's favourite stuffed chicken. There'll be plenty, so you're welcome to some."

"All right," Marva said. "I got to get the soup going. I didn't know you back on the island." She put a big pot on the stove to boil and pulled out the ham bone and turkey carcass from the fridge, then claimed some of the vegetables that Pearl still had out on the table. "How long you here for?"

"Not sure yet. I haven't made any plans. I want to see my daughter in a good way first."

"What you mean? She good. She happy. She got Desi. She got her work."

"Of course you'd say that," Pearl goaded. "A mother can tell. He is not the man for her. She's still young and there's plenty of time for her to get on the right track."

"Dunno 'bout that," Marva mumbled, offended. "They happy nuff. True, I didn't figure it would last long either, but here we is. He not the same man he was before, I can tell you that."

"You always have to take up for him, don't you? Well, I guess he pays you well enough to do so, eh?"

"Not-true, not-true," Marva whined. "Me? He don't own me! I telling you how I see it, and I here near every day. My eyes don't miss a thing neither. Yes, they had problems—"

"Really? Like what?"

Marva bit her lip. As much as she wanted to hold her tongue, she was anxious to put this woman in her place. "Nothing that don't all couples go through," she said simply.

"Like Marley?"

Marva felt trapped, only there was no holding back now. "What you know 'bout Marley?" she asked while turning the stove dial to simmer.

"I know him well," Pearl said, smiling. "A perfectly fine, young, decent man, don't you think? He adores Aya, and why shouldn't he? They make a perfect couple."

"Dunno 'bout that neither." Marva went over to Pearl. "The Missus happily married. He probably got women everywhere he go 'cause he don't stand one place too long. That is, if he don't prefer gentlemen."

Pearl burst out laughing. "He's not gay, Marva, that's wishful thinking. You should know better after practically raising Carlton all these years. I don't want to argue with you, so trust me: Desi's time is limited. He'll get some other girl living here soon enough."

"Not at all," Marva argued. "Not with the baby com—"

Pearl's eyes went wide with disbelief. "Who you think you're fooling? Desi can't have any more, and Aya certainly doesn't want children—not with him, anyway."

"We soon find out," Marva said, retreating to her pot.

Pearl got up and went to Marva. "You seriously believe Aya's pregnant?" Marva pushed out her bottom lip and would not look at her. "Well, if she is, it can't be Desi's, so that will be the end of things anyway. Thanks for telling me."

"You trying to get me fired!" Marva shrieked. "I never said for sure."

"Well, Desi isn't going to raise another man's baby, that's certain. Especially not Marley's! Ooh!"

"The Missus would never do that to Desi! Not ever! I don't wanna hear no more 'bout this," Marva cried.

Marva could not believe that her world was about to come crashing down on her, which kept happening to her time and again. As soon as her life seemed full of promise, something would come out of nowhere and snatch it away. The Lord had a lot of explaining to do.

Worse still, she had let the pregnancy slip! The Missus would be livid and might even want her fired. Desi might not be of much help to her either. Why couldn't she control her mouth?

Pearl must have sensed Marva's worry because she set out to calm her down. "Oh, Marva, don't worry. I won't say anything about what you've told me, I promise. I don't want to make any trouble for you or anyone. Really, not a word."

"Well, I hope not," Marva mumbled, not quite believing. "It better to wait and see if I'm right first."

"So Aya didn't tell you, then? Well, I suppose you would know best. She is looking a little puffy lately. Oh, I'd love a grandchild! I'm so tired of hearing about everyone else's."

"Well, the Missus might not keep it, the way she talk. She not changing her mind on babies at all."

"I wouldn't blame her if it was Desi's," Pearl joked. "A Wright baby would be too beautiful to miss."

Marva did not reply. She changed the subject by observing Pearl's recipe and describing her trip to Miami. Pearl made easy conversation and the hours trickled by until Marva finally breathed a sigh of relief, believing that Pearl would not out her. She did a surface cleaning of the house and kept an eye on the Mother, who remained either in the kitchen or family room or out on the balcony.

It was coming up to five o'clock before Aya came through the door.

"You sure took long at your meeting," Pearl said while winking at a flustered Marva.

"I didn't get in right away," Aya replied. With that, Marva knew she had gone to the doctor to take the test.

"You must be hungry, then," Marva said. "You wanna wait on the others or have some a my soup now?"

"I am starved. We might as well eat now," she said, making her way to the kitchen. "Desi called and told me they won't get home until late."

"Oh really?" Pearl said, and this time Marva gave her a look.

"And you don't like to be on the road when it's dark, Mother. You better get going soon."

"It will be dark long before we finish eating. Why don't I spend the night? I haven't got to see you at all," Pearl said, and Marva squirmed.

"Oh, Mother, really? I told you I'd come out and visit soon. I didn't mean to be gone so long, I went first thing hoping to get away early. I did try, and you could've let us know you were coming."

"I don't see why I can't stay. They won't be home until late, and Marva's leaving so we can have a proper visit. I'll disappear to my room as soon as they get back. I won't start any trouble with Desi," Pearl moaned.

Marva couldn't help noticing that Pearl was making a lot of promises. She hoped she would keep them.

Aya was too tired and hungry to argue. "Fine, you can stay out in my new cabin. It's been freshly decorated and is nice and cool. You'll get a good night's rest."

"Out there by myself? Anything could happen to me and you wouldn't even know it. Can't I have one of the rooms upstairs?" Pearl pressed.

"Junior is right across from you and all sound carries up to the house. Trust me, it's better this way. Besides, I haven't checked with Desi yet."

"Oh, you have to get his permission, do you?" Pearl frowned. "For your own mother to stay over? Boy, you really are only a guest in his house, aren't you?"

"That's enough," Aya said and looked to Marva, who nodded her head in approval. "You staying for dinner, Marv?"

"I took mine already," she answered. "I heading down the road now. See you all."

During dinner, Pearl studied her gorging daughter hard. She had not seen Aya eat so heartily since the breakup. Could Marley be the source of her angst? That seemed too much to hope for. Marva was probably right after all. They conversed at the table until the meal was finished, then Aya took her mother to get settled in her cabin while she went to shower.

They met up afterward on the couch in the family room to watch the evening news. Pearl figured it wouldn't be long now before the rest got home, so she delayed no longer.

"So? What are you going to do about Marley?"

"You can't be serious."

"Just talk to the man. What harm can that do? You must be curious." Pearl grinned.

"The only thing I'm curious about is what in hell you are up to? What's the real reason you hate Desi so much? It's almost like you're jealous. Why wouldn't you be happy that your daughter married a man who has been so good to us?"

"You don't know who he really is, Aya," Pearl warned.

"And you do? You sound just like Dad. In fact, you're acting just like him! Turning on Desi after all he's done for you."

"Now don't you dare take his side over mine!"

"Since when were you on different sides? You didn't give a damn that he lost his friendship with Dad after he took up for you. Or did he take up *with* you? Is that it?"

"Is that what he says?"

"I want to hear what you have to say," Aya challenged. "That's all that matters right now."

"I won't allow him to come between us. Don't you see that's what he's trying to do? Isolating you from all of your family, and you really don't have any friends here either with Nicola overseas getting her Masters. You'll be all alone and relying on him—completely. He's got you right where he wants you. It's not wrong to want you to work with Marley so that you can create a separate life for yourself," Pearl argued, hoping to return the topic back to safe territory.

"You still haven't answered my question," Aya said, uncompromising. "Are you angry that I have him and you don't?"

"What kind of question is that? I can tell he's been running his mouth about me. What arrogance! What conceit! Saying that I want him? He thinks every woman wants him. Any mother knowing his track record would want better for her daughter. You know how they all ended up. I don't know why you can't see that. That's what scares me most of all."

"You can't be objective when it comes to Desi because of your feelings for him. You knew all about his women before I married him, and you still adored him. Knowing him, you probably slept together. As much as he cared for you, he didn't fall in love like you probably did."

"Oh, you can't be serious," Pearl said under her breath, looking toward the window.

"Can you not answer a simple question?" Aya hollered, which gave her mother pause. "I am not unfeeling. I can understand what you must think about how things look. I am not blind about Desi, and he has been honest with me, eventually. He is not perfect and neither am I. You think he married me to get back at you or at Dad? I considered that, only it doesn't add up. He misses Dad, terribly, except he's been too hurt by him for things to go back now. Your history together makes him uncomfortable around you only because of how you are acting. He is not trying to isolate me. I know that man loves me and is determined to make our marriage work."

"More like desperate," Pearl said. "I've never seen a man more neurotically try to hold on to what does not belong to him. You really see yourself with him in the future? As he ages? Why settle for an old man when you can have a young, vibrant one? How can you trust him? How can you lay with him?"

"Yes, I know that's what really gets you, us sleeping together. Well, we do, so get over it. Leave it alone. Whether we stay together or not has nothing to do with you. I am living my life, he is living his, and we are both satisfied."

"Why you would want to live a merely satisfactory life is beyond me, with all of your strengths. You should have so much more."

"I will have everything I am meant to have. Nothing is stopping that. Not Desi. Not you," Aya said hotly.

"Fine! At the very least you could give Marley a call and get going on another book. You need to get your finances in order, girl. Get a property of your own and rent it out or something. Stop relying on Desi's money."

"I'm working on it," Aya said sharply as the front door opened and Desi and his boys came in cautiously. Desi shuddered when he saw Pearl's shoes still at the door.

Ricky was delighted to see his step-grandmother and greeted her warmly. Junior made brief, polite conversation before heading out to his pad. Desi came in after much stalling and warmly greeted his wife. He did not acknowledge Pearl at all and quickly made his way to his bathroom to clean up, with his wife following closely behind.

"That was quite rude," Aya said crisply to her husband as he started to undress. "You don't have to like each other, but you must give each other proper respect, Des. And in front of Ricky too."

Desi rolled his head from side to side and Aya heard his neck crack. "Aya, I dead tired. The last thing I wanted was to come home and have to deal with her. I wanted to cuddle up with my wife." He took off his dirty clothes and put them in the hamper. "I have tried and tried and she has been nothing but unreasonable and outright insolent. You can't ask me to take that."

"I don't expect either of you to take that. This needs to end now. You have to be pleasant and polite, and so does she. I've warned her. She's staying with us a few days so you guys can work it out."

"She what?" Desi gasped, all the muscles on his lean body tensing. "You never asked me?"

"You keep reminding me that this is my home too," Aya said, to which Desi replied by putting both his hands over his face. "She is staying in my studio so she will be out of the way, okay? I don't like the strain between her and me. She is my mother, remember?"

"I know it too well," Desi grumbled as he made his exit to the shower.

Aya was not finished with him, however. "So you'll come out and play nice, then?"

"Hon, I told you I'm tired. It's late. I just wanna relax. If she's here all weekend, then we can do it tomorrow, can't we?"

"You're not even going to eat, then?"

"I asked Marv to leave me some soup and that'll do. I've damn well lost my appetite."

Aya sighed. "Oh, Desi. Don't be like that."

Desi slid open the shower door, poked his soapy head out, and looked Aya dead in the eye. "Hey, you want me to play nice, I'll play nice. I got it."

"I'll go get your dinner," Aya said quietly. She returned to the kitchen and began to warm up his soup. Her mother and Ricky were hysterically laughing at the poor singers on a talent show.

Pearl came over to her daughter quietly and asked, "I take it the two of you had words, then?"

"Is that what you were hoping for?" Aya asked, not removing her attention from the soup.

"Of course not," she whispered. "I'm not trying to make trouble and I've said all I have to say about it. He could've at least acknowledged me."

"He's going to correct that," Aya said. "He didn't want to get in an argument with you, that's all. I promised him that you guys could hold a cease-fire, and he went along with that."

"Oh really?" Pearl said. Ricky shouted out for her to observe some character on the television and she went to him.

When Desi came in to get his supper, he nodded at Pearl and sat on the arm of the chair to embrace his son, who was excitedly telling him about the show they had seen. Desi faked interest for a time and then went over to his wife, who had set the table for him.

They didn't say too much. Desi smiled at her and Aya continued to imagine her husband and mother locked in a passionate embrace. She would not let on to her mother that she had strong doubts about her marriage, or that she was not uncomfortable enough to make a move yet. Or secure enough.

Once Desi finished eating, he insisted his wife sit as he put his dishes away. He informed his son that it was late and that he needed to head up to bed. Reluctantly and with much complaining, Ricky did so.

Pearl came into the kitchen and told Desi, "You have a wonderful son. You have a lot to be proud of."

"Well, thank you," he said hoarsely. "I could say the same thing 'bout your daughter." Aya sat at the kitchen table, observing them at the island.

"Yes. That's my baby and she means the world to me. She's made it clear that we need to get along, and I think we can do that for the New Year. Don't you?"

Desi smiled. "Indeed," he replied and returned to his wife's side at the table.

Aya sat still as he rubbed her back and asked if she was ready to turn in. She looked at him through her haze.

"Don't let me keep you. I'm going in now myself. I'll make you some corned beef and eggs in the morning," Pearl said.

"Mother, I haven't eaten like that in years. That food is poison."

"Marva makes breakfast, so don't trouble yourself," Desi intervened. "And you are a guest, so take it easy."

"Well, you both know how much I love to cook, and it was always your favourite, Desi." Pearl smiled.

Desi put his arm around Aya's waist. "You go on to bed and let me make love to my wife," he said flatly.

Aya's eyes bulged as her body shook. Pearl took the blow, then recovered enough to bow and make her way out the back door.

Aya forcefully removed herself from Desi's embrace. "Why the hell did you say that? Is this some sick game you're playing?" She sat down on the couch in front of the television.

"Now don't get upset. I didn't mean to—"

"You definitely meant to cut her with that remark. Not to mention how disrespectful it is to me!"

"Oh, darlin'. I'm sorry. She just makes me so—"

"I don't want to hear it. Just go to bed and leave me alone." She continued flipping through the channels, refusing to look at him.

"Let me say this." Desi said, rubbing his bald scalp. "I was wrong to go there. I have no excuse. She's not here a week and already building a wedge between us. Don't let her do that, Ay. I love you just as much as she does."

Aya pondered what he had said, but when she made no immediate reply, he went to bed.

She was up until the early hours re-reading Marley's letter. She didn't know what to do. Just a few more nights and it would be New Year's Eve and he would be there. Somehow that gave her great comfort.

Chapter 21

When Marva arrived the next morning, Aya was still sleeping and Desi and the boys were in the kitchen with Pearl. The boys were wolfing down the eggs and praising Pearl's cooking, but Desi was picking at his food and not saying much. Marva tucked herself around the corner to eavesdrop.

"You're getting very small, Des, you need to eat more," Pearl said. "A man should be bigger than his wife."

The boys chortled and finished their meal, then headed out back together.

Pearl continued to goad Desi. "You should be ravenous after a night of vigorous lovemaking! Don't worry, it's not poisoned."

"How you getting home?" Desi snapped.

"Why? You gonna take me?" She giggled. "I might turn up like Lucinda."

"Whatever you playing at, it ain't gonna work. I'm telling you, stop messing with me."

"I'm actually deeply concerned. Your appearance is a little alarming, Des. You're too thin. I can see it in your face and it's aging you. You on the bottle again or is it…"

Marva heard chair legs scraping across the floor as Desi rose from the table. "Hurry and tell your sister you coming home," he said bitingly and left her.

When Desi came around the corner, shoulders slumping, Marva pretended she had just come in. "You look miserable nuff," she said. "You got to stop letting that woman get to you. You got the baby coming, remember?"

At that he smiled and corrected his posture. He put his hand on her shoulder and said, "See if you can get rid of her for me."

Marva wondered where this about-face was coming from. The Missus didn't ever have much to say about her mother, and now the woman was always around. It was clear that the Missus wasn't too happy about the intrusion, yet she wasn't in a hurry to do anything about it.

Then there was Pearl to worry about. What was she playing at? Marva was determined to get to the bottom of it. She could smell the breakfast that had been prepared and got even more apprehensive. Pearl was a much better cook than Marva, even Desi used to rave about it back in the day. If she took up residence in the household, there would be little need for Marva—baby or no baby. The Missus would obviously prefer to have her mother's free help with the child than her own.

Although the Missus had made assurances that she would never put Marva out, Pearl might have other ideas. All Marva had was Desi to support her, and if it came to choosing between her and his wife, she would be the guaranteed loser. All this made her stomach cramp and her bottom lip protrude even farther than usual.

"Marva? Is that you?" Pearl asked while sticking her head around the corner.

"Mm-hmm," she mumbled and followed Pearl into the kitchen. She would have to get in between the Missus and her mother before they were able to fully reconcile. There was no other way. It's not that Marva didn't want them to have a proper relationship; she couldn't do that to the Missus. But she could not have Pearl usurping her hard-earned position. She could visit and care for the child on occasion, but the primary guardianship had to be with Marva. The little Franklyn would be the child she never had and would secure her comfort in her rapidly approaching old age.

"Come have some food, Desi didn't eat much," Pearl said and pulled out the seat next to her at the island.

Although Marva knew it was best that she be the most professional and efficient she had ever been until she was safe, the food was too tempting to miss. "Wrap it for me and I'll eat it on my break later."

"What? Come sit with me, I don't have anyone to talk to. Besides, it tastes best now when it's hot. You don't want to have to reheat this, do you?"

She couldn't be more right. Marva's mouth was already watering at the pile of sausage and scrambled eggs sitting in front of her. There was also freshly baked salt bread with a thick slice of honey ham stuffed in it and stringy slices of bacon on the side. Marva put down her several bags, took a seat, and began to eat. Pearl put away Marva's things in their usual place in the pantry. Little did she know that the reason for this practice was so that Marva could stuff those bags with items from within. No one seemed to question why she would need to bring an oversized purse, overnight bag, and duffle bag with her every day. Marva hadn't bought her own toilet paper in over a decade.

"It taste all right?" Pearl asked, returning to the island.

"Mm-hmm," Marva mumbled, trying to not appear as enthusiastic as she felt.

"Well, at least you'll eat it. Aya only craves sweets and Desi eats less than a sparrow. What's wrong with him? He's looking real old and boney. You're feeding him, aren't you?"

"Yes!" Marva said. "I make sure to leave good food for him, but he don't eat at regular times due to work. He gonna take it easy soon though."

"He's been saying that for as long as I've known him. He was going to ease up once Junior was able to manage, and now both he and Carlton are grown and he still won't let go. There's always some excuse. Not like there's anything wrong with loving your work, mind you. It's just that Aya needs more than a part-time husband."

That Desi was too set in his ways was not news to Marva. With the baby coming, things could surely change. "I tell you, he retiring in the new year. He just need a good rest, and a month home should do it. I'll make sure he get it and that he eat good and regular."

"It's funny that he doesn't want to be home all the time with his wife. I mean, he proclaims his undying love for her yet is not bothered that he doesn't see her much."

Marva knew she had to be careful with her remarks. She could not compromise Desi at any cost. "You wait," she replied cautiously.

"Yes," Pearl smiled. "Especially now that Marley is coming back and a baby is on the way."

"Marley?" Marva nearly choked on the ham in her mouth. "What he coming back for?"

"He lives here from time to time, you know? He can help motivate Aya to start writing again." She lowered her voice to a whisper. "Hopefully her condition won't get in the way."

Marva thought on that. If the Missus ended up leaving Desi, that would mean she would have to pick up the pieces: an even easier route to job security. Even though in her heart she would prefer to raise a child and be a part of a proper family.

It was clear Pearl was still trying to come between the Franklyns. Whether she was trying to oust her daughter to take her place remained to be seen. There was no going back with Desi as far as Marva was concerned. It was alarming how much he despised Pearl, while she seemed focused on living upon the razor thin line between love and hate.

"Thanks for the breakfast," Marva said finally. "I got to get to work. I want everything ready for Old Year's Night."

"Aren't they going out?"

"Yeah, but I'm gonna spend the night here with Ricky and watch the ball drop. We're sending for Chinese and all. Can't wait."

"Really? I would've thought you'd want to be with friends or family."

"Me? I don't wanna have to dress up to get somewhere and worry how to get back. I don't drink and can just put my feet up and relax. And I don't mind staying with him," she was quick to add so it would not seem as though she was doing it more for herself than anything else.

The two women hushed as Aya came into the room, still in the T-shirt she had slept in. She looked like hell and they were at a loss for words.

"You feeling all right?" her mother asked.

"I didn't sleep too well." Aya grabbed a cold bottle of water out of the fridge.

"Well, sit down here. You want some of this food?" Pearl asked.

"Look more like she need to go lie down," Marva added.

"I kept tossing and turning so I decided to come out for a bit," said Aya, who proceeded to eat all that remained of Pearl's breakfast.

Pearl and Marva looked at each other and nodded. She was definitely pregnant.

Chapter 22

Aya got some interesting news when she returned to her OBGYN for her results. She decided to sleep on it first to make up her own mind before informing her husband.

He had become amicable again after her mother had gone back to Bea's, except she had not yet told him that her mother had returned to the island for good.

New Year's Eve arrived, and though she was hardly in the mood to party, she knew Desi had spent a large sum to give her a night out, so she dressed sexy enough to make him proud. Forever preoccupied as Aya was with Marley, she had not realized how lean Desi had gotten again lately until she saw that his suit was falling off him.

They arrived at the village early to get a good parking space and prime seating. Neither Aya nor Desi ate much, but Desi drank pretty hard right from the beginning.

Aya kept asking her husband if anything was wrong, and although he was clearly troubled, he would brush her off and change the subject. He kept looking for someone, then fretted as though he did not actually want to see them.

Aya tried to alleviate his concerns by reminding him that her mother and aunt were coming with a group of people and would not be sitting with them. Shortly after, they did come to their table briefly and then made a hasty retreat, but not before Pearl asked why Aya was not drinking alcohol while her husband reeked of it, to which Aya replied that it would make her too hot and drowsy.

Associates of Desi's would come to the table offering greetings from time to time; however, the Franklyns were mostly left alone to sit in long silences. It wasn't until she heard Marley's laugh that Aya came to life. She made sure not to look in his direction as she was aware that Desi was astutely studying her face.

"If you not up to this we can go home, you know," he said innocently. "We could be back in time to see the fireworks from the balcony. Even get some of that Chinese before they finish it."

Aya was determined not to go anywhere. "Oh no," she answered quickly. "We haven't even danced yet. The night is cool and the stars are bright and beautiful. I'm fine. Besides, the way you've been drinking, you'd better rest a bit. Why don't you order a coffee?"

"Then I'll be up all night. You can handle that?" He smirked and leaned in to kiss her brow. "I'll go get some punch, you want some?"

Aya shook her head and was glad to get a moment away from him. She scanned the dance floor for Marley, who could not be found. When she turned to look about the seated area, she caught Desi studying her again. She decided to sit still. It was foolish of her to think of reconnecting with Marley where there were so many eyes about. It would be much better in private. She would email him at her first opportunity under the guise of wishing all her contacts a happy new year. It would be up to him to take the hint.

Desi returned with a drink for her even though she did not want it, then asked her to dance. It was creeping toward midnight, the music was bumping, and Aya was pleased to be able to circulate around the floor.

Desi was smooth on his feet, and she actually found herself enjoying him and even forgetting her condition, which threatened to ruin her evening. Pearl jokingly tried to intercept and dance with Desi, but he grimaced and ignored her. Both mother and daughter laughed at that.

The midnight countdown came, and Desi gave his wife a deeply embarrassing sloppy kiss. Aya could not imagine what had gotten into him to do that in front of everybody and put it down to the booze. Pearl, who did not miss a moment of their interaction, knew it was something else entirely. She came over to the couple, offered Desi champagne, and wished them all well for the year of new beginnings.

Desi stiffened and finished the glass in one shot, and said nothing. Aya hugged her mother, feeling deflated to have not once been able to lay her eyes on Marley.

Everyone proceeded down the path to the sea as the fireworks started. Aya was sandwiched between her mother and her husband as they watched the twelve-minute display and could not even look around. Aya knew Desi would not want to remain after they had finished and she was losing her chance, but thankfully, they were on the coast, where several hotels had boats lined up to stagger their shows, and they were able to witness another twenty-three minutes as fireworks went off down the shore.

A good portion of the crowd returned to the dance floor, while the majority headed for their cars. Desi wanted to join them, so Aya tried to convince him that it would be too busy to leave now and that they should wait until after the rush. Her husband was worried their vehicle would be blocked in as had happened in the past, so he decided to go check on things.

Aya let him go, and her mother quickly disappeared as well. Aya walked down to the sea and put both her swollen feet in, finding the cool water incredibly refreshing. Then all the hairs on her body stood up as she felt a presence. She turned to see Marley right behind her, looking as loveable as ever and with a pronounced grin on his face. He put his arms around her in his standard bear hug.

"Marley! I can't believe it," she said, keeping an eye on her surroundings for anyone who might be observing.

"Happy New Year, my dear. You look wonderful as usual, if a little tired. How are you feeling?"

"You can see in the dark?" She laughed. "I'm good. Really. I haven't been doing any writing, but I'll start back again in January. There are a few things I need to get sorted first."

"Well, I'm always here for you. I'm happy to help you get going in any way. I hope we can at least discuss some of the ideas you're working on. Did you get my card?" he asked, leaning in closer.

Aya had been waiting for this moment and now felt so flustered. "Yes, my mother brought it for me. How do you know her?"

"Changing the topic as usual," Marley quipped. "Your aunt put her on to me. She sent her down to one of my book signings to check me out. You know, since you and I had worked so well together. So, what did you think of my letter?"

"You gave me a lot to think about, to be honest. I'm a little confused. Sadly, now is not the time to talk about this, Marl," she said nervously.

"I agree. What are you doing tomorrow? I could swing by and take you for lunch."

Aya's mind raced and she stumbled through her reply. "I don't know. I think Desi has plans. I'll have to see how the day goes."

"You mean see if you can sneak away." Marley laughed. "No worries, I understand. I want to give you a draft of what I've been working on lately. I wrote it in six weeks! I've dedicated it to you, and I really want to know what you think, love."

Aya felt like she was floating on air—until the tide came in high and soaked her up to her thighs. She screamed, and the pair jumped up onto a rock.

Aya laughed wholeheartedly. "Of course I'll read it. We'll meet up soon. Oh man, that water is cold. I'm going to freeze sitting in this dress all the way home."

Marley reached down, lifted the bottom of her knee-high black chiffon dress, and rung it out for her. Desi appeared out of nowhere, yanking Aya off the rock and catching her in his arms.

"Des, what the hell?" Aya shrieked. "You twisted my wrist."

"Are you all right?" Marley asked, taking her arm and ignoring Desi altogether. "Does it hurt?"

"She's fine," Desi snapped, snatching her hand away. He turned to Aya. "I heard you screaming and didn't know who he was. I thought you were in trouble."

"No, the water came in and it startled us. Marley was just helping. You remember him, right? He's giving me a draft of his work to preview," Aya said, focusing on her dress.

Marley held out his hand to Desi. "Nice to see you again."

Desi ignored the proffered hand. "Yeah, hi." He turned back to his wife. "We better get you home and out of that wet, hon. Let's go."

Aya sighed. "Oh, all right." She turned her attention to Marley. "Please bring me the draft as soon as you can. Don't have too much fun now so you get home in one piece."

On the drive home, Aya nervously fussed over her wet dress and sandy feet.

"I didn't know he was back living here?" Desi said gingerly as the vehicle climbed up the last hill toward home.

"Who, Marley?" Aya said. "I don't think he's been here long. We only spoke briefly."

"So you all will be back at *it* again?"

"'It'? I told you, he's giving me his manuscript. I don't have mine yet. I haven't even begun to begin, so there's nothing for us to work on. Please hurry, I really have to go to the washroom."

Desi dropped the subject. He noticed she had used the restroom at least once an hour that evening and an awful lot the past couple of days. He was sure it was the result of being in her first trimester.

Aya rushed right into the bedroom to clean up while Desi looked in on the others. Marva was fast asleep on the couch with her head back and mouth wide open, snoring. Ricky was stuffing popcorn into his mouth while dancing with the performers on the television.

Upon seeing his father, Ricky rushed over to him, gave him a big hug, and showed him his dance moves, making Desi chuckle.

A hard snore shocked Marva awake. When she saw that Desi was home, she wriggled at being caught out. "So you home, then? Where the Missus?"

"In the washroom. Again," he stressed, giving her a wink.

"You get home later than expected. You all had a good time?" she asked.

"It was nice." He hiccupped. "I drank a little," he admitted while trying to copy his son's dance moves.

"Little? I can smell it from here. That not like you. The Mother get to ya?"

Desi simply shook his head and focused on his steps. Marva sat watching them another forty minutes, when they all decided they'd had enough. When Desi came into the bedroom, Aya was sleeping fitfully on her side with her hand on her swollen abdomen. After bathing, Desi lay down next to his wife and put his hand over hers. Her belly was hot like a fever and sporadically quivering. It was the best feeling.

Later that afternoon, the doorbell rang and Desi went to answer it. His eyes narrowed when Marley came in, grinning and asking for his wife. Aya, who was sitting at the breakfast table, jumped to her feet and rushed him outside the door, speaking in hushed tones. Desi moved to a position where he could hear and not be seen.

"Marley, I thought we would call first."

"Sorry, dear, I wanted to give you the draft before I go. I'm catching a plane to the States in a couple of hours as an unexpected opportunity may be coming my way. I went around back looking for you and discovered some half-naked thug in there. I was jealous!"

"Oh, that's Desi's eldest. I've moved over to the other side now. So how long will you be gone?"

"No more than a couple of weeks. I'm extending my stay here afterwards. We can catch up properly then, so try to finish reading it."

"That's fine, Marl, please call first and let me know when you get back. It's probably best that we meet someplace else in the future. I'll let you know." Desi thought she sounded nervous.

Marley promised he would. Aya stayed and watched him back out the driveway. Desi was waiting for her in the kitchen when she came in.

"He sure popping up a lot lately," he said, then swallowed his pills with a large glass of coconut water.

"He brought me the manuscript." Aya sat back down at the table. "He's going back overseas for a while and wanted me to have it. Come sit with me a minute. We need to talk."

Desi gave his wife a quizzical stare and slowly sat down next to her.

"You're looking real frail these days, Des. Several people have asked me about it, even last night. None of your clothes fit anymore. What's going on?"

"I've been working a little too hard, I know it. There's a lot of pressure in this business sometimes, Aya. But," he promised softly, "I'm taking time off as soon as this one finish."

"You're getting thin and hardly eat anything, Des. I'm getting concerned. And then all the hard drinking ..."

"You talking 'bout me? You were the one in and out of the bathroom all night. You didn't eat anything much either, or take the champagne I ordered for us to celebrate. What's going on with you?"

"Right now I'm dealing with you. I want you to go to the doctor and get a full checkup, and I'm coming with you to make sure."

"I don't need no doctor." He pushed back his chair and looked up at the ceiling. "You the one who should get the annual. You haven't been since we married."

"I've been twice already and I know what's going on," Aya blurted out, then looked as if she regretted it.

"What is it?" Desi smiled and took her hand.

"Well, I've got a few large fibroids that are messing with me. I've got some kind of hormonal imbalance to sort out. I'm still doing the research and seeking advice," she answered sullenly.

Desi was confused. "So that sends you to the washroom?"

"Well, my periods can be very heavy so I keep having to change or check that everything is okay. It never used to be like this, but lately, things are out of control. I didn't drink because alcohol thins the blood and that would exacerbate the issue. It explains a lot though. The doctor described things that I hadn't even realized were symptoms. Like uncomfortable intercourse due to the pressure. In many ways it's a relief to know."

Desi was stunned. He could not wrap his head around what he was hearing. His wife was menstruating heavily, so she surely wasn't pregnant. On top of that, she didn't enjoy his lovemaking. His head was reeling.

"Don't panic," Aya assured him. "I've weighed my options and I'm not having surgery. They wanted me to get a hysterectomy because of my age."

At that remark, Desi's eyes went wide and wild. He put his head down to rest in both of his hands to stop himself from collapsing. As it was, his ears were ringing so loudly he could barely hear her.

Aya moved her chair closer to him and rubbed his back. "There are other procedures that can be done. I have options, so I'm not doing anything drastic. It would only be urgent if we wanted to have children, and since we don't, I'm going to try the holistic approach for a year and maybe investigate a centre in Miami that offers treatment."

Desi raised his head to fight back the tears forming in his eyes.

"I'll be all right, Des, really. I just don't know what's been going on with me the past couple of months. I'm going to a specialist in February, who wants to see everything that I've been taking since my hormones are off the chart all of a sudden. I don't think its age either."

That remark gave Desi pause. He had to swallow his vomit, and he started sweating profusely.

"My God, Desi, don't take on so. You better lay down." Aya raised him and helped him to the couch. She then went to get him some cold water.

Desi drank it thirstily and slowly regained his composure. Now Aya was the one who looked confused.

"I just love you so much, Aya," he said finally. "Don't you think you should do something 'bout it now? I mean, to be bleeding so heavy and not enjoying my loving at all."

"I didn't say that. I work from home so I can handle the heavier flow for now. I mostly need to get to the bottom of why it is coming like this lately. I'm treating it and getting all the advice I can. So don't worry about me, you need to take care of yourself now. I know you like to keep busy, but you could do many things around the house. You've wanted to renovate for quite some time, remember? That'll keep you more than occupied. You need to take it easy, Des, we can't both be down."

"All right, hon," Desi agreed. "I'll get checked out and take time home."

"Thank you." Aya patted his hand and rose. "Now you lay here and rest. I need to go to the bathroom again."

The tears started falling once Aya left the room. Desi wiped them away quickly in case Marva or one of the boys showed up. He had never felt so completely desolate. Not only had he already been for a full medical, he had seen two specialists and an oncologist about his relapse. Although he'd be damned if he ever let anyone know it.

Chapter 23

Aya cherished every moment that she could find to be alone. She needed privacy to read Marley's words, which were clearly about his feelings for her. The working title was *Favoured*, and it was about a couple who had other attachments but kept being drawn to each other. They felt an immense attraction that neither of them could ignore and would not act on. The novel explored the outcomes of them getting together at different periods of their lives, and it came to the conclusion that the present is always the best time, for to delay causes serious trauma later on. It ended rather cleverly with the choice being left up to the reader, who is meant to be Aya.

It was a delicious read and showed how clearly Marley saw her without her ever knowing it. She could not believe the intensity that she had created in this man, and now she had to consider what her own reaction would be.

It was unfortunate that she had married the way that she did. She should have looked before she leaped, even though things had worked out halfway decent. Yes, Desi was a stick in the mud; still, they complemented each other well enough. He had kept up his end of the agreement and Aya didn't want for much. Except for the twinge of excitement and comfort she felt and the sexual desire that ran rampant throughout her body every time she was near Marley.

That was a line that she should never have crossed with Desi. He was a fatherly figure to her and she would never find herself getting excited by him. Although being naughty in this way had its initial pleasures, that had worn out long ago. She was now left with a man whose life force was dwindling before her eyes.

Aya felt a pang of guilt at that. She did not want Desi to be unhappy on account of her. After all, he had helped her out of a dire situation. He had given her a beautiful home and a sporty compact utility vehicle, he covered all the bills, and she didn't have to lift a finger. Although Marva's services were rarely consistent, she was helpful enough that Aya could focus on her writing all day and night if she wanted. When it came to what Aya had to offer Desi, she drew a blank.

Yes, he had a fine, sensuous wife to make him proud. He had an in-house supply of sex, only that had never been an issue for him anyway. He didn't even want her to be a mother to his children, and he was genuinely contented to buy her things or take her anywhere she had shown the slightest interest in.

So why did he marry her? Could it be that he was as crazy in love as one would have to be to give so much for so little? Or was he trying to get back at her parents as her mother repeatedly suggested?

Why would he be so in love with her? She had barely glanced at him growing up. He certainly didn't have to marry Aya as he could have tried seducing her the way he'd done so many women. No, he had insisted on marrying from the get-go. He coveted her, even though he had been with her mother. Perhaps that was why he bedded Pearl in the first place. No, Desi was a man who slept around. So then why tie himself to the daughter of his dearest friend and ex-lover?

Aya could not figure it out and wondered why it had taken her so long into the marriage to really consider the question. She did feel that Desi loved her, even if there was something more going on. It had to be the real reason behind his suffering and, although she did not cause it, she was of little help.

Aya did not feel that Desi was unhappy in the relationship. He liked that she was mostly home and to herself. He appreciated her efforts to help out in the house and how orderly she kept things. He praised her role as stepmother and adored her understated fashion sense.

These were all things Aya had thought she wanted in her man when she was single, only now she realized they didn't mean enough when the love was lacking. She would be happy to live above a rum shop as long as she was with the man she cherished. No matter how much he loved her, Aya needed to love passionately in return.

She had thought she had felt that with Bradley. She now realized it was some other needy, addictive emotion that had taken over her life when she was involved with him. It was giving real love that was the essence of a successful partnership. That was why she had been so distant with Desi lately, other than her imbalanced hormones. He kept throwing trinkets at her that had no meaning for her because she didn't truly love him.

Aya knew the grass always seems greener on the other side, and she could not imagine taking such a risk. Somehow, though, she also knew the opportunity to know and experience something real could not be ignored.

She had no idea how Marley would be as a partner or if she could give him all that he needed. What if she didn't satisfy him sexually, what then? There were too many moving parts. She had made a little money, although not enough to support herself. She could move in with Marley, except she wanted him to respect her as an independent woman, so she would have to get a job, which would put a damper on her writing at this crucial time as well as be a major step backward in her career. Moving in with her mother and aunt would be a humungous sacrifice. Could she really do it?

And what about Desi? How would he handle a separation? Would it turn nasty like it had with her parents? Would he throw out her things, change the locks, and empty all the accounts? Aya was certain he would be irate to be left for another man and put on a show for inquiring eyes to prove himself manly. She would have to leave the island.

Maybe he already sensed that something was up when he hired that firm to take over the accounts from her. He never included her in any business decision anymore when that used to be all he'd talk about. She hadn't known what to make of it at the time and had chosen to focus on her writing.

All these thoughts swirled around in Aya's head for many days and sleepless nights. She was able to cover by pretending to be working on her next novel, and the family gave her plenty of space. She needed to find an answer before Marley returned to the island at the end of the month.

Chapter 24

"Oh loss, Glenda! I dunno what I gonna do." Marva steadied herself to sit on a crate under the large frangipani tree in the back corner of her yard. It was a moonless night, and her heavily medicated mother was upfront watching her soap opera with the volume up to maximum.

"That mad woman in there on my last nerve. I can't take it no more! She cuss me hard and strong on the front porch for all to hear. She bawl that I trying to kill her and that my ninety-eight-pound self beat her. Me? You believe that? Her two-hundred-sixty-seven-pound flabby ass! She carry on so bad and I feel so shamed I could barely hold up my head.

"I was sure everyone could tell she gone off, but the way they look at me cut me cold. The whole gap come out to see what going on too, and that bucktooth Sally got the nerve to say she gonna call and report it and get that old bag put up safe in that home in Crestfield. Ain't that the one that near beat that blind man to death? ...

"As soon as she satisfied with the damage she done cause, she get quiet and wheel herself inside as calm as ever. She sit in the front room behind the drapes listening to everyone talking and all happy with herself. She make me sick! Lord forgive me but I have half a mind to throw some kerosene in there and light the place up. It just too much, Glenda. Too much …

"I don't wanna hear that! I got every right to be angry! Every right. How the ass can I stop letting her get to me? You know how she is, and she getting worse all the time. I'd be happy nuff for them to lock her up, then she could sell the place or rent it and have me put out. What kinda mother that is? Why I been cursed like this? The Lord must be real vexed with me.

"Then to make things worse, the Missus ain't even pregnant. Glenda, that near broke my heart. And Desi's too. Fact is, she can't even really get pregnant, or stay pregnant, with her condition. She got some woman trouble, and I here thinking I got a baby to raise. Even if she lucky, it could take years for her to breed, and I tell you, Desi don't got that much time.

"That Marley be sniffing 'round her again. He ain't got no business to come after a married woman like that. He wearing her down, and Desi too blasted foolish to do something 'bout it …

"Yes, he looking better these days. He put on a little weight when he stayed home those few weeks, but now some emergency come up and he right back working long again. Leaving the Missus at home to read that Rasta's book and texting, calling, or chatting to him on the computer. I saw them. She has on headphones to listen when he talks to her while she types her answers so I dunno what they talking 'bout. It ain't good, that for sure …

"How you mean, how I know? I know, is all. She light up these days, all giggly and excited. I never seen her like that and it got me so worried, Glenda. And Desi so wutless, he think it 'cause he getting better. He feel safe that Marley not on the island, but he couldn't be more on the Missus's mind. All hell gonna break loose when he finally do come, I know it …

"I mean she gonna start seeing him then. Desi won't be in the dark too much longer and he not gonna be easy. She a fool if she think he just gonna let her leave him like that. Desi can be real vindictive when he ready, and her mother could tell her nuff 'bout that. She another one who been circling like a vulture, that Pearl. I know she up to something. She in the midst a all this, stirring the pot. I'm ready for her though, you watch, Glenda. The Lord will help me …

"Girl, I hope you right. I can't see what the Missus thinking, messing with that ragamuffin. Maybe she'll get tired a him and stay

Franklyn before too long. I sure hope she not planning on keeping both a them though …

"Yeah, I know men do it all the time. Hell, it would serve Desi right to have it done to him like he done so many times. But, he ain't gonna see it like that. He would kill the Missus dead. Oh Lord, Glenda, I dunno what to do. No peace where I live or where I work. My future gone up in smoke. I can't even sleep at night for fretting. I shout at Ricky the other day so bad I make him cry. All I wanted to do was come home and get a good night's rest and the heifer had to offset everything …

"I know, I know. Trust in the Lord. But I so tired a struggling, Glenda. I tired, ya hear me? Why you life so easy and mine so shite? Not that I grudge you any, but it easy for you to keep telling me to be patient when you never had to …

"Ya lie! You leaving Marshall? Seem to me you left him long ago. You never forgave him for sending you children overseas to study when he was right to do it. You been too caught up in their lives for too long and he wanted his wife back. He wanted you to spend time together again, without it being all 'bout them. He told me so and I let you know it, remember? Still you ignore him and treat him bad, Glenda …

"Yes you did! You never gave him a chance. He loved you. You kids got good education, good jobs, and good lives 'cause a him. What you want them here doing? Sure, it might'a come out the same, but they happy and don't wanna come back. I think you more angry with them 'bout that than with Marshall for anything. You miss you babies, I know. They grown and got they own lives and starting they own families. You can't let that good man go, Glenda. You just can't …

"Stop yelling at me! I had nuff a that tonight already. Course I on you side, that why I telling you the truth. You gonna regret it if you don't fix things with you husband …

"It not too late. He still love you, he just tired a being hurt. I know he'll forgive you. Yes, forgive you for checking out on him …

"So what if he had other women? You cut him off, didn't you? What, you think he just gonna walk 'round with his legs cross? You know a woman that kept her man by making him go without? You just hurt yourself with all these things you been doing, Glenda, and blaming everyone else. I ain't never had a man love me, but if one did even half as much as Marshall did you, I'd never leave him. Me? ...

"I hear what you saying. I know love a two-way street. You know, I wonder if that what the problem be with the Missus too. Desi love her hard, and she okay with him until that Marley come confusing her head. He young and fine and sexy. She got another man to run to if Desi don't kill them first. But what you gonna do, Glenda? You gonna move into some small apartment and be by yourself? ...

"Wha'? You blackmailing me now? If I don't move in with you, you gonna leave and be with you children? That the worst mistake you make yet. Who says they want you 'round them all the time? Did they ask you to come? ...

"I thought so. You go down there and force yourself on them and they come 'round to resent you soon nuff. You asking to visit be one thing, packing to stay without telling them be another ...

"Okay, if you get you own apartment nearby, how you know you gonna like living up there? You hate the cold. You never been there a winter yet. They gonna be working all day and wanna be with their friends and family mostly. I not saying this to be cruel. You not the only one who pack up for their kids and end up lonely in a strange place. Then they don't have anywhere to come back to once the money gone. I just telling you straight. Visit them as often as you want, without movin' there. I ain't saying it to be selfish neither, if it was for you own good I'd pack you bags and you know it ...

"You may be right 'bout that, I dunno how this whole Franklyn thing gonna play out. I happy nuff to leave this hovel, so I may have to move in with you for true. We'll see what plans the ol' witch has for me. Even though I make you cuss me, you know I love you true nuff. I wouldn't put you wrong. Me? Think hard before leaving you husband, and I'd tell the Missus the same thing ...

"All right, all right. I not arguing with you no more. I done with that for one evening. I gotta get me a good night's sleep before I drop. We talk tomorrow."

Chapter 25

It was a drizzly afternoon and the sun had just set below the choppy Atlantic Ocean horizon as Aya drove down Old East Coast Road to a discreet villa. She pulled her silver Toyota Rush into the coral stone driveway and put it into park, flipping through a tabloid as she waited for Marley to arrive.

Her heart pounded in her ears when she observed Marley's black-and-white Mini Cooper pull in. The time had finally come. Thankfully, Desi was working that evening, giving her at least four hours to talk and get home before raising any alarm.

Only she was sure Marva was suspicious. She had told Marva she was going to watch the movie that she was tired of waiting on Desi to go to. Marva had offered to come along and sleep over, so Aya lied, saying she had other errands to run and was not sure whether she would even really get to the cinema in time. Since Desi and the boys were out working late on a Friday night and Desi was sure to treat the boys to dinner, she told Marva there was no point in her sticking around.

This created the perfect opportunity for Aya to meet Marley, and she hoped it would continue for weeks. As long as Marva was out of the house and she made it home before Desi and the boys, no one would be the wiser.

"My dear," Marley said. "Come, give me a hug."

Aya picked up his manuscript, which she had brought with her everywhere in his absence, and went to his arms. Marley gave her the usual warm bear hug, and then he put both his hands on her cheeks.

"You look better than ever, babe. You seem happy. Now, I wonder why that is?"

"I am happy to see you, Marley. I have so many ideas for the next book. You renting this villa?" she asked while he took out his luggage and forced open the front door.

"Nah, this belongs to a relative who lets it out. I stay here when I need a place to crash. With no neighbours nearby, it's a great place for finalizing a draft. I love listening to the pounding surf, and the smell of the sea spray is incredibly soothing. You know the next land mass is Africa? This place is where I feel most at home in the world."

"It is beautiful here," Aya agreed. "Is it safe though? It seems very isolated. I mean, there aren't even any street lights."

"You're always safe with me. Come, make yourself comfortable. It was a long flight and I need to wash up. Help yourself to whatever you want."

"I'm good," Aya said, taking in her surroundings. The sky-blue villa was quite rustic, and dry rot was everywhere. The furniture was deep mahogany, rugged and bare. Tiny transparent lizards could be found in many dark corners as they welcomed the gloom. Aya made her way out onto the front terrace and sat down to a view that overlooked mangroves and the sea.

A short while later, Marley emerged dripping wet with only his towel wrapped around his waist. His muscles glistening, he beamed with pride and joy. "You all right, love?"

"I'm fine, just waiting on you to get dressed."

"I like to air dry," he said, standing at the rail next to her. "So tell me what you think of my book?"

"I like it very much, I've told you that. I love your style, how every plot has layers within layers, how you describe subtle nuances. You are so creative. If I can be a tenth as good as you, I'll be happy," she gushed.

"Oh, you'll be better than me, love." He cuddled up next to her. "Right now we need to talk about us. Are you staying with me tonight?"

"Here? What do you mean?" Aya asked incredulously.

"Come on, Aya. I asked you here so we could be together. Really be together. You know what I mean?"

Aya gasped and stood up.

"No, no, not that." Marley stood to block her exit. "Well, yes, that too. Don't you have feelings for me?"

"I'm confused. I just don't know about, well …" Aya stammered.

"I didn't ask about your confusion, I asked how you feel about me. Look at me," he said, holding Aya's arms and making her face him.

"Please put your clothes on," was all she could say as she squirmed to look away. Marley dropped his towel entirely to reveal himself. A surge of arousal exploded throughout Aya's body as he pressed himself close to her. It was past dusk and she could only faintly make out his features. She knew she had to stay standing. For if he got her down, it would be over.

"I stand here before you naked. Like with my narrative, I have left myself vulnerable and exposed to you, and this time I must have an answer. I need you, can't you feel that? I've never wanted a woman so much," he said with great urgency.

"I'm married, Marley," she pleaded. "You can't do this, Desi doesn't deserve—"

"He deserves this and more! Can you tell me he makes you feel the way I do? Tell me honestly?"

"It's different." She hesitated before saying, "He's not all bad, Marley."

He let go of her arms. "Why are you here, then?"

"You asked me," Aya answered, choking up.

"You didn't have to come! I'm sure you had to lie about coming to see me, why hide it? Why did you need to meet me to discuss your ideas? We've been talking for weeks now. When I asked you to join me here, you jumped at the chance. You couldn't wait. I could tell." He picked up his towel and sat back down on the chair, covering himself.

"It's true," Aya said quietly, fighting back tears. "I wanted to see you. I read your work and was thrilled to know you felt that way about me. It gave me all kinds of ideas about what could be between us, and it was exciting. My life has not gone at all the way I thought it would, and you come along and offer me a glimpse of something extraordinary. You make me feel so special."

"You are special, love," he said. "So dear to me, you wouldn't believe."

"I needed to feel that way so badly. I used to know that before, but it left me, so I just went along with whatever came my way. I could only take that for so long and I jumped at a chance to make things happen. I packed up my life and came here for a change, only it didn't take long for me to realize that everything had followed me here too. So I tried to leave and go someplace else, and my efforts were constantly thwarted. I felt so defeated, Marley. Then Desi came along and ..."

"He offered you his island to run to."

"Yes," Aya answered. "He was kind to me, gentle and supportive. He never asked me for much, just to be there for him. He gives me everything and anything."

"I don't doubt he cares for you. He'd have to be a madman not to realize how fortunate he is and not try to hang on to you with every cent he can muster. Are you truly happy, love? Is he, for that matter? Would you be with him if he didn't have the money, honestly?"

"I didn't marry him for that, Marley." Aya sulked. "I didn't know what he had. I did it because I wanted to get out of Auntie's house. I was so tired of that tiny room, like a prison. And the constant parade of middle-aged women trying to act like their lives are not empty with the same conversations all the time. I did not want to end up like her, or like them. Every day the same routine. I was so sick of it, I had to get out before I went crazy."

Aya sat down next to Marley. "Desi gave me an out, and I took it. I knew him well enough to know that he would keep his word. He is the only man in my life who always has, and that was enough,"

"Are you happy?"

"I was satisfied," she answered. "It's not up to Desi to make me happy. He gave me the space to be creative and not have to worry about anything else. He's not perfect, but he's been good to me, and I'm not easy to get along with either."

Marley ran his hands through his drying dreads. "So you're saying that no matter what you feel for me—which you still refuse to admit— you will not leave your husband, who you feel you owe. Correct?"

"I do have strong feelings for you. I adore you, Marley, and love being around you. With you I'd never get bored, you stimulate me on all levels. Alas, love has not been good to me and you're probably better off with someone else. I don't know what I'm going to do about my husband. That's between him and me."

"That's why I wrote that chapter on going with the flow and not against the natural forces," Marley said. "You need to reread that, my dear. You don't believe you deserve to be happy, so you're still settling. Your heart was severely broken all those years ago, and you refuse to expose yourself again. I get that, it's happened to all of us. Desi can't hurt you since you don't care enough about him, so you'll stay with the devil you know instead of taking a chance on the one you don't. With me, you'll have to feel things and stretch muscles you've forgotten about. You can only stay stagnant for so long, Aya. Sooner or later you have to let go and grow. You have to know by now that you can do that safely with me."

"Marley, you're very dear to me, only you have to let this go. I'm in no position to be in a relationship with you—or anyone—right now. I have to sort out my life on my own."

Marley laced his fingers and rested his elbows on his knees. A sharp wind rose out of the west suddenly, and he wrapped himself in his towel and stared out at the coastline. Aya wanted to reach out to him in the dark but decided against it. She did not know what to do; in spite of this, she did not want to leave.

"I'll give you time," Marley said finally. "Are you asking me to stay away too?"

"I value your friendship so much, that's entirely up to you. If we can't be around each other, maybe we should just talk on the phone or online?"

He leaned in to kiss her and Aya could not resist; it felt as natural as breathing. He enveloped her body with his to shield her from the cooling February evening, and the world slipped away.

Chapter 26

Later that evening in bed, Desi gave his wife yet another inquisitive look. "Aya, you sure you all right? No matter what you say, I can see something troubling you. You won't look at me and you fidgeting like crazy. You hormones acting up again?"

Aya turned to look at her rapidly aging husband. As she studied his face, her mind transformed him into Marley, looking at her with loving eyes. She could still feel his warm strokes on her body. She did not hear anything that Desi was saying to her; it was as if he were merely a ghost. When he came close to her, she blocked out his smell and replaced it with one she found more rousing. He kissed her tenderly, and she sucked him in.

Aya nearly devoured her husband's body, stretching his briefs beyond repair and kissing him passionately. After four years of her contrived interest, Desi struggled to keep up with her. She rode him vigorously, trying not to get distracted by his heavy panting.

"Aya, you need to ease up some, I'm cramping."

When she didn't respond, he put his hand on the right side of her face and pulled her down closer to him. "Look at me. Look at me," he pleaded. "Say my name."

Aya threw her head back and rode him even harder. She hated that he always wanted her to say his name. Why? He didn't think she knew who he was? Had the pervert forgotten his own name? What was the point? She was hot with anger that now—when she was finally on the cusp of ecstasy—he was messing it up.

Desi persisted to pressure her and it stopped Aya cold in her tracks. She could no longer retain the fantasy and released him. She lay down with her back to him and sobbed. Any effort Desi made to comfort her was ignored. She screamed at him to shut up and leave her alone, but he kept trying and asking questions until she finally got up, put on her robe, and went to her cabin.

She collapsed on the ground the moment her slippers hit the studio floor. She knew her cries would carry, so she covered her mouth as her angst forced its way from the pit of her stomach. Mercifully, the singing of the frogs and the sporadic drizzle of the rain were loud enough to drown out the sound of her weeping.

A knot formed in her chest, so Aya massaged her heart as she gasped for breath in between her tears. Her eyes, nose, and mouth were all running, and as hard as she tried to wipe her face clean on her silk robe, the waters kept flowing. She whimpered and sobbed, only this time she didn't want to die. She simply wanted to live an authentic life.

The next morning, Aya woke naked, blurry eyed, and puffy faced after a night of bawling on the floor. Desi sat across from her and looked down at her with a hurt expression on his face. Aya moaned and turned away from him. *Why can't he just leave me alone?*

She was still tired from a restless sleep and did not want to deal with him right then. Desi came over to her and asked her to look at him. She reluctantly turned around, and when she saw his puffy red eyes, she felt mercy.

"Ay, please listen to me. You gotta know I love you, honey," he said. "I've never seen you so upset, and that hurt me so bad. Whatever I did, please forgive me. I am so sorry. I would never, ever, do anything to make you unhappy. You have to believe me. I just don't understand what's wrong, and you need to talk to me so this never happens again."

Aya sat up and pulled her knees to her chest to cover her nakedness. She could see that her husband wanted answers, and she really didn't have any to give him. What could she say? *I'm angry with you because you've given me very little sexual pleasure and you should know by now that I am not satisfied, and I have a man who can offer it to me on a silver platter but I had to deny him and come home to you?* Or maybe *I'm worried because I don't know where things stand between me and Marley now, and I don't want him to leave my life as he has lit a spark in me that I cannot let die?* Or how about *I'm furious with myself because I've royally jacked up my life and because my family was right all along?*

Desi sat down next to her on the cool tile floor and draped his arm around her shoulders. "There ain't anything you can't tell me, Aya," he said, rubbing her thigh. "Are you unhappy 'cause of me?"

That was a can of worms Aya was not ready to open with him yet. She was far too vulnerable, her head was throbbing, and she had to tell him in the right way.

"Is it your hormones setting you off?"

"Probably," she said tearfully. "I go back to the doctor on Thursday and I'll see what she recommends. I'm sorry I overreacted, Desi, I just couldn't get it. I was trying and trying and very little was happening. It's so frustrating!"

"I understand, and I wish I could do something for you. Maybe more foreplay, that could be a lot of fun." He smiled. "You really might need to reconsider the surgery, hon. I know you frightened of being cut, just I hate to see you suffering like this. Pearl went through the same thing and recovered fine. Have you talked to her 'bout this?"

Her shoulders tensed. "I'm not having the surgery, Desi," she said sternly. "There are other ways to handle this, it will take some time. I'll be careful to be more sensitive to you, so please be patient with me. I know you love doing it and everything ..."

"I thought *we* loved it. Who wouldn't wanna make love to his beautiful wife?" he asked gently, stroking her face and softly kissing her cheek.

Aya could not believe that he was actually trying to seduce her. Wasn't he tired? Yet the more he kept touching her, his erection pressing ever deeper into her hip, the more she found herself responding. She needed release badly. Before she could even believe it, her husband was on top of her, smoothly penetrating. *So much for foreplay*, she thought. She was still wide open from the previous night and he entered so quickly it was almost by accident.

His strokes were varied and regulated as he studied her expressions, and she noticed that he made an effort to contain himself and take his time, interested only in her pleasure. She breathed in deeply and let the waves of gratification wash over her. She was close this time, very close. Too tired to resist and too raw to feel shame, she fantasized that Marley's dreads were falling over her face and that his high, tight backside was surging into her. She remembered the feel of his soft, full lips and his fingers tracing designs over her welcoming body.

The momentum was in her favour, and Desi uncharacteristically kept his mouth shut. She opened her legs wider around him and thrust herself forcefully against his member. She started to cry out, and bit her lip to prevent herself from saying the wrong name. Desi had already peaked, which was of no matter to Aya, who kept on until she was spent. Her whole body was throbbing, and she struggled to keep Marley alive in her mind's eye while her husband repositioned his bony legs and kissed her.

She kept her eyes closed and savoured the moment. She felt minor discomfort after her surrender, and she rubbed her belly where the largest mass of fibroids resided. She was glad to hear Desi's hard breathing shortly after since it meant that he was asleep. She opened her eyes to observe the man she married sprawled out on the floor.

He was content in his rest and in life. He didn't want much, not even a loving wife. Until Marley came along, he'd had no complaints.

She wanted to talk to Marley and convince him not to be angry with her, only what could she possibly say after stimulating him and then running out before he could pounce on her? Aya didn't know how she had found the strength to deny him, as ready and willing as she was to be ravaged by him.

The fact of the matter was that Aya was not prepared to take the gamble with Marley yet. She was not about to jump into another relationship again without going in with her eyes wide open. She had to figure out what to do about her marriage. In fact, looking at Desi now, she knew that she could not divorce him. As shameful as it made her feel, she did not have her ducks in a row. She would have to be financially secure in her own right before she made that move. She remembered how her mother had struggled during her parents' divorce, working evenings in a bar for over a year until the settlement.

She would find a job somewhere and start working no matter how things looked or what Desi said. She would start building her security blanket in case she ever needed to begin an independent life. She would go to as many conventions as she could in order to interact with other creative people and make new friends so that the bulk of her social life would not revolve around Marley. This upcoming year would be about getting healthy and creating a personal space that would allow balance to come to her way of living.

Then there was Marley and her deep desire to be possessed by him. What could she possibly do about that?

Chapter 27

Desi retired from his technician position and focused on management. He took on two apprentices and would check in with them periodically throughout a day. He postponed doing any home renovations until the trainees were established with the company and he would not have to check up after them. Other than that, he focused on his wife and strengthening their relationship. He would not let her out of his sight, always wanting to be near her and generally driving her crazy.

He would rise at six in the morning to get Ricky ready for school, schedule the services for the day, and have his coffee with Aya when she was having her morning tea. He would then see Aya off to yoga, drop off Ricky at school, and go to whatever site the apprentices were at to check on them and customer satisfaction. He would return home by lunch and either offer to take his wife out or join her in the studio for their meal. He would then leave her to write and go to the carport to work on his pickup or organize his tools or shed. By 2:30 p.m. he would leave to pick up Ricky from school and take him to meet up with Junior wherever he was. Dividing up the work this way allowed them to be finished and home by 6:00 p.m. for supper most evenings.

Aya or Marva would have dinner ready and waiting on the table when they came in, and they would all eat as a family. The boys would clean the dishes while Aya drove Marva home as an excuse to get a breather. She stretched the thirty-minute return drive into forty minutes, enjoying the peace and quiet. If she took much longer, Desi would be on the cell to make sure his wife was safe.

One night about a month later, Marva and Aya stopped by the grocery store and ran smack dab into Marley. Aya's heart raced, and she quickly scanned the checkout line to make sure that Marva was still there and had not seen them. Marley gave her a welcoming smile, and Aya found the courage to pull him behind a beer display to talk to him.

"I wasn't sure you'd speak to me," she said softly, "after the way I acted the last time we were together."

"I'm sorry about that, my dear. I shouldn't have started with you. You asked me to give you space and I promised to do that. You were right to leave because I'd hate to have you angry with me if it wasn't what you wanted."

"Thank you, Marl. I didn't know whether to call you or not. I wasn't sure you'd ever want to hear from me again, and I felt like such a fool."

"You did the right thing. When we make love, I want it to be the right way with you as my woman. I need you to want to be with me as much as I want to be with you, and I won't limit us to a one-night stand. You're always welcome to call or come see me, although maybe we'd better not be alone for a while."

"Do you think we could ever be just friends?"

"So you've made your decision, then?"

"I'm not ready yet, Marley, and I don't know that I ever will be. I can't expect you to wait for me, but I do value your friendship so much. I'd like us to be the way we were."

"Things will never be the way they were, Aya," Marley said gently. "I can't go back to that. I'll respect your marriage if that's what you want. I don't know what our future will be, I can't promise you anything."

"I suppose that's fair," Aya said, downcast. She noticed Marva circling the rows to find her. "You let me know what you decide."

Aya turned to leave and Marley took her arm. "Can you at least give me a hug?" He smiled. Aya beamed and gave him a big embrace. She would have loved to stay in his welcoming arms, only she had to get on before Marva saw them. He kissed her on the cheek and released her, and that's when she saw Marva's steadfast glare on them.

"You'll hear from me again," he said as the two women walked away.

On the ride home Marva's bottom lip jutted out far enough to shroud her face. Aya knew that she had better get this conversation over with before she went talking to Desi.

"What's wrong, Marv? How come you didn't speak to Marley?"

"Me and him ain't friends," she said sternly. "You shouldn't be hugging him up like that for all to see neither. What people gonna think?"

"Who cares? I am greeting a friend I haven't seen in a while. What's so wrong with that? Why do you hate him so?"

"I dunno him, is all. I don't like what I see neither. He shouldn't be hanging 'round no married woman like you the way he do. People will talk."

"So let them. He is dear to me, and I owe him a lot, Marv. I can't have you not being nice to him when he comes by, he hasn't done anything to you or anyone. You know how important my book is to me, and I couldn't have done it without him."

"He want more than to help you with you book, Missus," Marva said sharply. "It ain't my business, but you looking for trouble if you get mixed up with him."

"If you knew him like I do, you'd know what a gentleman he is. He would never ..."

"It you I worried 'bout, not him," she huffed. "Keep focused on you own husband. He home a lot now, and the better man for you too. He wouldn't like this Rasta nonsense."

Aya wanted to put her in her place. However, she was still glowing about the few moments she got to spend with Marley and did not want Marva ruining it. She put her foot down on the gas to get the misery home faster.

Chapter 28

"This is a surprise!" Aya said when she opened the door to Pearl.

"I was passing and noticed Desi's truck was gone, so I thought I'd check in on you." She followed her daughter into the kitchen. "Are you alone?"

"Yeah, Marva's off today and the boys are out until dinner. You want something to eat?"

"You've finished cooking already? I'm fine for now," Pearl answered, planning to stay for dinner anyway. "So how's the book coming?"

"It's taking shape really well, thank you. I'm taking my time with this one though. I want it to be detailed and more of an experience."

"You mean more like Marley's work?" Pearl smiled. "You hear from him lately?"

"We check in with each other every now and then," Aya said, not taking the lure. "How's Auntie doing?"

"She's excited about her Mediterranean cruise this weekend with her friends. Aren't you and Marley working together on this one?"

"Oh yeah, I forgot about that. How come you didn't go?"

"I'm not going with that bunch of old fogies." She laughed. "So what's up with you and Marley?"

"Mother, there's nothing going on. He's my mentor, that's all! I don't even know if he'll have time for me. Desi told me about another woman that I should look into having represent me. She really knows her stuff, and at least she's readily available since she lives on the island. I'll see what happens. So, what are you going to do with Auntie gone?"

"I'm sure that he would make himself available to you any time, Aya. Don't you dare insult him by hiring some stranger. You know better than that! Your husband's got your head foolish."

"Wow! Not even in the door five minutes, and you're starting an argument. I didn't say I was replacing Marley, I'm simply looking into it. I'd also run it by him before I made any decision. I don't want him to feel obligated if he doesn't have the time. As for my husband, you were to make peace with him this year, remember?"

Pearl clicked her tongue. She was clearly not going to get an answer about the distance that was now prevalent between Marley and her daughter. She'd had such high expectations when he had returned, but they had come to nothing. Now that Desi had cut down his workload and was playing the doting husband, there was little chance of getting between them any time soon.

Worse still, Aya was not even pregnant by the writer and was firmly established as Mrs. Franklyn. There had to be some way, something that could be done. She had to find a ruse to bring Marley back into the equation.

"Okay, I get it. I didn't come to argue with you. I want you to be content with the right man for you. I do want us to be closer, which is why I was hoping you'd come stay with me while Bea is away."

"I don't know, Mother. I'd feel uncomfortable, and what about Desi?"

"What do you mean 'uncomfortable'? You used to live there. And what about Desi? You two joined at the hip or something? He can come visit if he likes, or he can take the week to work like I know he's dying to do."

"I'm sure you'd love him coming by for conjugal visits!" Aya laughed. "No, I don't think that'll work. Besides, I'm all set up here with the studio."

"Oh, a few weeks off won't kill you. If the work's so important, come spend the nights with me, then. I don't want to be on my own, it gets so dark down there. Won't you please come?"

"I'll think about it, even though Desi won't like it. If you don't want to be by yourself, maybe I could ask Marva ..."

"I don't want Marva! I'd like to be with my family, but of course Desi comes first."

"Now stop whining, he's my husband for Christ's sake. We'll work something out."

"Well, do, because I can't stay there by myself. All those locks and gates and bars, it's worse than Fort Knox. I'll never figure it out. I'd even put up with staying here if it came to that," she said, finally getting to the purpose of her visit.

"Then what would you do about Auntie's house?"

"She can lock it up!" Pearl said. "No one can get in there anyway, she's gone so overboard on security measures. Some church man in the neighborhood comes by every day to check on things whenever she goes away. It'll be fine. In fact, that might be the best thing."

"I'll discuss it with Desi and let you know," Aya said dismissively.

"Well, you can invite me for dinner and we both can tell him then," Pearl pushed.

"That's up to you, it might be better if you left it to me."

"I can defend myself, dear child," Pearl said with a smile, happy with her result.

Chapter 29

That weekend Pearl moved into Carlton's old room and set up shop. Although it was only for two weeks, she was determined to find a way to make it permanent as this was more of the lifestyle she wanted in retirement. She could help look after the boys as it was unlikely she would ever have grandchildren of her own, as well as be near her daughter—with Desi not able to do a thing to stop her.

She needed to make sure these weeks went as smoothly as possible so that her daughter would welcome it in the near future. She would also be certain to put Desi at ease by letting him believe that all was forgiven and the past would remain there. Pearl knew how to play to win.

She was surprised that Desi had not put up any resistance to the idea of her staying with them. Any irritation he must have felt was clearly masked or possibly non-existent. That worried Pearl, because that would mean Desi felt secure in his marriage and certain of its continued success. He probably figured she had emptied her bag of tricks and was defeated. However, Pearl had yet to begin to fight.

"You looking very comfortable there, Pearl," Desi said as he popped his head in the bedroom door. "You not up to something, are you?"

"I'm glad you mentioned it because we need to talk. Why don't you come in and shut the door?"

He smiled. "I'm fine where I am, thank you."

"Boy, you really don't trust me, do you?" She smiled back. "Fine, I didn't want to disturb Ricky. I want to apologize for the way I was acting. I still don't like what you did, though I can see that you do love Aya and treat her well. She wouldn't stay with you otherwise."

"You expect me to buy this?"

"I can't say that I blame you, Des," she said, sitting on the bed and bidding him to join her. "You'll see that I don't have the energy for fighting with you anymore. I'm retired now and want to enjoy what's left of my life by spending as much time as I can with my daughter, thank you very much. If I have to make peace with you to do it, I'll do it gladly. Life is too short, and I'll be damned if I lose her to you."

Desi squinted his eyes, looking unconvinced.

"It doesn't look like I'll ever have grandkids of my own, and I've always adored your Ricky. It would be nice to be a proper part of this family," she added.

"So you can tear it down from the inside?" He leaned on the chest of drawers beside the door. "That what you trying to do?"

"Nothing of the kind, Desi, I'm telling you, I'm done. Aya's old enough to make her own decisions, and suffer the consequences for them too. I'm all for living my own life now, maybe find a man of my own," she said, winking.

"Well, good luck to you," he said, straightening to leave. "It's 'bout time you did." He headed for the doorway.

"You don't think I'm still hung up on you, do you?" she goaded.

At that they both laughed, and Desi leaned on the door jamb. "You were always a classy lady, P, you shouldn't have any trouble sinking your fangs into some unsuspecting fella."

"Oh, is that what I did to you?"

Desi smirked and left the room, bouncing on his dangling long legs.

Got ya, Pearl thought. This was going to be easier than she'd expected.

Of course, Pearl was not factoring in Marva, who did not like the situation at all. She was very unsettled by Pearl's change of heart and could see that trouble was brewing. Even worse, it was clear that Pearl was quite comfortable living in Carlton's room, which she herself had already planned to take over.

Talking to either of the Franklyns about it was out of the question since she did not want to seem too eager. The Missus had been very short with her since the night they had met up with Marley at the grocers, so she would have to pick Desi's brain to come up with a solution.

Desi's temperament did not change one iota with his monster-in-law living under his roof. He maintained his schedule and made pleasant conversation with her during meals, in which she took great pleasure preparing for the family. It was clear she was trying to take Marva's place, although she showed no interest in cleaning and was untidier than any person had a right to be.

Mother and daughter decided to spend the day out together so Marva took advantage of the opportunity to feel Desi out. She found him on the family room couch, flicking through channels in the early afternoon.

"You got you foot up now that the ladies gone?"

"Yeah, I'm taking it easy today. Nothing on at all to watch though. You need something?"

"No, I good, Des. That Pearl got a right mess up in that room that took me all morning to finish. She got many things to be here a short while."

"She's always been like that, I don't know how Aya could come from her as fanatic she is 'bout cleanliness. Don't bother with that room until she's gone. She can clean up after herself, this is no hotel."

"Well, it don't look to me like she be gone when she say. She act like she fixing to stay."

"She don't wanna stay up in here with us for long, believe me. She's too happy down there with her sister," Desi countered. "Aya wouldn't have her here either."

Marva was not convinced, and it troubled her that he seemed to be giving Pearl a pass. "Trust me, she got plans, hear? Once she get a foot in the door, the rest will soon follow."

"Steady yourself, there's nothing she can do that I can't handle. She knows Aya and I are solid now. It'll take her some time to find another Marley."

"Not so," Marva challenged. "The Missus and me run into him the other night at Ruby's. He looked happy nuff to see her, hugging her up in the store."

Desi sat straight up and fixated on Marva. "Ya lie! I thought he went back to the States?"

"He there with a cart full a things. I dunno how long he staying here for, but he still 'round these parts and looking to keep 'round."

"Aya never mentioned that. Neither did you. How come you didn't tell me before?"

"As long as he wasn't coming here, I didn't think you'd be bothered."

"I ain't bothered," he said flatly. "I count on you to keep me informed, is all. Did you hear any of the conversation?"

"None, I cashing out when they talking. I only saw them hugging goodbye."

Desi placed both his hands on the counter and chewed on his lips. "It don't matter," he said finally. "Aya's committed to me. In the meantime, let's both keep an eye on her mother."

Marva agreed and decided to leave it at that, for now.

That evening, while Aya dropped Marva home and the boys were out with friends, Pearl joined Desi on the couch to watch the news. She had already been there two days and was anxious to get some alone time with the man of the house.

"So it's just you and me, then, Desi?" she asked as she sat gingerly next to him. "You wolfed down everything on your plate for dinner. I need to cook for you more often."

Desi laughed. "Well, when you keep making all the things I like, how can I resist? You trying to take over Marva's job?"

"Of course not. I do love cooking for a family though. I've never figured out how to do it for just myself or Bea. You boys make me feel real good when you eat up like that. Aya's been finicky and never cared much for most of the things I make, she's always done for herself. You're not one for cooking either."

"No, I was too busy earning to get much time in the kitchen. We had good church women who brought food for us," he said jovially, redirecting his attention to the news.

"You've been pretty lucky with women," she said lovingly. "You constantly manage to find those who take care of you."

"Oh yeah?" He returned his focus to Pearl. "You remember my first wife? The way I see it, I'm the one who takes care of my woman. Always have."

"You definitely provide financially, I'll give you that. On the other hand, you work all the time, which doesn't leave much of you for your woman. You should take them on jobs like you do your boys, that way you won't get easily distracted."

"I admit I've made that mistake, though not this time. I'm setting things up good and proper for my family, who won't want for nothing. I can ease up for the next couple of months until the casino job comes in."

"You're doing the casino? How'd you manage that?"

Desi snickered. "You don't think we could do it? Word of mouth is money in my pocket on this little rock. Me and my boys work long and hard to get every project done in less time for less money, everybody knows it. That strip mall on the coast was the best thing that ever happened to us. They're recommending Franklyns in all the right places now, and this company is growing well. I'm looking over an offer for the Bahamas that will put us head and shoulders above all the bigwigs here."

"You've come a long way, Desi, you should be very proud. Although your wife still needs you home sometime."

"I realize, and I am doing that now, P. I've hired help and even have a consultant and an operations manager to advise me now that we're expanding. Once things are in place, I'll take on more staff and be able to step back even more and let Junior ascend the throne. I have a plan, and everything is falling in place. I'll be home so much Aya will get sick of me."

Too right, Pearl thought. Aya was already annoyed with his constant attention, she could tell. The idea of so much wealth coming to Desi was hard for Pearl to swallow, yet it gave her hope. Maybe it was a good thing that Aya had stuck with him for so long; surely it would be better to divorce him at the height of his riches.

It was unusual for him to be so open with her, of all people, about his finances; he must be trying to rub it in. She would be sure to have the last laugh though: she would make Desi's first divorce settlement look trivial next to what she would get for her daughter. A broad smile spread across her face. "I'm glad to hear it," she lied. "Although you're looking better these days, you're still rather thin. Keep eating my meals and you'll be fine."

"It helps not to have a nasty mother-in-law and her sister trying to undermine me all the time," he said brusquely.

Pearl laughed so hard that she fought back tears and moistened her pantyliner. "Better us than her father, don't you think? As much an ass as he's been, I really hope he and Aya can make up before too long. She's so much like him and he adores his baby, as you well know. It's not natural for them to be estranged for so long, and you need to help them reconcile."

Desi frowned at that comment. "Don't know what I can do 'bout that. The man's been done with me for a long time now, and he don't go back on things."

"It's been years, Des, I'm sure he misses you. He's heard in a roundabout way that Aya has flourished being married to you. Maybe he's changed. It's worth a try, isn't it? Apparently, he wants to retire here as well, but he's troubled by being in such close proximity to his enemies." She laughed.

"So you here for good?"

"My daughter and sister are here, so this is where I belong. Listen, Herb's expected to visit this year and I'm going to have words with him about Aya, so you can too."

Desi didn't reply to her demand. They enjoyed a quiet evening in front of the tube, waiting for Aya and Ricky to return.

Aya was having trouble forgetting the image of her mother and husband sitting comfortably on the couch together when she came home. They had looked like a mature couple, so at ease with each other. It had made her feel so odd that she excused herself, like she used to do back in Canada, and went to her room to leave them to it. Desi followed her in shortly after to check if everything was fine—and of course to initiate sex.

He was pulling out all kinds of tricks to try to stimulate her, which left her feeling little of anything but dry. He wanted to play games, take on roles, and even dress up. Aya was frightened to think where this was going and tired of having to fake it. She would have agreed that she needed counselling if not for her night with Marley.

She was delighted to know she was more than able to experience rapture, and she explored all degrees of it in her writing. Her current novel was about a woman discovering her sexuality with several partners, some of them even strangers. Being able to delve every day into this freedom Aya herself had never known was as luxurious as cheesecake. Sadly, it was Desi she went to bed with every night, even though it was Marley who possessed her mind.

Marley had promised that she would hear from him again, yet he had been largely absent from her life for almost two months. She missed him dearly, but she realized she was the one who had made her bed. She kept her eyes and ears open for him, hoping somehow he would appear. She would think she saw his face or heard his voice everywhere and would end up disappointed. She had to admit that she was heartsick, and that was possibly what Marley was hoping for.

That Sunday morning, Aya rose early to do her yoga. She could already smell that her mother was up and cooking Sunday dinner, which was served at lunch. She then decided to take a long walk up and around the hill, which gave expansive views of the horizon.

The crisp, fresh air was invigorating and Aya was able to increase her pace. About fifty yards uphill, she made her way to a welcoming clearing and sat down at a picnic table under a large breadfruit tree. She took in the view of the rooftops, the main road, and the sailboats skimming across the surface of the sea. It was a calming sight.

This was a big year for her as she was turning forty in December and wanted to be settled in her heart, mind, and spirit by then. Of course, she would have to make several decisions and get her finances in order first.

By then, she hoped to accumulate at least seventy-five thousand dollars of her own. She had been putting aside a thousand dollars a month out of the living expenses that Desi had given to her to manage, and she kept most of the five hundred dollars a week he gave her as pocket money. Her surplus was hidden in the mini freezer of her studio, wrapped in a brown paper bag. She planned on finishing her draft in May and hoped it would be picked up by summer, giving her something of a cash windfall.

She would travel to promote her next book and take a trip to California for her birthday. Aya was desperate to be around the movers and shakers in the business of promoting positive stories for women of colour. It would be the best place to network, even if she would have to run that by Marley first.

Marley. Sooner or later, everything came back to him. Her mind cleared as a strong wind blew over her, bringing precipitation as she sat under the tree. She could not be with Marley now: the timing was off, or the stars had not aligned, as he loved to say. Whether they would find each other again would be up to the heavens. Right now, Aya was determined to get her life in order. After all, there was still time to fall in love with her husband.

By the time Aya made her way back down the hill and returned home, she was drenched and everyone was already eating. Desi jumped up and hugged her soaked body in relief. It was now half past one and Aya had been away over four hours! He had gone looking for her in the rain and was worried sick when he could not find her.

The family devoured Pearl's meal of roast pork, rice and peas, macaroni salad, steamed vegetables, corn on the cob, and salt bread. Knowing that Aya would not eat much of that, she had also prepared baked red snapper, pickled cucumber salad, and stir-fried turkey breast with egg noodles. Even Aya had to admit it was the best spread she had seen in quite some time. Once the boys started clearing the table, Pearl got right to whipping up her decadent coconut cake.

The day turned into a pleasant evening enjoyed by all. Junior and Ricky were sticking close to home now that Pearl was cooking, delighted to have her around. Even Desi, who had wanted nothing to do with her a few weeks before, seemed quite at ease in her presence now. Why wouldn't he? Pearl prepared all his favourites and doted on him as though he were her precious child—"Desi this" or "Desi that," and he lapped it all up. Aya found the whole matter sickening; she almost preferred the two of them fighting.

Ricky brought out a board game for all to play and Pearl would not let Aya escape that torment. It was all about a happy family for her mother all of a sudden, which made her daughter all the more suspicious. Nonetheless, she faked interest in the mundane contest and made it through the night without hurting anyone's feelings. Desi was delighted by these events as it was apparent that this was the way he wanted his dynasty to live: engaged and involved with each other, not shut up in separate areas throughout much of the day.

Aya escaped to her room just before 10:00 p.m., and when she turned off the television at midnight, her husband still had not come in to her. She shrugged her shoulders and went to sleep, and she did not feel him slip in next to her until nearly 2:00 a.m.

Chapter 30

By the following week, Pearl was fully ingrained in the Franklyn home. She prepared all the meals and they sat at the kitchen table as a family for every meal but lunch. She was even taking Ricky to school in the morning so that Desi could go in with Junior and the apprentices during the final stage of their project. She had taken Aya's place in the family room, watching television or playing games and joking with Marva, who kept as far from her as she could.

With Pearl always in her territory, Marva found it impossible to watch her soaps or even to make lengthy phone calls without nervously having to keep an eye out. She had to clean Pearl's zone at least three times a day, and Desi was of no help at all. He merely laughed and told her that the interloper would be gone soon. That was even more disconcerting to Marva—how well the two of them were getting on. Desi was delighted to be eating so well and had requested that Marva leave it all up to Pearl while she lived with them. Even the Missus could tell how hurt she was by that, while he was too busy stuffing his face.

Marva wasn't sure if the Missus would be of any help either since she was cooping herself up in the cottage now more than ever. She was simply leaving her mother and husband to it, which was a big mistake, for it had become quite clear that Pearl had designs on the man. Worse still was the fact that the boys treasured having something of a grandmother for once and had little need now for ugly, inadequate Marva.

These circumstances left Marva feeling very insecure and in need of answers. Even if the Mother did return to Bea's in Jackson, she would most definitely be visiting very often now, and when she became elderly, her daughter would be sure to move her in with them. There was little chance of the Franklyns wanting to care for two infirm women.

Junior did not have it in him and would be busy with his own conquests soon enough. Ricky, although very fond of Marva, clearly preferred having a distant stepmother with an affectionate grandmother. Although Desi would honour his obligations to her for a time, setting her up for retirement was another matter altogether. There were still the questions of the shack and whether she would be able to get any cash from it, what to do with her mother, and how to handle the expense of getting rid of her.

Sure, Glenda would be able to house Marva temporarily; however, what help would she be if they both became frail at the same time? What if Marshall (assuming there was no divorce) didn't want her around? What if the kids sent for their mother, what then?

Obviously, this wouldn't matter if she dropped dead tomorrow, which she had to consider with the way she was stressing herself out over her future. Marva had to laugh about that. Somehow, she was certain that she would live long, much like her decrepit mother. It wouldn't be like the Lord to take her from her misery any time soon.

Marva decided to prepare her celebrated split pea soup for Aya, who would be thrilled to have it that chilly afternoon.

"Oh, Marva, that was so sweet of you to bring this for me. It was just what I needed! Desi will be well pleased too."

"Well, you mother got so many bones there from her cooking, I thought I'd make myself useful," she said humbly.

"What do you mean? You're always needed around here, Marv. Don't let her make you feel put out, there's only a week more. Besides, you should be happy to take it easy a while. It's not like you're being paid less or anything."

Marva gulped. "True," she said slowly. "It not like me to take it easy, Missus. So how you book doing? I hardly see you these days."

"I'm taking my time with this one, but I like what's developing. I may even get myself a part-time job so I can absorb more culture."

"For wha'?" Marva shrieked. "You ain't gotta work no more. Desi not giving you nuff?"

Aya wanted to put Marva's mouth in check, even if she could appreciate her honesty and was grateful for it. Come to think of it, she was the closest friend Aya had ever known as she had little trust in most people. It's not as though Aya had confided in this ordinary woman intentionally, Marva just had a way of cutting to the heart of things. Initially, Aya had felt restrained in her dealings with Marva because she was certain that it was being reported to Desi. Although that had partly proven to be true, it was painfully clear that her housekeeper had protected her interests as well.

"I'm not doing it for money, and it won't be full-time either," she said. "I'm trying to develop my characters, Marva. I need to be out and about with people, you know? I think that was my mistake the last time, shutting myself off like that and living out of my head."

"Desi know?"

"I need permission?"

"Don't bark me down." Marva snorted. "Just, I know he not gonna like it. He gonna think it make him look bad to have you working."

"I haven't spoken to him about it yet as I was waiting to actually have a position first. You don't need to be warning him either."

"Why you always have to say that?" Marva sounded insulted. "Like I be running to him all the time on you. Me? That not the woman I is, and you know me now all these years."

"Okay, let's not argue. I don't need anyone getting in the way of me working again. It's very important that no one else know about this right now."

"So why you tell me, then?"

"As usual it slipped out," Aya said, laughing. "Because I obviously trust you, Marv, you should know that by now."

"Well, I sure don't see no other people 'round here checking for you besides you cousin," she replied. "You shamed a this family or something? How come you never bring people over?"

"My people are all out of the country," Aya lied. "We talk on Skype, and soon enough they'll come visit."

"You not going back there to visit, then? Been a mighty long time," Marva said skeptically.

"I'm sure I will one day, but right now I'd rather see new places. Especially now that my mother has relocated here."

"Mm-hmm," Marva said cautiously. "She'll be moving in here soon nuff."

"Why do you say that?"

"Well, she very comfortable here now that she and Desi getting along."

"We'll see how long that lasts." Aya smirked. "I admit they're making an effort and there's calm in the house. I doubt either of them would be able to handle each other permanently though."

"There are those who say a mother's place is with her daughter."

"Oh? And do you agree with that?" Aya replied, to which they both giggled.

"Just saying you mother come here to be with you in particular, and I think she looking to live here too, and that why she putting up with you husband."

"I'll deal with that if it comes, until then I won't worry about it."

"How you gonna turn her down if she ask? She birthed you."

"What are you so worried for? You're trying to sort out things that could take years to happen, if at all. My mother is no invalid and she's happy living with Auntie, so why even think about it? Right now, I need to focus on a job," she said, rising to return to her computer.

Aya was never able to get around to that job as the whole thing blew up in her face a few nights later. The boys were on the couch watching television, Desi was putting away the dishes, and Aya and her mother were reading different sections of the newspaper at the kitchen table. Aya circled a few vacancies that interested her, and that caught her mother's eye.

"What are you looking at want ads for?" Pearl asked, leaning in close to read the listing. "You looking for work or something?"

"Never mind that, I'm researching," Aya said nervously.

"An accounts manager? That's your field! What's going on? You need money?" Pearl exclaimed loudly, attracting Desi's attention. He came over and took the paper out of Aya's hand.

"What's this 'bout you looking for a job?" he asked suspiciously. "You got enough on your plate to be worrying 'bout, and we got plenty of money."

"I should hope so!" Pearl agreed.

Aya sent her mother a ferocious glare, grabbed the paper out of her husband's hands, and rose from the table. "I hoped to get into an office environment again to develop my storyline," she replied unconvincingly.

"What are you talking about?" Pearl asked. "You've worked in an office all your life, what more do you need to know?"

Aya wanted to strangle her mother and was so hot with anger that she could barely speak.

"Don't worry 'bout it, P," Desi said. "No wife of mine needs to be working. She has her writing career and this house and this family to oversee, and that is enough. We've got some major renovations going on later in the year and she is needed at home."

"Will the two of you stop?" Aya said harshly. "Am I a child or something? Don't talk about me like I'm not here."

"We're not treating you like a child, Aya," Pearl said. "But for what possible reason would you need an outside job?"

"Correct," Desi added. "I provide enough for— I mean, everything is provided for you here. You barely have time enough for us as it is with your writing. When you going to find time to work?"

Aya swallowed hard, completely unprepared for this assault. Damn them! Hell must have frozen over for those two to take sides against her. She was about to curse, but then she noticed the boys had turned their attention to the conversation.

"I'll find the time," Aya said carefully. "I'm not looking for a full-time position, just a few hours a week to get the pulse of what's going on. This has nothing to do with money—or either of you, for that matter."

"It has everything to do with our family. I don't approve at all. I've finally got everything sorted so we can spend more time together, and now you go and do this."

"Yes, Aya. What's the meaning of this?" Pearl said.

At this point the boys came to the table to be up close to the action so that Aya had four sets of accusing eyes on her. Seeing no way out, she escaped the best way she could. She excused herself and went for a drive.

Her head was still reeling nearly an hour later when she parked outside of the Wright cabin on Old East Coast Road. She put her head down on the steering wheel and wailed like an infant—so much so that her windows clouded up. Exhausted, she fell asleep.

The early morning crowing of a cock brought her out of her lethargy several hours later. Not remembering where she was, she rubbed the indent on her jaw and looked at her watch. It was 5:40 a.m.! Aya shook the fog from her mind and looked for her phone, realizing she had left it behind in her rush to get away. She could imagine how frantic Desi would be, not to mention the hell of a fight she would be in for.

How had her life come to this? She'd had so much promise. She was still young, talented, attractive, well educated, and adventurous. Yet her life had her caged in and she could not take it anymore.

She revved up the car's engine and drove to the nearest gas station to call her husband. He had been up all night and spoke to her tersely. He said he would deal with her when she got home.

Aya did not want to return a minute before half past seven, knowing that by then at least the boys would have left already, and hopefully

Desi with them. She took a long walk on a dark sand beach that was overcome with seaweed. The odd fisherman greeted her as she passed, eager for conversation. Aya kept moving with an eye on her watch.

She was relieved to see her husband's vehicle gone when she pulled in the driveway. She wanted to go straight to her studio, but she was starving and needed to get provisions first.

She found her mother sitting in a practically see-through white nighty, sipping her coffee at the table.

"They're gone," Pearl said, not turning to look at her daughter. "He probably won't be home for lunch either."

"That's up to him," Aya said shortly, putting the kettle on to boil.

"We were so worried about you! He hardly slept a wink. You could've called us, you know."

"Since when do you give a damn about Desi's comfort?"

"What the hell's going on with you? You're clearly in the wrong, and yet here you are all defiant and not caring what this family has been going through. We've been sick with worry, thanks for asking. Des thought you must be dead to be gone so long."

"I fell asleep where I was parked. I had no intention of staying out all evening, it was an accident."

"I can see you've been crying too," Pearl observed. "Your eyes are nearly swollen shut. Where'd you spend the night anyway, at Marley's?"

Aya slammed the fridge door. "I warned you to stay out of my marriage, didn't I? How dare you take Desi's side about me working! What's wrong with me getting out of the house and meeting new people?"

"Don't take that tone with me. I'm thinking of your own good. Let Desi pay for everything, he's not complaining. Get your book published and see how that goes. What if it becomes a bestseller? Don't tie yourself down right now. The time to go back into the workforce is when you leave him and need cash to carry you over until a settlement comes through. Is that what this all about, you leaving your husband?"

"I deserve to meet new people and have different experiences without being handcuffed to him. I want my own identity, and I will have it. The next time I'm trying to have a discussion with my husband, stay out of it."

"I didn't mean to upset you, I just don't understand. I'm here now, and you have your auntie, cousins, and other family. You don't have to shut yourself up in the house. There's always Marley—"

"Enough about Marley! I'm so sick of you bringing him up all the time."

"Fine! I won't mention him again. So where did you spend the night, then?"

"On the east coast," Aya said sullenly. "A nice spot I pass every night when I drop Marva home." She sat at the kitchen island with her toast and tea, facing her mother.

"Well, I'm glad you got home safely, so let that be the end of it," Pearl said as Marva came in the front door. She put her coffee cup in the sink without washing it and went up to have her shower.

Probably to come up with a new line of attack, Aya thought.

"Mornin', Missus," Marva greeted her. "Ooh, you face all swollen. Desi hit you or somethin'?"

Aya could only muster a faint mumble, to which Marva shouted, "Did he?"

"No, Marv, of course not," Aya said indifferently. "I had a late night, and I'm going in now to catch up on my sleep." She rose to leave.

"I think it more than that, but I'll let you rest if you say so."

"I don't have the energy to get into it now." She yawned and went to her room.

Aya awoke hours later feeling the heat of her husband's stare on her back. She rolled over and faced him, unafraid.

"Why'd you run out like that?"

"I didn't want to argue in front of the boys. This is between you and me, anyway," Aya said angrily. "We don't need her stirring things up, this has nothing to do with her."

"Why you so cross? That's what I don't understand, you just up and left me there like a fool," Desi said, hurt in his voice.

"I didn't mean to, I was furious and thought it best to leave. It's better that we settle this privately," she said sternly. "I've spoken to Mother about it already."

"How come you never told me 'bout wanting to get a job?"

"It was just an idea I was mulling over. I wanted to see what was offered to me before we had that discussion. I wasn't aware that I had to ask the master how to live my life."

"Not this again," Desi pleaded. "I ain't trying to control you, we're married and we need to be making decisions together. I should be included, or at least a consideration."

"You never include me in any business decision. I only found out about the new staff from Mother. You do what you think is best for our family, and I'm supposed to go along with it and trust that it's in our best interest. Why can't you do that for me? Why do I always have to run everything by you?"

"You really don't think I have a right to know?"

"Is this because you don't want my mother to think you're not providing? Forget her! It would only be a few hours a week. I'd find something during the mornings so we could still have our meals together. It doesn't have to be a big deal." Aya got right in her husband's face.

"There's no need for it," he said irritably. "Where'd you sleep last night?"

"I told you on the phone, in the car on Old East Coast Road."

"Was he with you?"

"He who?" Aya replied in disbelief.

"I left the house two hours after you called and you still weren't home. What were you doing all that time?"

"I went for a walk on the beach. *Alone.* You can check with the fishermen there if you like."

Desi was not amused. "Walking when I was here waiting for you?"

"I needed to clear my head," Aya explained. "I didn't want to come home angry and start the whole thing up again. I know my hormones make me testy at times, so I tried to relax a bit first. I didn't sleep well at all either."

"Just don't do that again," he said. "I was worried sick."

"I'm sorry about that, I didn't mean for it to happen. I'd never do that to you intentionally, especially with my mother here. Who'd you think I was with?"

"Let's not bother 'bout that now," he said, trying to change the subject. "I tired as hell, but I gotta go help them finish. I'll see you later and we can discuss this work business," he said crisply and left the room.

Aya lay back down and pulled the sheet over her head, listening to the whirring of the ceiling fan until she was able to drop back to sleep.

She was woken up by Marva's gentle knock on her door. She looked over to her clock and saw that it was 3:03 p.m. and beckoned her in.

"Just checkin' to see if you still breathing," Marva mumbled. "You mother making you another stir-fry. Desi and the boys not gonna be home 'til late."

"I can't believe I've been sleeping so long, what a waste of a day."

Marva began sweeping the tiled floor. "You feeling better now?"

"Good for now, I guess. I better get up or Mother'll accuse me of lying about while my hard-working husband has to be out all day after I kept him up all night."

"What you mean?" Marva asked, turning to her. "Why Desi up all night?"

Aya sighed. She got up and began making the bed, deciding that she might as well tell her. "We fought about me working. I went for a drive to blow off some steam and ended up falling asleep in my car."

"Mm-hmm," Marva said, giving Aya her full attention and waiting for more.

"So he was up worrying after me since I didn't get home until this morning."

"Mm-hmm," Marva repeated, pushing out her bottom lip.

"Mm-hmm," Aya mimicked. "That's why we're both so tired."

"You shouldn't be tired if you sleep in you car."

"Hunched over my steering wheel?" Aya raised her eyebrows. "It was not at all restful, believe me."

"Where you park?" Marva asked, clearly skeptical.

Aya finished making up her bed and went into the bathroom to wash up. "That clearing on Old East Coast Road. There was a beautiful breeze whipping around, and the sound of the waves crashing must've lulled me to slumber."

Marva nodded and pushed her thick glasses back to the bridge of her nose. "You love that spot nuff. It not safe being so dark and out the way, anything could happen to you."

"I know, I know," Aya moaned, drying her face. "I didn't mean to stay out all night and worry everyone."

"And leave you husband to the Mother? She must'a been well pleased," Marva muttered.

Aya stuck her head out of the bathroom. "What was that?"

"I said Desi must not have been pleased. He still vex?"

"I'm sure he is, hopefully he'll be too tired to start with me when he gets home. I already got into it with Mother," Aya said while changing her clothes.

"Oh?" Marva put down her broom. "She taking his side, I bet."

"Mm-hmm," Aya teased, coming back into the room. "I told her to keep her nose out. They're both adamant that I should not get a job."

"Well," Marva said carefully, "I agree with them on that. I told you he wasn't gonna like it."

"Yeah, yeah, I know. I'll see to that later, just you wait," Aya said and went out to her mother.

"You feeling better now?" Pearl asked innocently. "The food's about ready."

Aya had to admit that she was hungry and the aroma was enticing. She took out plates and poured herself a large glass of sorrel. "Thank you, I will have some. Desi didn't eat any lunch?"

"Poor man has to finish up today since they decided at the last minute that they wanted to open the restaurant early," Pearl said. "He's getting a premium for having to rush it, so I doubt you'll see him any time soon."

Aya had no idea about any of it. "How come you're so concerned about his welfare all of a sudden? It wasn't long ago you wanted to run him over with your car, remember?"

"Oh, Aya, I'm so tired of fighting all the time," she said, dishing out the food. "I see no point in swimming against the stream. I know there's a much better match available for you, but I also know you can't have it before you're ready. Everything will work out in the end, so I'm not running up my pressure to go to an early grave. Take as much from him as you can for as long as you can stand it and then get on with your life."

Aya chewed her meal thoroughly, taking her time to come up with a reply. They sat in silence until Marva passed through, turning down their offer to join them. She had too much to do.

Later that evening, Desi and the boys walked in looking exhilarated. Everything had gone well and they'd been handsomely paid. The restaurant owners had even allowed them to order off the menu, although they'd had to eat it in the staff quarters due to their attire.

Ricky hugged the women and offered them a box of sugary pastries before leaping on the couch to watch some television. Desi, although clearly tired, talked excitedly on and on about how they'd managed to pull it off, with Pearl clinging to his every word. Junior gave Aya a wink and grabbed some beers, which he took with him to his cabin to relax.

In bed later, Aya reminded her sleepy husband that they had unfinished business.

"There's nothing more to talk 'bout," he said firmly. "We made a mint on this job, so I'm putting enough cash in your hand to modernize this place. I've already put aside the funds to remodel the kitchen—you know the built-in oven and high-end range that you like? We can get all stainless-steel appliances, granite countertops, new cupboards, the whole works. I need you home to help stay on top of the contractors. Then we'll paint and get new fixtures and furnishings to match. You have great taste and you can make here more of our home."

Wow, Aya thought, speechless. He'd really covered all of his bases. How could she possibly argue with that?

Chapter 31

All were buckling under the hot, sticky weather that had been dragging on, and so they welcomed the intermittent rains that were far and few between that season. The months hurried by like days in Aya's mind. After her mother went back to Jackson, she'd experienced a severe bout of writer's block that had her put the project aside for almost three months. Not wanting to address her failure, she turned her attention elsewhere.

Aya kept herself busy with the renovations that took place throughout much of the year, while Marva became increasingly irritated by all the noise and disruption. Even though the work took six weeks longer than scheduled, it somehow managed to come in under budget.

Aya had to admit she had a beautiful home that would be the envy of many. From the outside, it appeared she was living a charmed life. She had a seemingly faithful husband, a property that was easily worth a million, no debts, more than fifty thousand dollars hidden away, a decent wardrobe, a maid, her own vehicle, occasional dinners at fancy restaurants, and just enough travel to keep island neurosis at bay.

A few years ago, she would have thought she had died and gone to heaven to be blessed with so much. Now her outlook was entirely different. Every few months, Desi would dangle a new bauble to keep her distracted and satisfied until reality set in once again. She wasn't happy; in fact, she was far from it. Her guilt kept her in denial as she did not want to appear ungrateful; however, the material things were of little significance to her anymore. What good was another inanimate piece of jewellery? Of what value was a romantic getaway with a man she had no desire for? Aya may have had very little money before Desi, but her life was her own and she didn't have to answer to anybody.

Her life had become monotonous, with her going through the motions and becoming ever more resentful of her spouse. She had not heard a word from Marley and it was now late August. His absence loomed greatly in her heart and left very little for anything else. Her creativity had fallen to the wayside and she now felt like a prisoner in her palace.

She knew she had to do something about it, and then the opportunity presented itself. The British syndicate offered Franklyn & Sons the job for a mall in the Bahamas by a familiar developer, and they accepted the project, which should take about a month to complete. Desi wanted to leave Marva at the house and go as a family, but Aya came up with excuse after excuse until she finally sold him on the idea of using the time to finish off her novel since he would be too busy to spend any real time with her anyway.

Reluctantly, her husband packed for the trip, only to insist that Marva stay on with Aya the entire time he was gone. But she still felt it would be something of a reprieve since she could shut herself up in the studio and decide how she was going to leave her husband. It wasn't as if she were seeking a divorce right away; she just needed some time on her own to figure things out. She would leave under the guise of some author's symposium and not return right away. She would take few belongings and her cash, quietly leaving the island.

Aya would be sure to keep in touch with her other half to let him know she was alive, though not where she was. Whether he would take her back if she decided to return to him was still an obstacle, yet the chance of her actually wanting to do that was beyond slim. In reality, she wanted to run to Marley's bed, have a vigorous affair to get it out of her system, and see where things stood between them. Somehow, though, she had the crushing feeling that ship had sailed and she had missed her best chance for happiness.

Marva was like a shark that smelled blood in the water, constantly circling Aya to ascertain the source of the wound.

"You awful quiet these days, Missus," Marva had the courage to ask on the third day of Desi's absence. "You not even writing, just walking from room to room and barely eating a thing. What bothering you?"

"I need to get out of this house for a while. I think I may take a trip of my own for a few days."

"Desi tell me to keep an eye on you, so wherever you going, I going too." Marva put her hands on her hips. "What you need to get away for? After all the work done on this place, I should think you'd never wanna leave here. What Desi done now?"

"I'm desperate to get outta here for a while, Marv," Aya tried to explain. "You wouldn't understand."

"Oh, I understand plenty," she said. "Anyone can see you so miserable you dunno what to do with yourself. Desi thought that fixing the house how you like it would help, and it did for 'bout a minute."

"Don't go looking for trouble where there isn't any."

"I see trouble written all over you face. You is a damn fool if you thinking to run off on you husband."

"What are you talking about now?" Aya asked, rubbing her temples. This was the last thing she needed, Marva insinuating herself into this private matter.

"I say that wherever you going, I going too."

Aya picked up her purse and headed for the door. "My cousin's back on the island. I'm simply going by to visit, if that's okay with you, Warden."

As Aya sped down the hill, she looked in her rear-view mirror and saw Marva shaking her head.

"What's he done now?" Nicola moaned as Aya hugged her at the door. Aya tried to shrug it off, only her relative was unconvinced. "It's plain as day on your face. You look incredibly glum."

Aya sighed. "I'm so tired of people telling me that." She followed Nicola out onto the front balcony, which gave expansive views of the pristine aquamarine beach a few miles below, and made herself comfortable on a plush chair.

Aya looked at her cousin with affection. Nicola's shoulder-length red braids perfectly complemented her golden-brown complexion. She had fine features, with a tall stature and a long neck that made her appear to be looking down over every one, which was deceptive because her warmth and kind disposition were very endearing and had earned her many friends.

Nicola's mother had died when she was young, and so she was raised by her overly strict father, only to get pregnant once she had attained her teaching certification. Her daughter's father did not stick around, yet she had never had a problem getting a man—it was keeping one. Tired of the cycle, the never-married forty-nine-year old had devoted her life to the caretaking of her daughter and father.

Nicola had to drag her daughter to join her in London while she completed her Masters in Education and was made to return to the island any time there was an extended break by her incessant whining.

Nicola handed her a large glass of fresh coconut water and the local dark rum, which was their standard refreshment. "Didn't Desi just go off to the Bahamas?" she asked. "I thought you'd be happy to get a break?"

"He's left Marva to scrutinize everything I do, and I can't get rid of her without it becoming a thing." She downed half her cup in one shot, at which her cousin chuckled.

"So, go off to your hut like you usually do. She can't trouble you there."

"Her eagle eyes don't miss a thing, and she's always asking questions. I'd actually prefer to get away for a while myself."

"So why didn't you go with him, then?"

Aya looked Nicola square in the face. "Because I'm leaving him, that's why."

Nicola rolled her eyes, put her drink down so she could cross her arms, and made no remark.

"I'm leaving him for real. I can't live like this anymore. I need to get away by myself for a while and figure out what to do next with my life. I should never have married him."

"Rushing into things is what got you into this mess in the first place. What is so awful about being married to the man?"

"Oh, we've been over this already," Aya huffed.

"Well, I don't understand it, Aya," Nicola tried to reason. "I mean, he pays for everything and he's hardly around. He puts cash right in your hand and doesn't ask what you spend it on or expect you to lift a finger. He renovated the house to make it how you like it, and he even made up with your mother! You're living an easy life. Do you realize how fortunate you are? Yes, you aren't in love and have to screw more than you'd like. That's not much for him to ask for, believe me."

"I would have thought so too not long ago, but now I know life is about more than that. The security money can give is important, just not the most important thing. I don't care about it anymore. I'd be happy to have my own little apartment and peace of mind. I'm tired of faking all the time. I yearn to be on my own and not have him or Marva or Mother in my face. I want to meet people and have experiences without having to justify it or ask for permission. I need to get on with my life. Oh, I can see by the look on your face you won't ever understand."

"You're right, I don't," Nicola agreed. "Why'd you marry him in the first place? Did you ever think on that?"

"I guess I was running away from my dreary Caribbean life," Aya said slowly. "I can admit that. Things here were not as exciting and new after the first year went by, and he really wanted me. It felt nice to be desired like that by a man."

"What are you talking about? Men wanted you wherever you went, you were just too picky."

"Oh yeah? Those idiots who are drunk before lunch, hardly working, and living with their mothers? Or the old fogies who want a young woman to be a nursemaid? The only guys who were age appropriate or halfway decent were primarily interested in 'hitting it' to add another notch to their belt. Desi wanted to commit to me, and I knew he could provide," Aya explained.

Nicola picked up her drink again. "Now he's accomplished just that, and even remained faithful. He's done okay by you, then, hasn't he? You couldn't ask for a better husband in this country. I know you want the sparks and fireworks that you get with Marley. Give it more time, you may actually come to love and appreciate the man you have before long. Men like Marley can cause a woman a lot of heartbreak. He may desire what he can't have until he has it, and then he'll be on to the next one."

"It's coming up to five years now, and Desi's wearing my nerves," Aya said with a look of disgust. "Now he's home a lot, and he's planning on retiring soon, and then he'll always be home. He needs to know that he should continue working since I can't handle spending more of my time with him."

"He wants to travel with you!" Nicola shook her head. "You've always wanted to do that, and you now have a willing partner who will even foot the bill. You can meet new people and have experiences then. Do you know how thankless you sound, dismissing all your blessings?"

"I can see why it would seem that way, I do. This should be a dream-come-true life for me, only I've learned an important lesson. None of it means anything unless there is love. I thought love didn't matter as long as I had all of the material things to make me comfortable. Until I had a taste of something real, and realized that if I was with the man I loved, I wouldn't care how we lived, or where we went, or what we had. It is being with my beloved that matters. Desi deserves to be with someone who can give him that love, and so do I. I thought I could settle, Nic, and I can't. The more time goes on, the more I know I've got to get out of this relationship no matter what it costs me."

"It could cost you everything, Aya," Nicola said, leaning forward and tapping Aya's knee. "Ride it out. If he's hanging around too much, simply go to your hut as usual. He'll get the message. You think you'll get much alimony if you leave him?"

Aya examined the floor. "I don't know, I haven't considered it."

"You haven't even talked to a lawyer yet, and you're planning on doing this foolish thing?"

"It will all get sorted out in the end," Aya said feebly.

"How do you know that?" Nicola said, crossing her hands. "Desi's got the means to tie you up for years, and things move slowly here.

He could hide his wealth so you get hardly a thing, taking back the car and whatever else he gave you. If you're going to do this, you've gotta do it right and have a plan. Get advice, and make sure to keep it confidential because people will talk. Get your hands on enough cash to tide you over for several years, and make sure that you have everything in order before you even consider making a move. Get an apartment, get a job, make sure what you need is in your name, for Christ's sake. There are so many ways this could go wrong, girl, you have to make sure you're protected."

Aya had to admit that her cousin was making a lot of sense. She was so anxious to get away when she clearly needed to get organized. That it never occurred to her to seek counsel was beyond careless. She was sure to get a settlement, even though she would feel guilty about accepting alimony. She still had a lot to figure out.

"You hear anything from Marley yet?" Nicola asked, pulling Aya out of her thoughts.

"Not a word. I doubt I'll see him again," she said quietly. She finished her drink.

"Oh, yes, you can. I saw him in town the other day and heard him say he's been up since Carnival."

Aya felt crushed. He had been here all this time and had not contacted her. It must really be over after all.

Nicola seemed to pick up on her pain and tried to cheer her up. "I'm only telling you, Mrs. Franklyn, since the cat is away the mouse can now play."

Aya gave her cousin a confused look.

"Go to the man! You need to resolve your feelings for him before you do anything else. Talk to him and see where he stands on things, and don't you dare tell him you want to leave your husband. You feel him out first. What do you really know about him anyway? You only ever hear him talk about his mother. Well, I'll find out what type of brother he really is, and you find out if he still wants you. Then go to a lawyer, and we'll meet up back here before you do anything to ruin your marriage," Nicola ordered.

Aya beamed and gave her cousin a hug. She was right; she had to see Marley again, and now was the perfect time. She could leave Marva home and spend hours by his side. Where would she find him, without anyone else knowing about it? She could ask her aunt, except that would bring her mother into the situation. She could go to his mother, only then she would look too eager. There had to be some other way. Of course, his family villa!

At the prospect of getting a second chance, Aya's spirit lifted to heights she had never known.

Marva was initially thrilled to see the change in Aya's demeanour upon her return. She had even brought Marva fried dolphin fillets with rice, beans, gravy, and coleslaw from her favourite food truck. The Missus was all smiles as she took numbers from the phone book, but she would not let Marva know what she was looking for.

Marva became suspicious when she observed Aya packing an overnight bag and stashing a large sum of money in it. What was the Missus up to now? The last time she had seen her so happy was when that Marley was involved, so it must be him she had just come from. With Desi out of the country, little could be done to stop them.

Marva racked her brain and paced the floors. She finally, reluctantly, picked up the phone to call Desi.

Chapter 32

It took Aya over two weeks to reconnect with Marley. She frequently visited her aunt and mother, but neither made any mention of him. She unnecessarily went to the same grocery store where she'd last seen him—sometimes three times a day—with no luck. She stalked his mother's home in the evenings in hopes of catching him, and she spent another night in her car on Old East Coast Road observing the villa, certain that he would appear.

When he finally came into her orbit, it was quite by chance. She walked into the waiting room of a lawyer's office, looking to get advice, and there Marley was. He jumped up and gave her his usual warm hug and bade her to sit next to him to catch up.

"You look lovely, my dear." He smiled. "I've missed you terribly and now see that you've clearly been doing very well without me."

"You promised you'd call when you were ready, so I waited. I heard you were back, how long will you stay?"

"Well, I can go now that I've seen you, and at my lawyer's office, no less. What's going on?" He put his arm around her shoulder, sending shivers along her spine.

Aya now knew the magic had not been lost between them.

"Getting some guidance on a personal matter, Marl." She wriggled in his embrace like a schoolgirl. "I've missed you too."

"Then let's have lunch after. I'm just here to sign some paperwork and shouldn't be too long. Why don't we try that Italian place by Buckley's Bay?"

"I'm not sure how long I'll be with Ms. Sullivan. Maybe we could meet someplace more private, like the last time," she said slowly.

"You remember what happened the last time?" He winked. "Ms. Sullivan wouldn't happen to be a divorce lawyer, now, would she?"

Aya's face flushed and Marley had his answer.

"Look, it's best we're not seen together right now. I mean, Desi's away for the month, and my mother and Auntie ..."

"Oh, I ran into them not too long ago. They invited me to some dinner they're hosting to raise money for the Alzheimer's society. Will you be there?"

"Yes, but that's not until this weekend, and I'd rather talk to you alone." Aya felt herself blush again. "It's better that we sort things out prior to meeting up in public, don't you think?"

"I'll wait for you downstairs and take you to a nice secluded spot."

Aya's meeting with the lawyer made little impression on her as all she could think about was getting to her man. She did not give Ms. Sullivan her real name and was satisfied with the options that were available to her. The lawyer had an excellent track record and came highly recommended. Aya was horrified to learn that it was in her best interest to make it seem as though she had tried everything to save the marriage before filing and that she should seek counselling first. As it was, Desi would seem the more sympathetic partner and could fight getting the divorce.

Even though it was going to be more challenging than Aya had realized, she had an ace up her sleeve. There was no way Desi would want her if she was with another man. He would definitely divorce her; however, the money would be slow to follow. Ms. Sullivan had offered her tools to cope until the matter could be resolved. It was a very delicate situation.

Putting those concerns aside, Aya happily stepped into Marley's vehicle less than an hour later. They made easy conversation during the ride, and then Marley parked under a row of coconut trees. He had brought her to a Rastafarian shanty that offered a variety of vegetarian meals and fresh fruit drinks. They both ordered curry rotis and sat down backing a handful of other diners.

"It's real nice to be with you again, Aya. I didn't call because it had to be you who initiated contact between us. It had to be your decision."

"I wasn't sure you still wanted to hear from me, I thought you'd moved on with your life. You're not married with kids, are you?"

"I've never been certain how that would fit into my life. I had to find my way to the right woman first, and I'm very picky. I need a lady who inspires me on all levels. Someone who excites me. Someone I can talk to about anything or be comfortable with in silence."

"You deserve all of that and more," Aya said, lost in his eyes.

"Regrettably, she is off limits at this time. Who knows what the future holds?"

Aya did not want to discuss her marriage now. In fact, it was as if Desi didn't exist. "So what are your plans? You going back to California?"

"My mother has been feeling a bit low lately. We've been running all kinds of tests to figure out exactly what the cause is, and we still don't have an answer. I'm waiting for her to see one more specialist, then I want to bring her back with me to get thoroughly checked out."

"I'm sorry to hear that." Aya put her hand on his shoulder. "What's the trouble?"

Marley took her hand in his. "Frankly, she doesn't have any energy and easily tires. She used to be energetic, up and about all the time, and now she can't be bothered or gets fed up. I knew something was off when I saw the state of her garden, she hadn't been out there in weeks!"

"Do they have any ideas?"

"They know very little right now. They offered to keep her in the hospital for observation, and of course she refused. Actually, that was where we ran into your husband," he said.

"Really? When was that?"

"When I was here earlier this year. He was being treated for something and I assumed you were there. But when I asked for you, he got all in my face. He went so far as to threaten me in front of my mother."

Aya completely disregarded the fact that her husband had needed care and had hidden the fact from her. "What did he say?"

"The usual." He chortled. "'Stay the hell away from my wife or else.' I let him rave on as my mother was with me and the waiting room loved the distraction. He was clearly not a well man, so I left it alone."

"He works too hard," Aya said, bewildered. "You should've told me about that. He blames you for our problems and that is not the real issue. I'm sorry about what happened."

"Hey, I don't blame the man for not wanting to lose you," he said as their food was brought to the table.

This was not the discussion Aya wanted to have at this time. She started to eat, taking in the ambience of finally being with the man she truly loved. She regretted that there was so little time until her husband's return—only ten days to luxuriate in Marley's presence. She intended to make the most of every moment.

Aya returned home that evening and repacked her overnight bag, to Marva's chagrin. She said that she had found a beautiful spot to alleviate her writer's block and that she wanted to spend the remainder of her time there before the family came home.

Marva pleaded with her to reconsider, and then relished the idea of having the place to herself. She'd always wanted to have Glenda over for dinner, and now she could. Actually, Glenda could come spend a couple of days with her to get away from the drama with her husband. Marva quickly took back her argument and promised not to mention anything to Desi, which she had not been able to do the last time she called him anyway. She had ended up lying and saying that the Missus had been feeling down since the family went away and that they should come back as soon as possible.

So, off Aya went to the sky-blue villa to be with Marley. He would dash away sporadically to check in on his mother, who was sick of his meddling, but they spent most of each day together. They would cuddle, order in, and talk away the hours. They would hold hands as they took long walks on isolated beaches. They would curl up beside each other in bed, kissing and fondling with their clothes on. It was glorious day after day.

Aya would check in with Marva periodically to make sure things were good, and the woman seemed only too happy to have the run of the house. She wouldn't take Desi's calls, instead she would text him in Marley's absence to let him know that she was okay and to confirm that the work he was doing was keeping to schedule. She was thrilled by the prospect that Desi needed more time; he said he was digging in his heels and working around the clock so that he could be home soon.

Aya fretted over how all this euphoria would come to an abrupt end once Desi came home. Nonetheless, she and Marley were both happy to remain in the moment until the end of the month.

Aya received several frantic calls that Sunday morning from her mother and Marva over her absence from the Alzheimer's banquet the night before. Marva tried to cover by saying that she had been cooped up in the cabin and had lost track of time. Unfortunately, Pearl showed up that morning and could tell Aya hadn't been home in days. As Marley was also AWOL, it didn't take her long to figure out that the two of them were probably together.

Aya rushed over to her aunt's house that afternoon to put out the fire.

"Well, finally!" Bea exclaimed as she let her niece in the door. "We've been calling and calling. Where've you been?"

"I've shut myself up to finish the book, Auntie. It's been a real struggle and I wanted to take advantage of my time alone to get it done."

"Take advantage is right," Bea scolded. "Where've you been staying?"

"Oh, it's only been a couple of days. I needed to get out of the house for a while, and I've always loved being up in the countryside. I found a little place there and the words started flowing, so I stayed on. I get caught up in my work sometimes, and I'm sorry I missed your fundraiser."

"Yes, I can see that. I haven't seen you so bright-eyed in a long time," Bea observed. "Funny thing, you in such high spirits with Desi gone."

Aya wrinkled her nose. "He'll be back soon enough. Did you raise much money last night?"

"We did, although it might've been more if Marley had shown up as promised. Have you seen much of him now that your book's nearly done?" Bea asked, steadying her gaze.

"We met up briefly, which is why I've been working so hard. I want to complete it while he's still here," she said, not making eye contact.

"Uh-hmm," Bea said with a raised eyebrow. "Well, your happiness is all that matters to me, dear. Just be careful, I hope you know what you're doing."

Aya did not offer any more information and left it at that, relieved that although skeptical, her aunt would not push the issue. Her mother might be a different matter; she would cross that bridge when she got to it. She made easy banter for an hour and a half, then rushed off to meet Marley before her mother returned.

The next seven days were a heavenly dream. Marley would wake before sunrise to go for a run on the beach, and Aya would call her husband, who was always very brief as he was rushing to get home in time. Marley would return to shower, and Aya would prepare breakfast for him while she drank tea. He would then make the half-hour drive to his mother's place, and Aya would do her yoga, then eat her fruit and yogurt. She would call Marva to talk a bit and then go for a swim until Marley came to meet her.

They would splash about in the surf, and he taught her how to dive and hold her breath underwater. They would then eat the food he had picked up on the way through town and head back to their cozy quarters. Any discussion would run them until evening, when Marley would leave again to see his mother to bed, allowing Aya to have another brief chat with her husband.

Sometimes Marley would bring home dinner, and sometimes he brought groceries to prepare a meal. He was a fabulous cook, and Aya felt nourished on so many levels that she never wanted to be without him again. They talked into the early hours that Monday night, and Aya slept fitfully beside him and wondered why. She sat up to look at him, his dreads gently cascading over his face as he slept. He was a blessed sight.

They had only three days left together, and Aya was beside herself. She simply could not go back to being with Desi again after experiencing this. To hell with counselling! Then she imagined a glimpse of her husband's reaction to learning that she wanted to leave him, which gave her pause. He would be so very angry, but mostly hurt.

She had to admit she had been terribly unfair to him. She would have to remember to be gentle and patient no matter what the future held. He must never know that her intention was to be with Marley, although the hospital confrontation clearly indicated his suspicions.

The love of her life had bought her a ticket to join him in the States in a little over two weeks, and she was delirious with joy at the thought of beginning her new life with him. She would simply separate from her husband and, after two years of never returning to the island, file for divorce. Marley would cover expenses, and she had her savings as pocket money until her book was published or she was able to find work.

Even if her relationship with Marley didn't pan out, at least Aya would have had the encounter and be able to move on with her life. Living a continent away from the Franklyns would ease Desi's shame and help him move forward with his life. Marva would stay on as support, and he never had a problem finding a woman. He might even sign off on their divorce quickly to be out of it.

Her mother and aunt would be another issue. They would not be happy that she'd taken off on them without notice, especially since her mother had packed up her life to spend her twilight years with her. Aya could deal with them later; right now, it was all about Marley.

She felt pangs of desire at the prospect of finally being with him, and she thought that he must be thinking the same thing as she noticed his organ start to expand. She wanted to unwrap his package and ride him as long as he could stand it. But Desi was in the way. He was still her husband, and although she had been unfaithful in every other way, she could not do that to him. She also did not want Marley to think of her as an adulterer, and when asked in court if she'd had an affair, it would be in her best interest to be able to say no.

The buzzing of her cellphone jolted her out of her thoughts, and she jumped to grab it before it woke her darling. She was surprised to see that she had sixteen missed calls. Thankfully none were from her husband. Marva had called eleven times, and the others were from an unknown overseas number. *Why the hell would Marva be calling at this time in the morning?*

Aya went out into the chilly air on the balcony to return her call. "Marva, what's going on?"

"Oh, Missus. I so glad you finally call me. I got horrible news!"

"What happened?"

"It Desi. He done collapsed and been rushed to the hospital!"

"What?" Aya crumpled onto a chair. "What do you mean?"

"I dunno all the details yet," Marva continued. "It seem like he drop on the job and they take him to emergency. It so bad they wanna airlift him back to his doctors here."

"But what happened? Is it food poisoning? A virus? What?"

"Won't know 'til we get him back here, Missus, and he arriving early this afternoon. I just had to reach you so we could meet them there. Little Ricky scared so bad he hysterical. Maybe we should have you mother come for him?"

Aya was astounded. Desi was coming home and ruining her last moments with Marley. Why was he always getting in the way? It was of no matter, for in a few weeks he would be a distant memory.

"I'll be right home, Marva." She ended the call and went in to wake Marley.

Her husband was unconscious and heavily medicated due to his severe stomach pain when the nurse wheeled him by the waiting room. Pearl, Marva, and Ricky were deeply concerned, whereas Aya was trying to figure out how to get back to the villa. There was no way she could explain spending the night away from home again without causing alarm. What to do?

After several hours, the doctor came out and informed the family that Desi was stable and that they could go in. Aya told the others she wanted to see him alone, but in reality, she wanted to use the opportunity to make contact with Marley.

Desi was very weak and tired when she finally made it into his shared room. His skin lacked all moisture and his mouth was white and crusty. He was clenching his jaw and biting his lip. He looked like a menacing stranger.

Aya was taken aback by the sight of this horror, but she tried to cover her alarm. "Why Desi, I ... I ... Are you in any pain?"

"I good for now, Mrs. Franklyn," he said harshly. "The first one I ask for is the last one to reach. Where you been?"

"I let the others go on ahead so that we could be alone. Ricky was so frantic that I didn't think he should have to wait any longer. I'm here now, Desi. What happened to you?"

"Nothing I can't handle."

Aya swallowed hard and looked toward the window. It was pointless to try to talk to him when he was acting so foul. She continued to avoid his gaze, waiting for him to either curse or dismiss her.

They sat that way until the nurse came in to check him. She had a thick French accent, which broke the tension as she tried to joke with Desi. She was successful in getting him to smile, even though he was clearly irate. Aya racked her brain to discover how he could possibly know about her shacking up with Marley. It wasn't possible, yet he was furious about something.

"This here my wife, Aya *Franklyn*," he said bitingly as he emphasized her surname. "She was brought up in Canada and living here shortly before we married. She trying to be a writer since she don't think I'm good enough for her."

Aya's head spun and her face flushed. The nurse raised her hand to caution her reply, and she held her tongue.

"Oh, now, Monsieur Franklyn, that cannot be true. I saw this lovely woman out there and she was so worried and upset. Anybody can see how she loves you, I must need to change your medication." She laughed.

Tears filled Aya's eyes and she gave the dark-skinned, nearly six-foot-tall, over 200-pound woman an appreciative look.

"I should hope so." Desi turned his focus back to his wife. "I damn near give her anything she wants and she's still not satisfied. She can't see how easy she has it since she's too busy looking in other directions. You see, she can't even look at me.

"You know," he continued gruffly, "my father never wanted to get tied up with any woman. He used to say that women would be a man's undoing, and I now see that he was right."

Aya rose to her feet and met her husband's stare.

The kindly nurse intervened again on her behalf while checking Desi's pulse. "Now do not take on so, you!" she admonished. "You are uncomfortable, miserable, and out of your element, so we do not blame you for being riled up. Now do not take it out on this sweet young thing. She is here to hold your hand through this, monsieur. She is not here for her health."

"You think so, Marguerite? Is that true, Mrs. Franklyn?"

Aya's tears overflowed and her guilty conscience exploded. He must know everything that had been going on. She fled from the room and heard the nurse call after her, only she kept running until she collapsed on a bench outside. She had difficulty catching her breath and wanted to scream, but there were too many people coming and going from the parking lot to make such a scene.

"Madame Franklyn, Madame Franklyn." Marguerite was panting when she caught up with Aya. "Do not pay him no mind, ma cherie. He does not know what he is saying."

"He's knows very well or he wouldn't have said it. Why would he act like that if he didn't mean to?"

Marguerite adjusted her blue uniform, which was riding up her enormous backside, and took Aya in her arms. "There, there, ma cherie. Listen to me. It is quite common the way he is reacting—yes? Most people, especially men, get very angry with this diagnosis. They lash out at those they love most. Believe me, I have seen it many times. He is looking for someone to blame for his situation, and he is taking it out on you this time. He is still devastated about leaving you, so please be patient with him—yes? I think he feels he has failed you, ma cherie. Do not take it personal, just love him and hold him no matter what he says. He needs you so much."

She encouraged Aya to sit down and wiped her tears with a handkerchief. Aya stared blankly back at her, not understanding. "Leaving me? What do you mean?"

"He is in the final stages of colon cancer, Madame Franklyn. Now that we have run out of options for him, all we can do is make him as comfortable as possible. This disease can be so vicious, ma cherie, it even affects brain cells—yes? He will start getting paranoid and accuse you of everything and nothing, so do not take it on. It is not him, it is the sickness."

There was a distant crack of thunder before a sudden torrent of rain came down from the rapidly darkening sky. Aya's world went black.

Chapter 33

"Oh Lord, Glenda, I got terrible news. Desi only got up to six months to live! ...

"Yes-yes, he got cancer! He got it for some time but didn't say nothing. When last we speak you was rushing to pack up you things before the Missus come back and we go off to the hospital. You didn't say nothing 'bout her staying out to write those few days, did you? ...

"No, I just asking. She didn't say nothing and don't suspect you was staying with me. Even if she did, she got too many other things on her mind to worry 'bout that now.

"So we go to the hospital and Desi looking real-real bad when they wheel him by, even still I never think it as bad as all that, Glenda. Even the Missus antsy to get him home so she could get on with her work. The Mother real sullen and teary when she sitting with Ricky, who as dumb as a mute ...

"It turn out Desi went up north not just to run from the divorce, but he got some obstruction in his bowels that needed seeing to. The Mother got him in a good facility and bring him back by her since the Missus was down here for the summer. Desi stayed by the Mother so much that the ex-husband get suspicious and finish with him. You believe that? ...

"When she come in with Ricky and me, the Mother take Desi's hand like she his wife, and he let her. They talk in code 'bout making plans since they didn't want Ricky to know he dying. He tell her the arrangements been long planned for, and I just get to figuring out he mean his funeral.

"No wonder the Mother love and hate him so! Imagine, you help the man recover from disease and divorce, and he still don't want you? He then go after and marry you only child? Even I feel that low for him to stoop ...

"She love him true nuff, that was clear to see. That the love he have for the Missus, though. But he treat the Mother very nice. They done had each other, for certain. She lay with him and still want him and it eating her up. She cry-cry so hard when we leave that I wanna slap her ...

"Ricky know, but he don't. He don't wanna believe he gonna be without either parent, so he in denial. He gonna be hard to deal with, but he get on good with the Mother, and hopefully she stick with him after Desi gone ...

"Junior still in the Bahamas since he gotta finish the contract before he can get home. As it is they was working 'round the clock, and with Desi out, they set back. He aiming to get here by next week though. And then Carlton not coming neither. He wrapped up in doing his exams and can't make it 'til they finish. He call most every day, and Desi light up and tell him not to bother to come since his education the most important thing.

"So now Carlotta wanna swoop down like the witch she is on his behalf. She crying and begging to come see Desi, but the Missus not having it. Carlton ask her to wait 'til his exams done to visit, but she nasty as hell so Lord knows she not gonna wait too much longer ...

"Who? The Missus? She a zombie, you'd never recognize her. She cry and cry that first time back from the hospital when she find out. I'd'a never thought she could carry on so. I thinking she love Desi after all only she not one to show it, or she now realizing how much she love he and it too late. Poor thing. She so devastated and then she don't wanna go to the hospital no more and won't tell me why. Later, I get it outta her ...

"When she go in to see Desi by herself, he treat her bad-bad, Glenda. He snap at her and she say if looks could kill she be gone. She don't understand why he being so cruel 'til the nurse explain his sickness and that he dying. He been going back and forth to the hospital for eighteen months and not telling a soul, so this nurse know him good. He not working as much as we thought, but making everyone believe so to cover ...

"Desi know he a lost cause months before he go to the Bahamas, and he still go anyway, the blasted fool! I dunno why he refuse surgery or getting chemo when it could'a saved him ...

"Too right, Glenda. He got so much to live for. I know he must'a done everything else he could to be cured since he come to know Marguerite well. She a real kind lady and helping the Missus a lot, even calling most every day to make sure she holding up ...

"The house don't feel like a home no more, girl, it feel real heavy here now. I been staying on since this all happen, and ain't nobody said boo. The Mother in Junior's old room next to Ricky, and I in at Carlton for now. Cicely tending to my old bag since she gone and catch pneumonia. She gonna give it a few days before she take her to the hospital. Well, that her business! As nasty as she treat me every day, you imagine how she be sick? Me? I not going anywhere near she ...

"The Franklyns need me too much right now, so don't you start. The Missus all shut up in her studio, not sleeping or eating or talking. Her mother can't reach her, and she don't wanna scare Ricky by letting him see how bad off she is so he know his father dying. It gonna be plain nuff when Desi come home this week, looking the way he do ...

"The Mother gonna nurse him, you believe that? The Missus in no state to take up for me, so the woman just push in and take over. She need to remember her place and know that she ain't the wife or the boy's family neither. I the one who been with them all these years, and she ain't gonna push me out ...

"The Missus just gotta get better and sort out this nonsense once Desi come home. I bring her food and I find it the same way every evening, not even touched. I had to force-feed her my soup last evening to stop her from wasting away. The Mother bring her tea, fruit, toast, and biscuits, and she throw them out. I not sure if it to hide that she not eating or that she don't want nothing to do with that woman since she block her out completely ...

"She acknowledge me and look at me when I talking, but not the Mother. She look the opposite direction and hide under the sheets a the bed. The Mother wanna bring in some counsellor to talk to her since she can't get a hold a that Marley, but the cousin back from England in a couple a days, so I hoping she do the trick. She the only one I hear the Missus talking to other than me."

"No, I dunno much 'bout her other than she studying up near Carlton in England. She older than the Missus and treats me good, not like help, you know?

"So, for now, every morning the Mother and Ricky go to the hospital and the Missus and I go every evening. Most times, I the one doing all the talking as they don't have much to say, but the one time she didn't show up, he so vex. What kinda madness is this? When she there he ain't got a word to say, but he watch her hard. I figure if I leave things would be different, but they say even less when I gone. Desi mind like it gone too. Marguerite keep telling me to be patient and let him deal the best he can even though I feel to cuss him to act right most every day.

"He nice as pie to the Mother though. After all the maliciousness she done bring him to? I can't understand it, Glenda. The Missus take his side over her own mother and auntie, her father still not speaking to her, and he don't give a damn all a sudden? You just wait 'til he get home, good and comfortable. Me and him gonna have words, I don't care what the nurse say ...

"Yes, I trying to take it easy, Glenda, and I know my pressure up, but I ain't studying that right now. I taking my medication and eating the food the Missus don't, but my mind mixed up so much I don't sleep at night neither. I take naps when the Mother gone to the hospital, but she come and catch me the other morning and make a remark like she the one paying me. That ain't none a her business! She acting too much like the lady a the house, and not even the Missus be like that, ever ...

"Too right, Glenda. It gonna be hard when Desi not living, I don't even wanna think 'bout it. Lemme change the subject. What Marshall say when you finally come home? He think you off having some fling like you hoped? ...

"Woo-hooh, ha! Oh Lord, Glenda, you too much. I thank you for that laugh, girl, I needed it bad. I keep telling you to stop playing with that man and tell him how you feel. Why he ain't left you yet, then? I'm telling you, he loves you and is waiting for you to love him back. You better not make him wait too long ...

"Don't you worry 'bout Marva, the Lord is my shelter. Me? I gonna be there for Desi and pray he come through. I gonna hold the Missus's hand 'til she can walk on her own again and be the proper family to Ricky that I always been. I gonna beat the Mother at her own game and get her outta my way, for good. I know the Missus will take up for me when the time come and send the Mother packing.

"Now to get my own sorted. If I live in, I don't have many expenses and can afford to put the devil in that home you told me 'bout and done with that. The Missus don't need so much space and won't argue 'bout me staying for good ...

"Mmm, you may be right. But why should the Missus wanna leave to get a place a her own? She got the cabin and she got me. She can't go off and leave the boy ...

"Yes, I there to watch after him, but what she gonna leave and do? I dunno what Desi gonna give her, or any a us. Remember, she not working, that Marley done run off, and she ain't gonna go back to living with her auntie. No, Glenda, she gonna stay on where she is, this her home now. This where we belong ...

"Now don't get upset 'cause you hoping I have to come take up with you. You thinking Marshall gonna leave you in that house, big as it is, and go find someplace else to park? He not gonna walk away from all that land, Glenda. He buy you out first, if you asking me. You really wanna leave there with all them acres you got? You rather dead than shift yourself for some nice lady to come in and treat Marshall right ...

"Oooh, that got you good now, huh? You stay there and push yourself out you own house and then where will we be? It looking more like you gonna be the one to come and stay with me, then, missy ..."

"Yes, I thinking Junior'll become the man a the house if Desi gone. He might take his father room as his own too. That good nuff since the Missus prefer out back anyway, and with the amount a women he got coming and going, it better he be as close to the front door as possible.

"The only thing now is Carlton, if he come. I hoping he not under his mother influence to try to suck out as much cash as possible. The land in all their names and I don't see them growing old together here, especially with Carlton's ways. That could be a problem if Junior get nasty. They might sell it once Ricky old nuff and go they own way, you could be right. Not if the Missus got any say, and that what we gotta wait to see ...

"Why you that way 'bout the Missus? You jealous? I'd never put her before you, if that what you thinking. You so nasty when you talk a her, like she done Desi wrong. Is there something I dunno 'bout? ...

"Well, you acting like she don't deserve nothing from him, but they married near five years and he happy nuff. None a his other women treat him so good, and she didn't spend off all his money neither ...

"Yes, the house get a makeover, but he wanted that more for her than she did. The Missus always telling him she don't want no fancy things and for him to slow down and take it easy. That why she wanna write so bad and be a success, so she can help take the pressure off Desi. She never planned to sit back and live off him, she wanted a business a her own ...

"Now, I know all 'bout that Marley, looking as fine as no man got the right to be. I know the Missus very well and she faithful to her husband, she not leaving him. And it ain't just for the perks neither, since they both got 'bout the same. The Missus love travel and the arts and that all a Marley, but she stick to Desi anyway. You got to give her that. Who you to talk with the way you treat you own husband? You forget 'bout glass houses? ...

"Don't be like that, Glenda! I not making sport at you expense. Me? You forget that you marry Marshall 'cause he got a good education, that land you sitting on, and a big inheritance coming to him from his daddy? You forget that the man you really loved was that yella fool who always had that guitar? Wasn't he a Rasta? ...

"You could'a had him and been happy, but you went for the money! You focus on how big a house you gonna build, what kinda car you gonna be able to drive, and how many times a year you gonna be able to go to London, Miami, or New York to shop. You forget? You make you bed and then don't want him to come in it! ...

"Come now, Glenda. I just playing with you, trying to make you laugh 'cause Lord knows we need it. We got some long, dark days ahead a us to get through and dunno which way the wind gonna blow. I gotta tell you, sometimes I think my head gonna burst trying to figure it all out. How I gonna live without Desi? How I gonna be able to watch him waste away in front a my two bad eyes? How I gonna bury the only man that been with me for all a these years? My only family outside a you.

"Then I gotta figure out what to do with my own home, if the bitch ain't signed it over to Cicely already. The Missus tell me to rent it out so I can have a little coin in my pocket every month, but I thinking I'd like to be rid a the whole thing and take what little I can for it. You interested? Lord knows you gonna need a place a you own soon nuff ...

"Too right, we still gotta see if I can get my hands on it first. As soon as I get her in that home, I'll get to the bottom a things. The Missus tell me that since she feeble, I as her daughter can get control a things at last. I guess I too frightened to find out all this time, since I doubt she got anything for me. Lord knows I deserve something and maybe he see fit to let me catch a break.

"Cicely treating me real foul these days too, like she believing everything she being told even though she know my life been hell in that shack with that woman. She must be feeling sorry for the ol' cow now that she finally coming to the end, and hoping to get a little something for her time. She need to think again ...

"I know, I know. We been through all this before—many times—and you don't like to hear me go on and get worked up. But my time coming, Glenda. I can feel it. If I can just make it through these next few months. And Lord forgive me, she better beat Desi to the grave 'cause I through with her and her nasty ways. I done!"

Chapter 34

"I came as soon as I could," Nicola said as she entered Aya's cabin. "I hope you're feeling a little better now, cousin, since you sounded awful the last time we spoke. Where's your husband?"

"They're not releasing him until the end of the week. My mother's going to care for him once he gets home," Aya answered weakly, closing the door.

"Why are you allowing that? She could barely stand the man not too long ago. She may finish him off before his time, the way she is. Desi's okay with that?"

"He doesn't want a stranger all up in his business, so he's keeping it in the family." Aya slumped in the chair next to her cousin.

"Since when are they family? Is she really going to wipe his ass, bathe him, and—"

"I suppose if it becomes as bad as all of that, we'll get someone in," Aya said crisply. "We're taking it one day at a time, Nic, I can't think about that right now. They made the agreement and—"

"*They* made it?" a skeptical Nicola asked. "That's exactly what I don't understand. They seem to be making all the decisions together, doesn't that seem strange to you?"

"No," she answered, rising to fix their usual rum and coconut water. "He doesn't want to bother me."

Nicola remained unconvinced. She knew her cousin only too well and knew where her mind was really focused. "And I suppose you haven't heard anything from Marley yet either?"

Aya took her time filling the glasses. Nicola could tell from how her shoulders slumped that she was carrying a heavy load that needed to be unburdened. The tears started to fall fast, and before long she had to help Aya's head up off the ground and onto her lap while she stroked her face.

"Come on now, Aya, he's not worth this. You've got to pull yourself together. I know you think you love him—"

Aya shot straight up and glared. "*Think* I love him? You know that I do, how could you think otherwise? If you only knew how wonderful it was going to bed with him every night and waking to his smile in the morning. And those lips!"

"So it's lust? He's your sexual fantasy come to life. How was he in the sack, then? Anything worth writing about?"

"We've never slept together!"

"So you went to bed with him every night and didn't jump his bones?" Nicola raised both eyebrows. "This man you love so much and are so horny for?"

"I'm still married and I want to wait until I am his alone."

"Bitch, that don't make no sense!" Nicola said. "There has to be some other reason. Are you afraid he won't live up to your expectations, or vice versa?"

"You're asking a lot of questions for someone who's supposed to be here to help me," Aya said, clearly irritated. "Desi's still my husband and I'm not able to cheat on him like that."

"You've cheated in the only way that matters," Nicola said. "You all spoon?"

"A little." Aya looked down at her feet. "We never took off our clothes or let things go too far, we respect each other too much for that."

"So you were fake lovemaking?" Nicola bellowed while wiping away tears of laughter. Even Aya had to smile at that.

"We wanted it to be over between Desi and me before we took it to that level. He doesn't like the idea of messing around with another man's wife any more than I do. It's just that things happened and we never meant for them to. We tried to fight it and I wanted to ignore it, you know that. I can't be with Desi anymore. Even if Marley weren't in the picture, I still would want a separation to get my mind right, he didn't tip the scales in that direction."

"So, is he pissed that you didn't run off with him and leave your husband for dead?"

"He left me a ticket that's valid for a few months to come join him when I can. He didn't want any explanation or promises from me once he found out, either. He told me it has to be my decision and he would not force the issue. Both he and his mother went to California."

"She know about you?" Nicola asked.

"I'm not sure, we've never discussed it." Aya raised herself from the kitchenette floor. "She's been polite the few times we've crossed paths, although I can tell she doesn't like me much."

"I see," Nicola said, also rising and walking to the table to take a drink. "She doesn't have the nicest reputation."

"Really? You did find out something about the Wright family since you flew back yesterday?"

Nicola smirked. "She's not his real mother, he's her sister's child. She took him as her own to land the father and live in the US. He sent her packing as soon as he found out, as I hear. He's made millions in real estate, so I'm sure that villa you love so much must be his. Back to her, though—you know they are Trinidadians? She got plenty of clothes, jewellery, and a few free trips out of this Wright man. When he set his mind on his marriage to another woman, he stopped coming back to the island.

"So, she becomes pregnant—or says she is, no one's really sure. The sister was only thirteen and knocked up, so she somehow took it and told the man that it was his child, even though everyone saw her sister's big belly but no one ever saw hers."

"You're kidding me?" Aya said as she slowly sat down at the table. "Does Marley know about this?"

"You're asking me?" Nicola laughed. "You're the one sleeping next to the man! When you should've been riding that pecker into the—"

"Okay, okay." Aya shook her head. "He's never called her anything other than 'Mother.' I did realize she had something of an accent but never thought much about it. I find it odd that he never mentioned this to me, considering all we've shared. He must not know."

"How could he not know? It didn't take much for me to find out, he could not be that obtuse."

"Well, what difference does it make anyway, after all this time? She still mothered him, didn't she?"

Nicola laughed out loud. "His real mother was the worst piece of work, from what I've been told from their old neighborhood. She outed the whole thing to the man when she came to find out she wasn't getting her fair share of the money that Mr. Wright was sending to her sister. It was a big scandal and the family split up. Clarissa—that's the woman claiming to be Marley's mother—had to leave the parish for many years. She had the smarts to get US residency for the boy so they did end up hiding in California after all, until the money ran out."

"Wait a minute," Aya interrupted. "Marley still refers to an American as his father from California, could it be a different man?"

"No, the man does live in California," Nicola said with a nod. "He was in the papers only a few months ago for the opening ceremony of that medical clinic out in the country. He's not Marley's father, though the man is named Wright."

"He told me he never knew his father as he died before he was born. Parents lie to their kids all the time. She was probably trying to protect him."

Nicola nodded and whistled. "Could be. Something's not quite right about all this, Aya. It reeks of dishonesty, and if he's been raised by such a conniver, could the fruit have fallen far from the tree?"

"Yes, I know you think I should stick it out with Desi—"

"It's not that at all, Ay. I know you're fed up in your marriage, I can see that. I just want you to be very careful with this man. It's to your advantage that Desi is kicking off now to leave you to him, so simply have fun for a while and don't make it into anything serious. Get in, get your sex, and get out."

"Oh, Nic, how can you say that? Marley's such a sweet, generous man. He's done so much for me, and I've given him little in return."

"Well, I feel a payback expected from you, and quick. This is the last time I'm going to warn you."

"Listen," Aya put her arm over Nicola's shoulder. "I know you're watching out for me, but I can look after myself. Marley does well for himself financially and is in the process of setting up a company of his own. He doesn't have women everywhere, or a single baby momma. Auntie's network has checked him out thoroughly and couldn't find a thing against his character."

Nicola became pensive as she thought Aya was making some very astute observations. "Well, why don't you call and ask the man about what you've been hearing? That would solve the mystery, wouldn't it?"

"He made it very clear he only wants to hear from me when I am coming to him. The last time I tried to see how he was doing, he became so upset with me for getting his hopes up. At this point my whole life is a mess and I have to be here for Desi."

"Why, when you have your mother lurking about? It could be months yet, even a year. Then what? You expect Marley to wait?"

"So you think I should leave him?"

"I'm saying you have a decision to make. Stop waiting to see what is dished out for you and take it your damn self."

"If Marley really loves me, he'll wait. We've had separations before and it's made no difference in our feelings. He's the one for me. I know it every time I'm with him. I just need to make it through these next months. I can't abandon Desi now."

"You mean you can't abandon your stake in the Franklyn estate. Don't cut your eyes at me! Listen, I don't blame you. If you left now, you could wind up with nothing, while waiting may allow you to have it all. There's no way in hell I want you running off to America with no funds of your own, relying only on Marley. You have to protect your interests."

"It's not that, Nic," Aya said, clearly hurt. "I've managed to put aside a little to carry me, and I still have my book to publish. It's that I wouldn't be able commit myself to Marley properly with Desi's sickness lingering over him."

"That's another thing I don't understand. You couldn't wait to leave him not long ago, what's the difference? His dying? Now you feel guilty and want to do the right thing when it's wrong too? I tell you, all-a-wunna lives are too messy for me."

Aya sighed loud and long. "I wish I knew what to do," she said finally.

"Make a decision!" Nicola snapped.

Chapter 35

Desi's return home went relatively smoothly. Marva tidied the master bedroom to sparkling perfection even though Desi had requested to be set up in his wife's cabin, to everyone's surprise. Aya heard his request but needed to make no comment as her mother and Marva were so fervent with their chastising.

Pearl explained that the bathroom was far too tiny to accommodate him properly and that his room was a much brighter and more comfortable space. Marva, not to be outspoken, added that he was better off close to her and that he could sit out on his balcony at any time to overlook the same area. Ricky put in his two cents as well, saying that the cabin didn't have many electrical outlets and that they were in awkward places. His room was far better organized.

Desi made no argument, keeping a steady gaze on his wife. Aya knew he was gauging her expression, testing her for something in his heavily medicated mind that she could not ascertain. She continued to stand back and watch them fuss over her husband, and stared right back at him. After a time, Desi grinned, and she assumed it was because he was amused by her moxie.

Although weak, Desi was still able to gingerly walk for some distance, but he made no effort to do so. He did not leave his room, and his curtains were left wide open all day long so he could watch the comings and goings of his wife.

After a couple of days, the excitement and panic of the changes in the household wore through and everyone settled into a routine. Initially Marva and Pearl had their eyes on Desi around the clock, but he quickly tired of their incessant fussing and now they only intruded every three hours. During that time, Desi was left on his own, and Aya would try to time it to be with him when he was drowsy or sleeping to keep up the appearance of an involved wife.

Aya quickly retreated whenever Ricky would appear as he seemed to be the only one to give his father any genuine comfort. Desi did his best to put on the façade of health for his youngest, and they even set up the Wii system in his room so that the two could play together.

About thirty days later, Aya felt relaxed enough in Desi's presence to test the waters and initiate a conversation with him.

"You're really starting to come back to yourself lately, Desi," she said. "You may beat this thing yet."

Desi fixed his eyes on her and cleared his throat. "Sorry to disappoint you, Mrs. Franklyn."

"Why in hell do you keep calling me that? That's all I am to you now, is that it? Why don't you come out and say whatever it is you are getting at?"

Desi cleared his throat once again. "Just a reminder of who you are, since you seem to be forgetting."

"And what is that supposed to mean?" Aya said, throwing her head back to look at the ceiling and rolling her eyes. "You don't feel that I am being a proper wife to you now?"

Desi squinted his eyes and curled his lips. "Your next book ready for review yet? I hear you been working real hard on it."

So, he knew then! Somehow, he had found out that she had been living elsewhere in his absence and probably with Marley. She wanted to wring Marva's neck. Aya recognized that he was ready to spring a trap on her and didn't take the bait by steadying herself. She squared her shoulders to look down at him.

"Yes, I have a draft ready," she answered coolly, pretending to organize his meds on the bureau. "Though clearly, other things are a priority right now."

"What he think of it?"

"He who?" she asked quickly, knowing perfectly well who he meant.

"Who else be looking over your work and creeping 'bout here?"

"Marley?" she asked sarcastically as she sat on the lounger to face him at last. "You can't call him by his proper name? Well, he hasn't been here in ages. I doubt he's even on the island."

"I know exactly where he is," Desi said cryptically.

Aya tried to remain calm and not let him ruffle her feathers. "So why don't you ask him, then?" she shot back, meeting him stare for stare.

"You asking a lot of questions when I looking for answers."

"As I said, the manuscript's not a priority right now, I have other concerns."

"Your husband for once?"

"Primarily," she said bluntly.

Desi cleared his throat, lay back on the bed, put his hands behind his neck to cradle his head, and closed his eyes.

"Stay out of this, Mother!"

Aya's shout drew Marva's attention, and she made her way down to the bottom of the stairs to be within earshot.

"You need to cut him some slack, Aya. You're so short with him! Can't you be kinder?" Pearl said.

Aya moaned. "You're supposed to be here to help me, remember?"

"I've been trying to help you with your mind lost in space. All you do is stare at the sea or the clouds and hardly eat a thing. You're nearly as sick as your husband! Have you looked at yourself lately?"

"I have no appetite, so leave me alone! We're all under a lot of pressure, and I'm coping the best I can."

"Well, you need to focus on your husband and get that damned Marley out of your mind. Sleeping out and meeting in out-of-the-way locations. Really, Aya?"

"What? You're actually saying this to me? Weren't you desperate for me to take off with the man, or have I lost my mind like you clearly have?"

"That was then, Ay. Things are different now with Desi's condition, and you're not giving him proper care."

"Excuse me?" Aya shouted, rising from the kitchen table.

"Oh, don't take on so. You're not being very loving to Desi when he needs it most. If it weren't for me encouraging him, he wouldn't get any nurturing at all. I mean, Marva-the-mouth does try, even if she can hardly keep the place tidy, what with her three-hour breaks."

Marva got so angry at that remark that she dropped the laundry bag she was carrying and all its contents spilled out and onto the floor. She was ready to cuss the Mother, only the Missus got to the heart of the matter first.

"Don't you say another thing against Marva. It's none of your business what goes on between me and my husband, and I've warned you on that already."

"You're taking the maid's side over mine?"

"She is not the maid! She is family. Ever since Desi got his prognosis, you've been insufferable. Everything he does is good or golden, and you despised the man for years, you hypocrite!"

Marva stopped picking up the clothes and stood up straight. She wanted to applaud. The Missus was back and true to form! She decided to ease her way out of such a visible spot and hoped that Desi was still sleeping and not hearing any of this.

"Stop yelling at me, Aya!" Pearl shouted, rising to meet her daughter. "I'm your mother."

"Well, you're in my house and making me crazy. I want you out!"

Marva gasped so loud that she was certain they must have heard her, and she scampered for cover in the laundry room. Although a part of her was delirious with joy at this outcome, something else was very troubled.

"You're putting me out?" a teary Pearl asked, truly shaken. "What have I done? Try to help you and our family get through this difficult time? You couldn't even put two words together a few days ago, and I was here at my wit's end holding things down for you. Hell, I'm the only grandmother the boy has ever known. He needs me, Aya! And Desi, he won't make it without me. Or is that what you want?"

She shouldn't have said that, Marva thought, and Pearl seemed to realize it too.

"You only care about what you want," Aya said acidly. "And I can clearly see what you want is to be with my husband, above all else. You are not here out of concern for me, you are here to be next to him."

"Aya, we're tired, stressed, and sick with worry over this whole situation and saying crazy things we don't mean. Let's call it a day and try to get some rest, and we'll talk about this later."

"Who says I even want to see you later?" Aya laughed. "Pack your things! I'm calling Auntie to come for you."

Marva pushed her head out of the laundry room door in time to see Aya storm into the still-sleeping Desi's room so the Mother could have no parting words with him. Marva, who should have loved this scene, could take no pleasure in it. She was glad that Ricky was at school and not around to hear the Mother fall to pieces at the kitchen table.

Ricky was crushed to return home and find that Pearl had left with no explanation. Junior was held up in the Bahamas, so he had no one to turn to for answers. Marva told him to ask the Missus, who blew him off by saying she would be happy to bring him to visit his grandma at any time but that she had needed to return home to her sister in Jackson. Desi was highly suspicious but said nothing.

Marva was relieved to have the meddler gone, even though the brunt of the responsibility now fell to her. Aya took her to collect her belongings and moved her in permanently, giving her a sizeable raise to cover the expense of putting her mother in care. Marva was so grateful for the Missus's support that she was willing to work around the clock if need be. Aya had ensured that she was to remain a part of the family unit no matter what the future had in store. Marva was one to never forget a kindness.

Marva would rise by 5:00 a.m. to begin her day. She would wake Desi to give him his medication and coffee, which he would enjoy on the lounger as she changed the sheets he had sweat through since he could no longer tolerate air conditioning. When that was done, she would put the laundry in, mop the lower level of the house, and open up all the windows. She would then allow herself twenty minutes to eat and check in with Glenda, who was becoming more and more distant since Marva had moved in to Frankly Fine full time. At 7:00 a.m., she would wake Ricky for school and take the daily morning call from Carlton before passing him through to his father. By quarter to eight, the Mother would honk for Ricky to come out so she could drive him to school. She would not give Marva the satisfaction of making her wait outside the door, so she remained in her car.

Marva would prepare bone broth soups, arrange and administer the daily meds for Desi, wipe him down twice a day, and help him in the bath. She ran errands, went to the market for supplies, continued to tend to the kitchen garden Aya had encouraged her to start, and oversaw the crew that maintained the acres of land.

The Mother did her part to pick Ricky up by 2:30 p.m. and return him back home with messages for his father. On Fridays, she would even take him out for pizza and ice cream and return him home just before dark.

It was on one of those Fridays two weeks later that Desi decided to appeal to Marva once again. Marva was doing the last vinegar wipe of his room before he went down for the evening. She was exhausted from being up since dawn and from missing her usual twelve-to-three nap because she had been anxious about hearing from the lawyer the Missus had found to handle her mother's affairs.

"So why you not keeping me up on what going on in my own house?"

Marva put down the vinegar. "What's that? What you think going on?"

"I mean, you been keeping me out the loop and you was never like that before. You got you head turned now since you got that pay raise?"

Marva took off her gloves and faced her employer. "What you mean, Desi?"

"What going on with Pearl and Aya, then? You haven't said a thing to me 'bout it in all this time."

"Well, she you wife and the Mother you new best friend so I didn't think it my place," Marva replied stoically, picking up a dirty towel. Desi had wiped his mouth with it and there was a distressing amount of bloody residue. "Besides, I dunno much 'bout it," she lied.

"Since when you don't know all 'bout everything going on in this house? Pearl call my cell and tell me you were nearby when it happen," he said through gritted teeth.

"Since when you start taking her word over mine?" Marva shot back. "I gotta tell you, Desi, I don't like you attitude since you come back from the hospital. You treating you wife like a stranger, and she suffering just as much as you. Ain't you got no feelings no more? I know this got nothing to do with the medicine neither!"

"You don't dictate how I oughtta to behave. I counted on you to look after things when I was away, and I come back to hear a bunch of garbage 'bout my wife while you here covering for her!"

"I ain't covering for nobody!" Marva said. "You let that wicked woman who been trying to ruin you turn you head."

"Where was my wife when Junior and the hospital was trying to reach her, then, huh? Why couldn't anyone get hold of her?"

"I tell you, the Missus shut herself up to focus on her work, you know how she is."

"How come she couldn't come to the phone? And don't you dare lie!"

"Des, it was the middle a the night—"

"She wasn't nowhere 'round, that's why!" he boomed.

He was so loud that Marva nearly jumped out of her skin.

"Oh, so that what you on 'bout? What kinda mother would talk so 'bout her own child?" Marva said, trying to change the subject and buy time.

"Pearl ain't got nothing to do with this and you know that. The minute I leave, my wife run off to another man—don't you lie to me!"

"That not so!" Marva argued, standing over a grimacing Desi. "Only toward the end when she was rushing to finish before you come back did she go, and Marley was nowhere near these parts. You think I could do that to you, after all these years? I wouldn't never stand for fuckery, as you well know. How many times I been on you for that foolishness?"

"I know very well that prick was with her, no matter what you say. Why would she have to leave this place to go and pay for another one to write in? That don't make no sense. She had to go so she could be with him and you not report 'bout it. That is, if you telling the truth."

"I ain't one to lie, not 'bout something like this. You working yourself up for nothing, the Missus not cheating on you—never. I see how she cry when she waiting for you at the hospital, she a mess. Only a woman who love you would carry on so. You see how small she is? She worried sick 'bout you, and you don't give a damn. Trying to put the Mother in her place, is it any wonder she get put out?"

Desi clenched his teeth and sat up in his bed. "The way I see it, you the one need putting out."

"Who needs putting out?" Aya said as she made her way into the room and stood at the foot of her husband's bed. Nobody moved or said anything. "Marva, it's getting late, you both need your rest. What are you still doing in here?"

"Desi here trying to fire me," she said, pushing out her bottom lip and crossing her arms. Desi's eyes flashed with fury and he pointed his finger at her to keep her mouth shut.

"Fire you?" Aya laughed. "No one's firing you, Marva, now go on to bed."

"No, you don't," Desi countered. "Me and her got unfinished business. Me and you, too, but I'll get to that later."

"Oh?" said an amused Aya. "You want to put me out of the house too?"

Desi chewed on his bottom lip and glared at his dictatorial wife. "You not the boss in this house now that I in this bed. If I say she goes, she goes, ya understand?"

Aya disregarded his remarks and turned to smile at Marva. "Marv, go on to bed. You've had a long day, and you don't need this after how hard you've had to work. When Mr. Franklyn is fully rested, I am sure he will apologize."

Marva was not so sure. But she was amazed by the strength the Missus was displaying, clearly ready for whatever was coming her way. As proud as she was of her, she knew Desi would not like this side of her at all.

"Don't you talk 'bout me like I ain't here or I some blasted child!" he shouted. "I ain't dead yet, and nothing's for certain. Your place is in this bed with me, not down there in that cabin. And even that not good enough, you had to go off and find yourself another one the minute my back is turned. I bet you didn't leave him alone in his bed, did you?"

Marva cast Aya a glance that said she had not broken her promise to keep quiet. Aya simply smiled and lay down with her raging husband. "Go on to bed, Marv. It's Saturday tomorrow so you can sleep in. I'll get breakfast ready for the family."

Marva gave her Missus an unbelieving squint, but Aya looked unconcerned. She took the washcloth from the bedside table and wiped her husband's brow. He immediately calmed and lay down. Although he was boiling hot, she cuddled up to him and closed her eyes to sleep. "Good night, Mr. Franklyn."

"Good night, Ay."

Chapter 36

Things calmed down for a bit once Junior returned. Although concerned over his father's welfare, he had his hands full taking over the business and satisfying his women and left Aya and Marva to run things. Desi was barely speaking to Marva, but he kept the peace.

Marva had hoped Junior would take more of an interest in Ricky but he preferred to not acknowledge what was happening until he was forced to. It would be over a month before Carlton was able to come back, and he was only staying for a brief two weeks before returning to his studies.

Marva was appalled that Carlton would not consider spending quality time with his father at this critical juncture; however, he seemed convinced that his father was recovering, and Desi was active in encouraging that falsehood. Although well accomplished at masking his searing pains, his bodily discharges were getting harder to hide, which was a large part of why he didn't want Marva tending to him and running back to tell his wife.

Aya kept to herself and did not confide in Marva at all anymore. Nicola returned for good, having completed her studies, and they would have hushed conversations in the cabin that Marva could not pick up on, no matter how hard she tried. Aya had become rail thin, so Nicola took her out to lunch or dinner one day a week and made sure that she ate. Marva intercepted a call from the Mother that was meant for Ricky and asked how to make her stir-fries, only to be fiercely cursed out.

Marva called Glenda to discuss that conversation but once again got the answering machine. It had been over a week since Glenda had returned any of her calls, and for the life of her, she could not understand why. She decided that as soon as she could get some time off, she would get a van up there to have it out once and for all.

That afternoon, while Marva was having her nap on the couch in front of the television, Aya got the call from her aunt.

She had been helping Desi wipe himself down and had noticed that he got an erection when she reached his thigh. She tried to ignore it, but he took her hand and guided it to his penis. She was not certain she could hide her repulsion from his harsh stare, but she did not remove herself from his grip.

He held her on his shaft and tried to climax. His hot, foul breath was on her forehead as he vigorously squeezed her with a strength that she would not have thought him still capable of. She was terrified that he would try to make her use her mouth where her hand was failing and wanted to vomit.

Although his forehead was dripping wet and she was worried that his lungs were about to collapse from the pressure, he failed to peak. After eight long minutes, he released her to rest his head in his hands.

Aya did not have words to offer and simply wiped him down and left to clean up. The universe granted her an escape from any follow up when the phone rang and she excused herself from the room to answer it.

"Aya Daniels!" Bea yelled into the phone.

"*Franklyn*, Auntie," Aya said, regretting having picked up. She walked out to the front gallery to have a private conversation.

"How could you do this to your own mother? You know you are her whole world, and you throw her out?"

"That happened weeks ago, Auntie, why bring it up now? You want rid of her too?"

"How can you be so heartless, Aya? What has happened to you? You know her only thought is to be there for you, and this is how you treat her?"

"I will not be disrespected in my own house."

"That's Desi's house you're living in, so don't be ridiculous. He is not gonna leave a thing to you the way you been carrying on either. Besides, you could've talked it out with P and been reasonable, you didn't have to let things go so far."

"I'm capable of taking care of him, Auntie, he'll be just fine. It's better this way, with her not living here. It's bad enough that they slept together, I will not have her pining over him."

"What do you mean?"

"You know very well what I mean. She's still in love with him, and always will be. She makes me sick!"

"Aya, you need to choose your words carefully. One can't help who they fall for. She loves you most of all, so don't be like that. Him, too, for that matter."

"I have enough to deal with, Auntie, and I don't need her adding to things. She was making Marva miserable and—"

"So, Marva is more important than your own mother? Are you hearing yourself, Ay? Because you're talking pure poop!"

"Just stay out of this, Auntie! Things will work themselves out in their own time."

"How's that supposed to happen when you won't even talk to us? You need us now more than ever."

"I don't need anyone taking over. She knew all this time that he had cancer and never thought to tell me!"

"He had a polyp removed back then, is all we knew. If P committed any offense, she's sorry for it and you need to work it out. We'll be all you have soon, you know?"

"I won't be alone," Aya said shortly.

"You still meaning to run off with Marley then?"

Aya would have no part of that conversation. "Auntie, I love you too and I know you're worried about me. Trust that everything's going to work out in the best interests of everyone. I know mother wants to help, but I can't deal with her and she needs to leave it at that for now. I take things day by day."

"Well, I'm coming by to visit tomorrow, and that's that."

"Auntie, you and Desi haven't gotten along in ages, why do you want to come now?"

"I can make my peace with him and visit you, can't I? I won't mention anything to P and we can talk properly. Don't even think of not being home because I will make myself a nuisance until I get in to see you."

Aya, knowing she was beaten, hung up.

Later that evening, Aya received a text message from Marley that animated every cell in her body.

Dearest: I am breaking my own rule to let you know that I am thinking of nothing but you.

Knowing that she was still in his heart and on his mind was a source of resuscitating strength for Aya. She had been feeling as if he were slipping away from her like two ships passing in the night, and she had to return the favour with a simple reply.

Don't ever give up on us.

She lay down next to her husband, the tastes and aromas of Marley filling her mind as she drifted off to sleep. She imagined him caressing her inner thighs and relaxed under his touch. He gently made his way to her vagina and massaged her clitoris, and she moaned with the ripples of pleasure.

He removed her panties, parted her legs with his right hand, and penetrated her. She lifted her right leg to rest on his, and took in every inch of him, gradually becoming aware that something was off. For one, she could not feel Marley's long locks dangling over her or the smoothness of his largely hairless body. This man's skin was hairy and coarse. This man's breathing was laboured and he smelled like liniment.

Aya was beginning to think and did not want to lose the fantasy. She had gone without for too long and refused to deny her body this.

Then Desi muttered louder and struggled to catch his breath, and Aya became anxious. She tried to assure herself that this was only a dream, even if the evidence to the contrary was mounting. She squeezed her eyes tighter and tried to block everything out, but Desi's foul breath in her nostrils could not be denied.

Aya played dead, and wished that she were.

Aya rose early the next morning and rushed to cover the late-night betrayal before Marva came in. She would not look at her husband as she cleaned him up. Then she took a bath to remove any trace of him from her body. When she was dressed, she removed the bedsheets with minor difficulty as Desi was sleeping so heavily, and she was in the process of setting up his medications when she heard movement in the kitchen.

"You up very early," a curious Marva stated. "Desi poking wake you up?"

Aya swallowed hard, trying not to confirm Marva's suspicions. "Hungry, is all."

"You still look sleepy, though I glad to hear you want food. What you feel like eating?"

"Don't bother yourself, I've got leftovers at the studio I can nibble on."

"You need proper food, you wasting away, ya know? I'll make you something and bring it over."

"I told you not to bother. Auntie is coming later today, so maybe make a little something for her if she stays long enough. Don't put your face like that. Send her out to me whenever she comes, I'll make sure she stays out of your way. Oh, and I've already wiped Desi down, taken off the sheets, and setup his morning meds so you don't have to worry about him this morning."

Marva could not mask her surprise or her suspicions, though she did not say anything and refocused her efforts on making the place spotless so the aunt could not report back to the Mother that things had fallen apart since her departure.

When Marva opened the door to Bea later that afternoon, Bea barely acknowledged her presence and went straight to Desi's room, ignoring Marva's demands to go out to the cabin first and let him rest.

Marva need not have worried since Desi was wide awake and sitting on his lounger, reading the newspaper with his glasses swung low on his nose. He welcomed the interruption from his boredom since his wife had been avoiding him.

"Hello, Desi, I'm here to see my niece, and of course I couldn't pass by without checking in on you. How're you feeling?"

"I good for now, Bea," he said, putting down the paper and giving her his full attention. "Aya didn't tell me you was coming, people trying to keep me in the dark these days."

"You're always scowling, that's why," Bea said. "What're you doing sitting in here when it's such a lovely day?"

"I good where I am," he said shortly. "I wanna keep an eye on things."

"You mean your wife?" she said, smirking. "Well, that's what I want to talk to you about. What are your intentions in her regard?" She turned and closed the door.

Marva took a quick look around to make sure she was alone and pressed her ear to Desi's bedroom door.

"Intentions to what?"

"Not to be blunt, but you're leaving Aya in the lurch here. I want to make sure you will protect her interests and not let the boys push her out in the event of your untimely ..."

"Death?" Desi snarled. "You here trying to give Aya the heads-up on how she gonna profit if and when I gone?"

Marva's face flushed and her heart throbbed in her ears. She could not believe the gall of the woman to ask such a delicate question in such brute fashion. She was liable to get the Missus cut out entirely.

"Now, Aya doesn't have anything to do with this, Des," Bea said. "I'm concerned for her like anyone would be. There's this large house to look after, then your boys—and don't tell me that Junior is grown because he don't do a damn around here. Then there's that uppity maid who doesn't know her place, and the business ..."

Marva pushed out her bottom lip and crossed her hands in a snit. She then heard Ricky coming down the stairs and had to duck out of sight, although not out of earshot.

"You got a hell of a lot of nerve to come in here with this mess. The way I see it, I done real good by Aya for these five years and she shouldn't expect no more. I made arrangements for everything and it's none of your damn business what I do with the legacy I worked my ass off for."

"That's not good enough!" Bea shot back. "She has been a good wife to you and deserves to not have to worry about her future."

"Oh, she worried 'bout that, is she? Well, she should be," he said cryptically.

"What the hell is that supposed to mean?"

"Mind your business."

The door shot open and Ricky ran in and hugged his father. He greeted Bea warmly, asked after her sister, and made polite conversation, to Desi's delight.

After unsuccessfully trying to get the boy to leave, Bea retreated to find Aya. "This isn't over, Desi," she fired back upon her exit.

"Yes, it is," he said softly, beaming.

"I'm telling you, Aya, you need to get this sorted out," Bea said.

"Honestly, do you think he would tell you anything different? You think he's concerned about what's troubling you right now? No, Auntie, he wanted to rile you up, to make you panic. He's probably hoping I'll do the same and start kissing up to him, and that's not going to happen."

"Why don't you suck up to him, then? Or suck *on* him for that matter? You need to secure your future, girl, and that book isn't gonna cut it. He's got plenty of money and property, he can leave you a little something. In fact, no matter what he does, you are entitled to your fair share, Aya. Go seek advice on how to challenge a will if need be."

"Well, listen to you," said a disbelieving Aya. "'Suck on him,' are you kidding me? I'll get by fine. Desi's going to do what Desi's going to do—and he's right, it is up to him to do what he sees fit. I can't think about that now."

"And Marley?"

"Marley is Marley. I can't think about him now either," Aya said, wondering what he was doing at that moment.

"Well, your mother and I are worried sick about you and that man. He looks godawful, and you don't look much better. Here. I brought you some food, and I'm gonna sit here and watch you eat it. I will come by like Nicola to check on you too."

Instead of replying, Aya nibbled on the fried fish that her aunt always managed to get so crisp without tasting oily.

"You and your mother need to get sorted out too, missy. Don't trust that Marva as far as you can throw her either. She a gossipy troll, ya know? Don't think that everything that goes on in this house hasn't been spoken on from her to several villages about here. Don't think she's not up in here robbing you blind when you're not looking. Don't think she gives a damn about you more than what you can do for her, ya hear?"

Aya rolled her eyes and continued to eat her food.

"You listening to me? She's all for Desi and always will be. Every move you make he knows full well about, and then you go and bring Marley into the equation and don't even keep him from the house. Really, Aya?"

"Auntie, you're getting dangerously close to being booted from here yourself. I don't want to hear any more of this. You all have made it perfectly clear how you feel about Desi, about Marva, and about me. You've had your say, now leave it alone. I'm not ready to deal with

Mother right now. I told you, I have enough going on. If you expect to keep coming here, I won't listen to any more of this talk."

"Why don't you listen? We have warned you and warned you—"

"Did you hear what I just said? I'm sick of the two of you trying to run my life. Has yours turned out so great that you think you can judge?"

"I don't want you to make the same mistakes, Aya," Bea appealed. "We wouldn't listen either and it cost us dearly."

"Well, you managed to thrive, so get over it. Leave us be, I'm warning you."

Marva finished getting a brooding Desi to take his medication, which he hated since they made him feel nauseous and drowsy to the point of passing out. Although they were nowhere near as cordial as they used to be, they had thawed to a difficult banter.

Marva had made it very clear to Desi that Bea was a nuisance and that the Missus had to relent to let her visit since she was threatened. She had told him that the Missus wasn't interested in his money and that Bea was acting on behalf of the Mother. Although Desi hadn't said much, she could see that he was taking it in and appreciative of the information.

Marva closed his door gently and gave a deep sigh. She was exhausted and looked forward to relaxing on the couch and listening to her soaps while she drifted in and out of sleep. She found this much better than going to her bed as she didn't like to be out of earshot of the goings on of the house.

She had just pushed her glasses up to her forehead, put her head back, and closed her eyes when she heard the back door swing open.

"Working hard as usual," Bea said sarcastically.

Marva pushed out her lip and sat up in the chair, then shook her head.

"You think I don't know what you're up to?" Bea leaned against the door jamb and crossed her arms. "You may have them fooled, but not me, lady! You've got them thinking you're here working, and you're not doing a damn. You're not ashamed to have Aya tidying up after you? Now that you've got Pearl out the house, Aya in the back, and Desi on his way home, you think you're the queen of Frankly Fine?"

"I been up since all hours this morning and I on my proper break. Not like it's anything to do with you, but when Desi sleep, I sleep. You dunno what go on in this house."

"I know you're one lazy old goat. I can't believe you have them paying you more money to rob them left, right, and sideways. I have half a mind to send my girl up here to show them what a decent day of work looks like."

"You can do whatever you please, I ain't leaving here. I as good as Franklyn for all these years and no one want me to go. I know that if the Missus hear how you talking to me she'd shift you right on outta here, just like you sister."

"Yes, I can see you're banking on that," Bea said wryly. "I know Desi's outraged that you've moved in without his permission and that he's having to pay you more while you're not looking out for his interests, so to speak. He's simply biding his time, you should know him well enough by now."

Marva eyes began to twitch.

"You relying on Aya is a foolish decision," she continued. "Things between them will combust sooner or later, and she'll move on without you one way or the other. The boys don't need you, Desi's already asked P to take over guardianship of Ricky, and the other two will continue living their lives. You're here all proud of yourself, living in a fool's paradise."

Marva's head was swirling with thoughts and she started to feel sick. She knew too well that Bea was trying to torment her and could not be trusted, only where had she gotten so much information?

Bea grinned. "No one in their right mind would hire the likes of you, as slow and lazy as you are. I don't blame you for enjoying every minute of this while you can, because you gonna be on the streets soon enough."

Marva pushed her glasses back down to cover her tearing eyes and focused on the television.

They heard Aya slam the cabin door, but that didn't stop Bea from putting the final nail in the coffin. "You think Aya cares about you? You think she's gonna put herself out for you? As long as Desi's footing the bill, she's not bothered, but she's not gonna pay for your nonsense out of her pocket. You can suck up to her all you like, you're as good as finished, and it serves you right."

She picked up her shoes and looked at Marva. "You think you're a Franklyn? Don't make me laugh," she spat, then headed out the door before her niece caught her.

As Aya came in, Marva turned off the television, careful to keep her back to her so Aya did not see her tears. She mumbled a few words and practically ran up to her room.

Chapter 37

The next three months dragged on with the Franklyns in a deadlock. Desi continued to bark orders and be short with everyone. He didn't even get much joy from Ricky anymore and shut himself up in his room. Marguerite explained that he was in the angry phase of his diagnosis, still in denial about how frail he was and irate about having to wear diapers and be babied when he was the man of the house.

His eyes were jaundiced as he wasted away before their eyes. His digestive system had stopped functioning for the most part, and he could only tolerate soft, bland foods and liquids. Even though his belly was protruding, Desi was a scrawny 138 pounds, and his teeth were rotten. He looked decades older than he should have, and his face was in a constant grimace from the pain in his rotting guts.

Aya wanted to run away from the monster he had become. Marva paid no attention and tended to him just as she did her own mother: matching all of his coarse remarks, handling his lanky body with ease, and putting him in the bathtub while threatening to push his feeble head under water one of these days. She worked harder than she had in all of her life. Aya was most grateful to her, yet Marva remained distant. Aya figured this was her way of dealing with her grief and didn't push.

Each day rolled into the other and the exciting life with Marley seemed to Aya like a disappearing mirage. She had heard only cryptic messages from him over the past few months, mainly letting her know that he was nursing his dying mother, who also did not have much longer to live. He did not elaborate much beyond that and would not return Aya's calls.

Carlton had come at last and was more effeminate than ever, who even wore lip gloss in front of his father; however, Desi's mind was too far removed to bear witness to it. Although he sat by his father's side the whole time he was home, he nevertheless was eager to leave and return to his studies. He could not face watching his father deteriorate further and wanted to see him out of his pain. Junior pretty much agreed that he wanted it done and over with, and he offered to buy Carlton's share of the business.

Carlton initially considered the offer, figuring that the business was as profitable as it would ever be and would quickly fall in stature with Junior's spendthrift ways and no one there to keep it in check. Only Carlotta soon talked him out of it. She asserted that the corporation had a business manager that would stay on top of things and that he should keep his hand in the game.

All of this incensed Junior, who did not think it fair that he should be doing all the hard work while the pansy enjoyed the spoils, especially since there would be no business if it were not for him. He then tried to force Carlton's hand by countering with a request to be bought out so he could do his own thing, only Carlotta remained firm.

Both sons' complaints to their father fell on deaf ears as he couldn't care less about the spoils now. Aya couldn't stand the additional tension and bickering and asked them to wait until their inheritance was fully disclosed before discussing the matter further, to which they both agreed.

Carlotta was aggressive in seeking time alone with Desi. To her great disappointment, neither Aya nor Marva would allow that in his delicate condition. Even Carlton blocked her efforts, fearing her greediness could isolate him further. She kept insisting that she had something urgent to discuss and would cry and carry on, only to be escorted roughly from the house by Junior.

Ricky got very quiet and increased his misbehaviour. The complaints from teachers and other parents were coming in rapidly, and he was sent to the school counsellor, who suggested quite aggressive therapy, alarming Aya. Pearl took him most weekends, and Carlton suggested he go to a boarding school near him so that he could look after his brother. Neither Marva nor Pearl approved of that idea. Aya had to agree that it was an option for the future, even though it seemed better to heal his wounds where they were born.

Aya and her mother had still not reconciled since Pearl was furious that she could not get access to Desi, except for the occasional brief conversation.

Bea continued to come by every week to check on things and bring food, trying to discover what Aya's plans were for the future in the event that she had no share in the property nor any money being left to her, but she would consistently draw a blank. Aya did not seem to care about the funds and sought no legal counsel to protect her interests.

Aya kept to her studio and her simple routine. She never returned to sleep with her husband again after their last encounter. She would prepare his cream of wheat and feed it to him until he grabbed the spoon out of her hands and fed himself.

She gave him his pills and helped Marva position him on the lounger to look out over the sea and her quarters. She would bring him the newspaper, leave the television on the only local station, and return again at lunch. This time he would spill the soup while fighting her to feed himself.

Aya would let him do what he wanted and not get angry as she was far beyond caring. When he made his usual accusations and complaints, she would ignore him. Desi hated her indifference and tried all the harder to get a reaction.

Aya had never been around a dying person and by some means managed to keep her cool while her world was crumbling all around her. She continued to pocket her share of the house money, and she was granted guardianship over her husband in his delicate condition. She made sure not to spend a cent more than normal so that all could see she was above board when his sons looked into their father's finances.

She moved a large portion of her things into a series of trunks in Nicola's spare room, keeping the bare minimum in the cabin and close to seventy-six thousand dollars safely stashed away. She was hoping to get at least a hundred thousand dollars to rebuild her life, since it worked out to less than half of that in American currency.

It was clear that things were going to be nasty between the boys when all was said and done, and Aya didn't want to be anywhere around all that. She planned to leave Marva in charge of Ricky, even though she thought there was a strong chance Desi may have legally put her mother in that position.

Aya wanted to take some time to travel before making her way to California. She needed to get away by herself for a while before taking up with another man. She would tell Marley when she was free and he was welcome to join her. That is, if the man was still up for the taking. That, more than anything, wore on Aya's mind, and her nerves were shot. She worried that whatever he found beautiful about her had faded considerably. Even she could not believe how empty her once bursting brassiere had become.

She should have run off on Desi long ago, yet she could not bring herself to do it. Something unknown was holding her there until the end, and she could never quite place what it was.

That morning, Aya found her husband sleeping soundly when she brought him his breakfast and chose not to wake him since he had been in so much discomfort that morphine had little effect. When lunchtime came around, he was snoring and had not moved an inch. Marva decided to wake him so he could take his medication, but she could not rouse him.

Aya screamed for Junior and the three of them poked, pushed, and prodded but got no response. Marva called an ambulance and Desi was rushed to the hospital. He had slipped into a coma.

Desi was stable a few hours later, much to everyone's relief, and he remained in Marguerite's care for a week. She advised the family that it was time to start saying goodbye as it would not be long now. He was on such high doses of medication that he was half out of his mind. There was blood around his teeth and he reeked of imminent death. He could no longer eat any food whatsoever and was on a drip for nourishment. His body was so hard and rigid it was as if rigor mortis had already set in.

Aya informed Carlton, who said he did not wish to see his father in such a state, and she could not blame him. Desi's frightening appearance made the hairs on her body stand on end. She wanted it all over with too. She wanted to pack up this part of her life for once and for all.

When her mother showed up at the hospital, Aya did not deny her access and waited with Marva in the corridor. Ricky, who could no longer deny the situation, had a major breakdown and would not leave his father's side. Neither Junior nor Marva could calm him any better than Aya could, so she hoped that her mother would be more successful.

"How are you feeling, Marva?" Aya asked. "You've been so quiet lately, not like yourself at all. I can understand how you feel. Why don't we talk about it?"

Marva only mumbled and crossed her arms, her bottom lip protruding.

Aya tried again. "Are you angry with me? Do you blame me for this, like the others?"

Marva whipped around to face her employer. "Who blame you? This not on you, Desi got this long before you was near these parts."

"So what is it, then?" Aya pleaded. "You barely talk to me anymore, and I miss you. You've been working so hard, I don't know what I would've done without you."

"That ain't nothing, Missus. You make a place for me in you house and pay me good so I can put my mother up."

"So, what is going on about the house, then?"

"I get access to her accounts, though she ain't got much, hardly nuff to cover expenses. The lawyer still checking on the title," Marva said sullenly.

"Your home is with us, Marv, the boys won't put you out. They need you and you are family."

"What 'bout you, Missus? You don't need me too?"

"Of course I do, I just don't know what the future has in store. The boys are already at it over the money, and there's little chance Desi left me much of anything."

"You leaving, then? Going back to you auntie's or getting you own place like out back?"

"I honestly don't know what I'm going to do, Marv."

"I concern 'bout you too, Missus, 'bout what gonna come a you. You don't talk to you family other than you cousin, and you spend too much time alone in you head. You need to keep people 'round you, even when they ride you last nerve." She patted Aya's hand and looked up. "Wait, ain't that Marley? And Carlotta? What they doing here?" She rose to follow them, Aya trailing behind.

Aya could tell it was her man, and her heart leapt with joy that he had come to rescue her. Before she could reach him, he went into one of three elevators and was gone. Aya ran up the stairwell after him with an energy she had not felt in ages, but try as she might she could not find him.

She should have tried her husband's ward.

"What are you doing here?" an astonished Pearl asked upon Carlotta's and Marley's arrival at Desi's bedside.

"We have important business to discuss with Desi before it's too late. Darling, take the boy and give us a few minutes," Carlotta ordered.

"I will not!" Pearl looked into Desi's canary-yellow eyes. "The man is exhausted and cannot handle any of your drama."

"That's not for you to decide, darling," Carlotta said harshly. "Your daughter wants you, and we need a minute with him."

Pearl was puzzled by the pained look on Marley's face, but she got no answers from him. Desi, on the other hand, seemed to know exactly what was going on and waved at her, a signal to leave them alone.

Ricky whimpered as Pearl took his hand and made one last glance at Desi, who took no heed. She decided to take the boy to the on-site counsellor that Marguerite had recommended instead of having words with her daughter.

"Desi, darling, it's Carlotta. You hear me? You understand me?"
Desi shook his head and steadied his gaze on Marley.
"This here is Marlon. Marlon, remember? My first child I told you 'bout."
Marva could not believe her ears! After the Missus had fled off, she decided to return to Desi, and that's when she saw Pearl and Ricky leaving. Desi shared a semi-private ward with two other men, whose spaces were partitioned off. One man was missing and the other was sedated, so Marva slipped into the unconscious man's area so that she could listen to the conversation.
"My sister dead, and we just come from burying her. She tell Marlon the truth and I couldn't deny it any longer, so I bring him here to you. He says you know each other already."
Desi focused on his nemesis, clenched his jaw, and nodded.
"Darling, he came here to learn about his family—his father in particular," Carlotta prodded. She was standing on Desi's left while Marley stood in a daze at the foot of his bed with his arms crossed.
"Des? Desi, you hear me?" Carlotta snapped her fingers and he turned to her.
He cleared his throat and struggled to keep his head from shaking. "What would I know 'bout that?" he said gruffly.
Carlotta let out a frustrated lament. "Well, you looking right at him, aren't you? He look just like him, as fine as he ever was back in the day. I know you must recognize him, darling."
"So what if I do?" Desi grumbled. "I don't know nothing 'bout his father."

Desi laid his weary head back down and closed his eyes as if to dismiss them.

Carlotta wasn't having it. "Desi, don't play the fool, man!" she barked. "This is your half-brother, and he wants to know about your father, Levi. You can't even do that for the woman who birthed you Carlton? We come all this way to talk to you properly before it's too ... late."

Desi continued to ignore her.

"Speaking of Carlton, you're gonna take care of him, aren't you, darling? He will finish his schooling next year and be ready to come back and take the company to high levels. He's a well-educated businessman now and has every right to be running things. Des? Desi? I know you can hear me!"

Marley started to sneeze and left the room so swiftly that the curtain blew open and he would have seen Marva had he been looking. He leaned back against the wall in the hallway and covered his mouth. He could hear his recently discovered mother screaming at his half-brother in the distance and swallowed hard.

Marley could not believe that no more than fifteen days ago, he had been at his supposed mother's bedside in California when she told him the story that many had hinted at but none had the guts to tell him properly. She was actually his aunt Clarissa, not his biological mother. Her sister, Carlotta, had a fling with Levi Franklyn that resulted in her shocking pregnancy at fourteen years of age. Clarissa, who was dating a wealthy man who lived in San Diego, took him to raise as their child while using the man's money to help maintain her mother's and younger sister's lifestyle back in Trinidad so that no one would be the wiser.

At some point, Carlotta's father exposed both daughters to the wealthy man, whose name Marley still carries. Levi bailed on Marley's birth mother as he did with all of his sons, only Carlotta was slick enough to get her hooks into Desi many years later, finding some kind of sick revenge on her sister, who made out well for herself by taking advantage of her immaturity and precious firstborn.

All of these details made Marley sick to his stomach, though he could hardly hate the woman who had given him such loving care, even if initially it was to benefit herself. As tumors took over her body, she was so weak and frail that she could barely open her eyes to witness her nephew's disgust.

When Carlotta was contacted, she gloated about her sister getting what she deserved and hastily insisted that Marley send her the fare so that she could be reunited with him. He reluctantly did so—and had since regretted every moment in her presence. She was rude, inconsiderate, and bitchy. Worse still, he not only had the same blood as Desi, the husband of the woman he coveted, but he was also the brother of one of Desi's sons! His whole world came crumbling down, and he hardly knew what to do with himself. He needed Aya, he realized. He had to find her and hold her again. They had to be together; he couldn't wait any longer.

But first, there was something he had to do.

Marguerite had never heard such a racket and yanked a shrieking Carlotta right out of the ward. Marva cowered in her corner and praised the Lord that Desi's roommate did not wake up with all that noise. She was eying the exit to make a quick escape and soak in the news when she saw Marley storming back.

He shook Desi to get his attention, leaned in close, and whispered softly, "I want you to know I love Aya and she means the world to me. She was never unfaithful to you, but it's obvious we are meant for each other. You don't have to worry about her being lonely or about telling her anything in reference to us being blood."

Desi bolted up in his bed. "Stay the hell away from her, you've ruined her life."

"Ruined her? I love her—for what she truly is, not what I want her to be. Don't you want her to be happy? God knows you haven't been a comfort to her in years."

At that remark, Desi smiled and his pupils dilated. "You nothing but a con artist, and I can see right through you. You think she gonna want you knowing how Bea put you up to seducing her to break us up? Knowing that Bea and you been laying together? Knowing you in cahoots with Carlotta, who she despises?"

Marley backed up and nearly choked on his saliva. "What the f—"

"Watch yourself." Desi grinned and waved his emaciated hand. "*My* wife could walk through the door any minute."

"To hell with you!" Marley snapped. "I can't believe I came here wanting to make peace and try to get to know you. I thought I could help you understand me and Aya so that we would get your blessing."

"Ya never!" Desi said, crossing his arms, lying back down, and closing his eyes.

"I have never been with Bea, you damn liar, and I sure as hell never agreed to get in between a man and his wife. Aya will never believe that. We are in love!"

"Then why ain't she with you all this time, then?" Desi said to the ceiling. "You think she only with me 'cause I in this bed? Naw, here where she wanna be, and you know it."

Marley winced and clenched his fist as Marva's eyes bulged wide and her jaw dropped. Marley opened his mouth to quarrel but reconsidered when he heard Marguerite approaching. "What's the point? You'll be pushing up daisies soon enough," he said as he angrily passed Marva and the incoming nurse.

Marva took this opportunity to dash out behind him.

"Who's that?" Marguerite asked Desi.

"Get the wife for me."

Marva's legs took her as fast as they could down two flights of stairs and to the very same bench that her Missus had caught her breath on all those months ago. She simply could not believe what she had just witnessed. Marley was the child of Carlotta and Levi Franklyn? Unbelievable! And Desi knew?

All this time, Marley and Desi were brothers? How could she not have noticed it before? They had many of the same features as their incredibly fine father. Fortunately, Marley had not been raised under the evil influence of Carlotta, though Marva loathed him all the same. How could he come to a dying man's bed and threaten to take his wife?

Good for Desi for standing up to that punk! What was that about Marley bedding down the auntie? Could he really have no feelings for the Missus and be working for the Mother and the Bee-yotch after all? What would the Missus do if she knew? Oh Lord!

And there was no one she could talk to about all of this now. Glenda had been indifferent to her for so long that Marva eventually decided to leave her alone and focus on her own household. Then out of the blue, Glenda had called, acting like nothing had ever happened, and Marva had been so grateful to hear from her that she did not let on how hurt she had been and gossiped all over her face until well into the night.

She was sadly disappointed when Glenda returned to keeping her at arm's length shortly after. Marva just could not figure it out and knew that she could not divulge this new information to Glenda and betray the Missus any further.

Marva uncrossed her legs, leaned her head back, looked up to the heavens, and cried.

Aya was like a madwoman, racing up and down the main-floor lobby hoping to catch a glimpse of Marley only to run smack dab into her mother and an exhausted Ricky instead.

"Oh, there you are," Pearl said. "You were looking for me?"

"Uh no, I was looking for ... Marva."

"Well, I haven't seen her. That nasty Carlotta told me you wanted to speak to me. She's up there with your husband and Marley, did you know about that?"

Aya gasped. "So he's up there right now, then?" she asked, thinking only of being in his arms again and not of what he must be saying to Desi.

"They are up there with him now," Pearl said with a frown. "Ricky needs to rest, so I'm bringing him home. You and me need to talk, so I'll wait until you reach."

"Yeah, fine. Go on, I'll see you later."

Pearl took Ricky's hand. "We need the key to get in as my boy has forgotten his," she said gently.

Aya had already walked away, so when she saw Marva coming in the doorway, she motioned her over to Pearl and Ricky and kept going.

Marley was here! He had come for her at last! Only what could he and Desi possibly be talking about, and with Carlotta no less? Aya thought her heart would explode, but when she made it to Desi's ward, there was no sign of her beloved.

Aya's disappointment registered with Desi as he examined her through his haze. "You come at last," he said quietly.

Aya looked around the room and sat with a thump on the stool next to her husband's bedside.

"You looking for something?" Desi asked, raising his right eyebrow.

Aya was panting heavily and he watched her make an effort to slow her breath. "Oh, no. Mother and Ricky just left, so here I am."

Desi sat up in his bed and looked her square in the eyes. "I want out this place," he said, lifting off the sheet and attempting to rise. "Take me home right now. A man belongs on his own land, dammit!"

Aya jumped up and held Desi down. "Oh, no, Desi! It's not time yet, the doctor has to run more tests, remember? When you get stronger you can—"

"You know too well I ain't gonna!" he said with all his strength and began trembling. "You not here looking for me neither, you looking for your *friend*, aren't you? Well, he's gone and ain't coming back, so forget 'bout him."

"Why?" Aya cried, as if taken aback. "What do you mean?"

Desi grinned and lay back down to look up at the ceiling. "The bastard and his bitch mama have left 'round here. They're both the same, hustling and out to take what don't belong to them. They didn't fool me! No, sir! He can't sweet talk me like he did you," he said, giving her the side eye.

Aya was speechless and sat down again.

Desi, happy to have her full attention at last, went for the jugular. "You let him turn your blasted fool head from me, and he don't even want you. He don't even know you! He's only doing your family bidding. You a smart girl but don't question how Bea come to know and set him up with you all of a sudden? You never wondered 'bout their history, if you get my meaning? It wasn't strange to you that he show up the same time you mother come trying to stir things up?"

Aya's face flushed.

"He's doing Bea's bidding," Desi chided. "Can you imagine how close they got to be for him to do that for her sake?"

Aya's eyes grew large. She looked as if she were struck dumb, and Desi savoured every moment.

"You thinking he gonna come and the two of you sail off into the sunset with all my money? Not so! I let him know you ain't got nothing that ain't mine, and he done left. What you think 'bout you fine young gentleman now?" He chuckled, nearly choking.

His last, cutting words seemed to bring Aya to her senses. "I don't care about the money or anything you've given me. It was okay to have nice things, but I don't need them. I lived without before and I can live without again. It was never about things, only it seems to me you never believed that, even now. What did you marry me for?"

Desi wiped his running eyes. "I wish I knew." The day's events had taken their toll and he was worn out. He had finally put his wife in her place and wanted to be left alone, only she wasn't having it.

"That's a bullshit answer!" Aya rose from her stool and sat on her husband's bed so hard that he jumped. "What did you marry me for? Obviously, you and Mother share many secrets, especially about your disease. You kept me in the dark regarding most things and compensated by buying me stuff. Why bring me into this in the first place?"

Desi could see from her pursed lips that he was not going to get out of an answer. "I thought we would be happy together," he said slowly, squinting his eyes. "We were both so miserable, and I hoped we could comfort each other."

"And didn't we?"

"Yeah," Desi said, rolling his eyes, laying his head back, and playing with his fingers in contemplation. "Until you decided what we had wasn't good enough."

"You see, that's where you're wrong, I felt that *I* wasn't good enough, and that didn't have anything to do with you. I needed to do more with my life: I have a degree, I'm a trained professional, and I have skills and interests I want to explore. I needed to grow, and you assumed that meant away from you."

"Because it took you away from me!" Desi said. "You were all 'bout him and that book and shut up out back. You weren't interested in nothing else, and you can't deny that."

"I admit I got excited and caught up for bit, but again, it had nothing to do with you."

"Exactly." Desi nodded. "Nothing was 'bout me no more, or us. It was 'bout what Marley was doing for you, and even that was a lie and you couldn't see it."

"That's not true," Aya said quietly. "The same way you were working hard to get the business set for your boys, I was trying to get myself established so I wouldn't have to make you feel pressured to support me. I wanted to be an independent woman."

"You just wanted to be independent," Desi said, tears welling in his eyes. "Admit it, you wanted it more so that you could get away from me, Bea, and Pearl."

"I wanted to feel like a woman," Aya tried to assure him.

"I didn't make you feel like a woman?"

"I mean, I didn't like living off of you, and I told you that many times. Stop making this about Marley."

"You know damn well that things took a turn when he came into the picture."

"I know it did for you because you wrongly accused him for the changes in me. It was all me, Desi. I wanted to evolve and he—"

"So why you sleep with him, then?" Desi asked, the tears flowing freely now.

Tears surged from Aya's eyes. "I told you, I fell asleep in the car that night. I wasn't with him."

"I didn't ask you that." He sniffed and wiped off his face with his hands. "I know you been fucking him, and you ain't got the guts to be honest even now."

"I am looking you in the eye, Desi, and telling you that I did not have sex with that man. I do have strong feelings for him, only I was never able to figure them out, something always got in the way," Aya said quietly.

"No point thinking 'bout those things now." Desi sniffed again and sat up in the bed. Unburdening his heart had cleared his mind and made his pain more bearable. "He's gone off to cheat some other woman. He was only out to stick it to me the whole time. That dread's my father's son, and takes issue with me like the others 'cause I got all Dadad's land and businesses."

"What do you mean, 'your father's son'?"

"You heard me."

Aya was quiet for a moment, then realization dawned on her face. "I can't believe I never saw the resemblance. So, you knew all this time and let me keep him around? Is that how you treat your wife?" she said angrily.

"I thought I could trust you," Desi said, equally angry. "I figured you'd send him packing soon enough. You the one who kept holding on."

"And you didn't think I should know he's your brother? That he's a part of the family?"

"He ain't never been my family. He only come 'round to get his hands on my money through you. Bea and you mother put him up to it. I didn't wanna come between you and them, so I let it go and I kept my eyes on him. On both of you."

"You son of a bitch!" she said, standing over her him. "How could you? Don't you see that what you did is so much worse than whatever it is they were trying to do?"

"Don't put this on me!"

"It is on you!" Aya snapped. "You could've put an end to all this foolishness but chose to play this sick game. You sound just like the man Mother always said you were."

"Now, you shut your mouth! You ain't got no business talking to me like that after all I done for you. You ain't got nothing without me! Everything you are is 'cause of me!"

Fresh tears fell down Aya's face as she backed away from Desi. "I finally see who you really are, and that is no better than me," she said, picking up her bag and readying to leave. "It has always been about what's best for Desi. I don't owe you for giving me things I never asked for."

"I deserve respect. I am your husband! You didn't respect me!"

"That's just it," Aya said as she left the ward. "I don't respect you."

"Aya, don't you walk away from me, dammit! Aya! Aya!" Desi barked. However, she was already down the stairs.

Desi could only hope that his lie would put an end to any thought his wife had of reconciliation with Marley after his demise. Even though there wasn't much time left, he could breathe easy now since Aya would know soon enough how much he truly loved her.

Aya raised her head from the newspaper to brace herself when she heard Ricky plead "Daddieeeee, don't go. Please Daddieeeeeeee!" coupled with her mother's howl from all the way down the hall. Marguerite came out and signalled for her and Marva to rise from their bench, except Aya couldn't move.

Each woman took one of Aya's arms and led her to where her husband lay. Once they got her to the door, Aya stopped abruptly and timidly peeked in. She could not blink, breathe, or budge until they literally pulled her inside. Desi's wet, bulbous, sightless eyes gaped at the fluorescent light above him while his mouth remained propped open as if he was about to speak.

This disturbing image would torment Aya's mind for many months. She had refused to see him again after their last argument, despite continuing to come to the hospital daily to sit for hours in reflective solitude.

Ricky continued to wail at his father's shoulder while Pearl crouched down next to him, blubbering prayers over the body. The medical team completed their work and moved on to the next patient as Marguerite closed Desi's eyes and sang a French hymn so exquisitely that all present became silent with awe.

Once finished, Aya's prolonged exhalation let out the air in her lungs. Marguerite held her all the closer so that Aya's head laid on her ample bosom. Marva released Aya's right hand and went to whisper her own devotions into Desi's ear as Pearl glared at her and then her daughter. Aya raised her head to meet her mother's eyes and caution her. She said nothing because she felt nothing and quickly left the room to call the other boys and meet with the undertaker. For Desi had wanted no funeral, preferring to be cremated unceremoniously and placed in the tomb next to his revered Dadad.

Chapter 38

Marva was taken aback when she received Glenda's call of condolence three days after Desi's service. It was a stormy mid-December afternoon, she had the run of an empty house, and she felt a hopeless sadness since it did not hold pleasant memories anymore. She had once been so desperate to live there, and now that she was, she desperately wanted to run away.

She was sitting at the kitchen table, looking out toward the sea and the cabin where the Missus was no longer, when the sharp noise of the phone ringing made her jump from her seat.

"Glenda? I thought you forget all 'bout me, it been months …

"I holding up all right. It's better this way. Him not suffering no more. He got real scary at the end …

"How I mean? Well, his nasty attitude get worse. As miserable as shite! He go down real fast after the Missus stop seeing him. He even scare off Ricky, who would only come when his father sleeping …

"I dunno nothing 'bout that. The Missus faithful and loyal to her husband to the end. She there with me at the hospital every day and talking with that nurse Marguerite. Her entire fortieth birthday, no less. She lost, I tell you, she didn't know what to do with herself …

"Me? What you worried 'bout me for? You ain't called for the longest time. Why you care now? …

"Yeah, I know you got you divorce troubles, but you could still pick up the phone, Glenda. So you really gone and done this dumb-ass thing? You left you husband over some nonsense?"

"Yes, I know you don't wanna hear that so you keeping you distance, but you can't never say I didn't warn you. You gonna regret it, Glenda. You gonna regret it …

"What? Me? No, I don't need no place to live, I gonna be just fine, thank you. The Missus lawyer come through for me true nuff. No, I don't wanna talk 'bout her now, I talking 'bout me …

"I been telling you the lawyer look into things and find out my father leave that shack for me, not her! I the rightful owner, the daughter a Jefferson Forde a the Forde Funeral Home family upcountry. You believe that? …

"All this time she been telling me he don't give a damn, and he left the house to me. That not all neither! The lawyer find out he left some money for me too, that ol' cow didn't tell me 'bout. She real vex that she couldn't put her hands on nothing, so if she couldn't get it, I wouldn't get it neither.

"But the Fordes real nice and they keep and invest it for me. They figured that once I come a age I'd come looking for them, only I didn't know where to look. So, my lawyer get a call from a Lesley Forde-Sanchez to go see pictures a my family, and it turn out she my half-sister!

"I couldn't believe it that such good things happening to me, and everyone 'round me so miserable. I had no one to talk to 'bout this and wanted you so bad, Glenda, it hurt like hell.

"Lesley real sweet and wanna introduce me to everybody, but I tell her I ain't ready yet, and she understand. I see pictures a my dead father, who as sharp as a man could be, 'cept I look like his sister. We both got that bumpety-type face, thick lips, and glasses. I got two brothers, one killed a few years back and the other over in America. My sister got twin daughters that are gonna be thirteen and a husband from Cuba. She invite me to dinner many times, but I been too caught up with Franklyn business …

"No, I not moving in with them. Me? We still getting to know each other first, getting friendly. I gonna sell the shack, and with the money my father leave me I gonna be just fine. I even got people to love and watch out for me, so I grateful to the Lord. He see all my suffering and wait for when I done gone past hope to give me salvation …

"No, I dunno nothing 'bout the will, it only been a few days. Junior wanna sell this place to buy out Carlton's share a the business and build on that nice piece a land Desi grandfather got by the harbour …

"It still gonna be awhile before this house get sell, so I gonna stay here and keep after it until it done, like I know Desi want me to. Then I figure I need a change and might go meet up with the Missus for a while and make sure she all right …

"What you mean, it not my place to look after her? She and I had a long talk the other day and come to an understanding. When I need help, she help me. She find the lawyer, she move me in here, she give me the raise so I could put the ol' bat in that home so she can make someone else miserable. She never talk down to me, she treat me like an equal. She even make Desi send me away for Christmas that time. She always there for me and I appreciate her for it. I was right there for her too, and that make us family.

"There ain't nothing I wouldn't do for the Missus, and she the same for me. She only gone for now 'cause she know I good. Even still, she gonna check in with me and make sure I stay good. She'd never leave me hanging for months without a word or not return my calls. Never! …

"You hold on, I ain't finished yet! Since when you and Queen Bea good friends? …

"I know you heard what I said, Glenda. There's no point pretending you didn't or denying it. I found it strange that Bea or Desi come to know things that only me and the Missus should know. I hadn't figured you and all the times you call wanting information …

"Now you wait, I to blame too. I trusted you and wanted advice on how to handle them, and we did enjoy the talk. I can't lie. Before, when you call asking me what going on with the Missus, I'd'a given you hours a chat. Only I didn't know you was turning 'round and telling the worst possible person ever. How could you, Glenda? Didn't you take no consideration into what it could do to me? Do you know how much trouble you caused between the Franklyns? …

"Yes, you! It's bad nuff you milked me for every update, you didn't even share what you knew, like you did with Bea. I know for a fact you saw the Missus and that writer on the beach together and didn't think to tell me a thing 'bout it, but you went to Bea, who went to the Mother who ran to Desi. You wicked wretch! ...

"Don't even try it, Glenda! Desi already told me all 'bout it, and even Bea admit that you told her things in passing when he confronted her. She didn't protect you, missy! She say you keep calling her for advice 'bout Marshall and pass on anything you hear ... What happen? ... Cat got you tongue? You too damn foolish with you prissy new friend to notice she not taking any notice a you. She love her niece and curse you every time you try to put the Missus down. She keep you 'round to get information to try to protect the Missus, not hurt her. But the blasted Mother ...

"Why didn't you come to me with you troubles? You angry 'cause you think I taking Marshall's side over you, Glenda? After all these years a me loving you as my only family, you could think so little a me? You could go and run you mouth to a woman I told you time and again I don't like or trust and who hate me? I could'a been fired! Is that what you trying to do? Make me lose my job so I'd have to come take care a you? Answer me! ...

"Never mind all that talk and big words. There ain't no excusing what you still trying to weasel out of. I told you I done talked to Desi. He yell at me one a he last days in bed 173 and curse me for talking Franklyn business to everyone but him. Said that he would'a gotten rid a me ever since if he didn't get such goodies 'bout what go on underneath his nose.

"I argue, until he tell me things he got no right knowing. Like how you spend those five nights with me when the Missus shut herself up to finish her book. Like things the Missus and me say when she call me during those days, it could only be you. Trust, I start to panic, thinking Desi got the place bugged, then he tell me flat out that he get it from the Mother, who get it from someone close to me. You know how much that hurt my heart?

"Then Bea come in looking for the Missus, and she out and admit everything to add to my shame. Worse still, I had to sit there and listen to him call me every name in the book, and she tried to defend me since she come to see I been protecting the Missus, like she was.

"I wanted to crawl into the ground and die. To think you could'a done this to me when I'd'a done anything for you. Even now, knowing all I know 'bout you, I'll never tell it. Me? The Missus say you ain't worth it, and I thank the Lord I come to find out now so I can make a fresh start too.

"Desi gone and buried, my mother still hanging on but I ain't got no room for her in my life no more, and you just as good as dead to me, Glenda. That's right! ...

"What you mean, I dunno what I saying? Me? My mind never been so clear. Like I tell you, me and the Missus had a long talk after I confess 'bout this whole mess, and she forgive me. She not even angry. The Missus always trying to lift me outta my situation and give me hope, while you keeping me down by telling me to stay in my place since I don't deserve no better ...

"No, you never say it like that, but you mean it just the same, Glenda. The moment I start to rise, you hold back on me and leave me high and dry ...

"Yes, you did! Not my Missus. And not even my sister. She happy nuff to train me a little so I can be a small part a the family business and have a job when she hardly know me. I the daughter of a whore who live her whole life in sin, but she raise me up and say we the same blood and our father would want all a us together. I got my own family now, and you done pissed away yours ...

"I can't say I feel sorry you so miserable now after all you done. Since the Lord watching me so close these days, I gotta forgive and let you go. It a new day for Marva Forde. That's right! I changing my name and all. My lawyer gonna take care a it for me. Marva Beccles as good as dead to you now 'cause there's no room for her in this body. I done talk."

Chapter 39

Aya sat stoically at her departure gate, feeling every minute of the two hours she would have to wait to board her flight. She was emotionally exhausted and looked forward to finally getting away on her own and leaving the past behind her. Much like Marva, her legal name was no longer appropriate. She wasn't *Aya Daniels*, nor *Aya Franklyn* anymore. She would now go by her pen name, *Dee Ayana*, and hope for better things in her next forty years.

She was returning to Canada for a few days to secure her valuables before heading to Botswana for the safari that Desi had wanted them to take together. She needed to be away from people and out in the wild for as long as she could stand it.

Only Marva knew her travel plans, and Aya was to check in with her every couple of weeks or be ratted out to her family. Her mother and aunt would learn soon enough as she planned to have it out with her father in short order upon her return visit. She would deal with the rest once she could stand the sight of them.

She'd slept deeply and soundly the night of her husband's passing for the first in a very long time. There were constant calls and messages from Marley; however, she was not ready to face him. A frantic Marva had run in to wake her from another deep sleep the following day to warn her that he had stormed into the house shouting for her and that she and her mother had had a hell of a time getting him out.

Marva had then revealed what she'd overheard in the hospital, which backed up Desi's story that Aya had been certain was a lie. Aya felt her spirit beginning to sink to depths from which she would not be able to recover, and she made the desperate decision to get away.

Pearl had stayed on to look after Ricky as Carlton was to return to England by week's end to find a halfway decent boarding school for his youngest sibling. Junior stayed high, whereas Marva needed to keep busy by working her fingers to the bone.

Aya packed all of Desi's things into his closet for the boys to review and cleaned out his astonishingly unlocked safe, which contained stacks of various currencies in bundles of ten thousand.

She prepared a foreign bank draft of the British pounds for Ricky to take with him, and she had US dollar drafts prepared for herself. She gave Marva half of the local currency outright for her unwavering service during the difficult times, as well as insisting she finally get her license by gifting her the Toyota that she would no longer be using. She cleaned out her local bank account and transferred a substantial amount to the overseas account she had used to pay off her debts all those years ago.

The majority of her garments were already packed and in Nicola's possession to forward to her at a later date. She travelled with a handful of clothes and gifted jewellery, which she was prepared to sell since they weren't her style.

The business was handed to Junior, most properties went to Ricky, and the bulk of the money was left to Carlton. The account Desi had shared with Aya was emptied, yet his entire life insurance policy was hers alone. Aya was certain that he must have forgotten about it or he would have changed the benefactor. Nevertheless, she was grateful for the couple hundred thousand dollars she had coming to her in the near future.

It was sure to take eight to ten months for all the paperwork to go through, and Marva would keep her posted, giving Aya more than enough time to be able to return to the island and settle scores.

Junior was going to be a father—was actually excited about it—and wanted to quickly build his own house in time for the birth. The women were happy that he had something positive to focus on and, hopefully, a new direction for his life. He assumed Marva would look after the child, but she was no longer sure that was what she wanted.

The Franklyn boys loved each other, only they were living in different worlds. Desi had wanted them to stick together, and Marva was convinced that it could happen in time. Carlton was at his wit's end with his mother and the news of his half-brother and couldn't wait to get away from them all and back to his books. He saw clearly that Ricky was in danger of falling through the cracks of a dysfunctional family. He thought a change of scenery would work wonders instead of realizing how crushing so much change in so little time among strangers could be.

Pearl was incensed Ricky was to be removed from her care at this difficult time. Desi had not made any legal arrangements for him to be with her as she had hoped, and it was made fervently clear that she was not blood and had no claim or say in the matter. Marva wanted to help, but she could not manage the boy on her own and truly needed her life to go in a different direction.

They were all skeptical about how he would fare with Carlton as his legal guardian in Britain. Nonetheless, they were desperate to try anything to get him through his grief. Pearl would continue to take him for counselling until she flew out with him in time for the spring semester. She wanted to check out his arrangements for herself and see that he was protected on Desi's behalf.

Aya said nothing and the Franklyn brothers did not argue with Pearl on that point. It seemed strange to all that she was so much more concerned about Ricky than her own daughter. It was of no matter since it worked to the benefit of everyone involved.

Aya and her mother were still keeping each other at arm's length with Bea as the go between. Aya could not get over Bea's newfound support of Marva as she recalled the conversation they'd shared earlier.

Before Marva would let Aya leave, she insisted they have an honest talk. Aya's bags were packed and at the door of her studio when Marva dragged her weary body inside and looked around for her. Aya was sitting solemnly on the chair, face drawn and lost in her thoughts.

"You 'bout ready to leave here for true, then, Missus? I never believed we'd see this day." Marva slipped off her cheap sandals, wiped the perspiration from her neck with her handkerchief, and pulled out a wooden chair to face her.

Aya forced a smile and clasped her hands, causing her bangles to jingle with the movement. "It's time, Marv. I gotta go."

Marva sniffled and looked out at the sea. "Why you stop going in to see you husband, Missus? You chat with me and Marguerite but didn't want nothing to do with him. And now you don't want nothing to do with that Marley neither. I tell you, I gonna call the police if he keep showing up here at all hours."

Aya took a long, slow breath and faced her friend. Dressed in jeans and a blouse for her travels, she was sweating profusely in the room but hardly noticed it. Then the whole story started coming out of her mouth before she could censor herself.

"I was frigid with Desi, Marva. He never brought me to ... Well, I deserved to have it. It's not all his fault. He wasn't lousy, he just didn't do it for me. I didn't desire him in that way. Like I do Marley. I thought it was me until he showed me different."

Marva squinted and leaned in closer.

"No, we never had actual sex. But we made love in so many other ways and I am not ashamed to say it. I've wanted to get away from Desi for the longest time, Marv. I'm sure you could tell. I was waiting for the right moment. It just never seemed to come. There was always some obstacle in the way."

Marva chewed on her lips and leaned back on her chair.

"Desi did his best, I know! I know I was no better! I just couldn't take it anymore though. It was all a lie. And then when I knew he'd had my mother!"

Marva scooted the chair closer and put her hand on Aya's leg. "She didn't get him that night. She was trying to seduce him, rubbing up on his leg when you in bed asleep. I saw her. He done with her though.

He been waiting for her to try something and catch her out. She got no shame! I'm sorry, Missus, but I told you she had eyes on being the woman a Frankly Fine, didn't I?"

Aya shrugged her shoulders and got up to walk to the window. "I meant before that. Anyway, I didn't want him, so what does it matter?"

"Well, I gotta tell you, Missus, I so glad you stood up to Desi for me when he got so mean and nasty. 'Specially knowing what you do now 'bout how Glenda played me."

Aya turned and smiled. "It was me he wanted to put out, not you."

"Not so, Missus. He love you 'til the end. And I thinking you love he right back. Why else you stay with him all these years? For money? When he never even make you wet and you got a dreadlocked stallion aiming at you with hose in hand?"

The women laughed, which broke the tension.

"With Desi gone most a the time and fading fast, you still stay," Marva said. "You even loss you father over him. Look, you mother could'a taken him off you hands and ya know it. You spurn you family and take his side—even when you come to know some a his dirty ways. You stayed Franklyn Missus when you could'a left him ever since. That stands for something."

Aya glanced back out the open door to see if Nicola was arriving. "I was such a two-faced wife. I could hardly stand to be around him and was happiest when he was away. He could tell I didn't like him much, so he would try harder and it made things worse. It was so selfish—just like he said. He should have left *me* long ago."

"Oh no, Missus." Marva got up and joined her at the window. "You forget I seen you all together and how you get on. Yes, you was best busy with other things, but when Desi come home 'pon an evening and see you, he be so happy and young. And then he hug and kiss you and ask 'bout you book—you light up too. You act like a little girl. Y'all was sweet together. It's not as simple as you wanting a father or getting at you family. That is *love*. You *loved* that man."

"My love is for Marley and is something entirely different." A tear formed in Aya's tired eyes and she turned her back to Marva.

"If you so in love why you ain't taking his calls, then? Why'd you duck him when he looking for you at the hospital and coming 'round here? I tell you it's 'cause Desi got you—that's what. Yeah, he got his faults, but he did good by you, didn't he? That Marley just a fog in you mind. You can't see him for what he really is. Christ! You know whose child he is!"

Aya turned slowly and met Marva's eyes. After reviewing Marley's Franklyn connection, Marva said she thought that it appeared he truly had not known his parentage and was just as appalled as they were. Aya questioned the true nature of his relationship with her aunt but was not able to imagine that they could have been lovers no matter what Desi said. Marva tried to convince her to go to the horse's mouth to find out before making any decision. After all, running away from him now could be a big mistake if there was a chance of finally getting a proper orgasm.

Aya changed the subject. "What will you do now that I will be gone? I worry that you don't have Glenda anymore and your mother getting deeper into madness."

It was then that Marva had revealed the wonderful news about the property, her family, and new name. Aya could not have been happier if it were happening to herself, and she hugged Marva so hard she nearly broke her glasses.

"I just want to thank you for all you done for me Missus," she said while wiping her face. "I dunno what I gonna to do without you, but the Lord never fails. I been so wrecked 'bout Glenda's doings I never realized that I got something with you so much better. I feel like a rich woman."

Aya put her arm around her and smiled through her own sniffles. "It is a decent amount of money you have now, but you still need to be careful, Marv. I'm glad your family is willing to give you a little work so you don't have to keep dipping into your savings. Does Junior know you are moving on from the family once the house sells?"

"I'll always look out for Desi's boys, Missus, you know that. And if he need help with the child when it come, I gonna get him sorted.

But Junior gotta be a man now and stop playing the fool. He got nuff responsibility to live up to, and Carlton's gonna have his hands full once Ricky get over there. You sure you don't wanna say a proper goodbye to him? You mother and him coming back from the clinic soon."

"I said my goodbyes to them at the luncheon for Desi's service. Junior understands and is too happy that we'll both be out of his way. Fortunately, Ricky is not really bothered about what happens to me one way or the other. I've gotta get out of here, Marv. Even Nicola thinks so—for once."

"I agree that you could stand a break away from the madness for a bit, but don't lock yourself away like you father. I'm a try and come see you when you finish the safari 'cause I get the feeling you not gonna come back to this land if you running from Marley."

Aya's posture deflated as she looked toward the floor. "No, I'll be back, Marv. I promise. I've still got things to attend to here."

"What 'bout Marley, then? Don't you wanna find out for sure?"

Nicola's horn beeped twice as she approached and Aya ran to collect her luggage. She kissed her dear friend and ran up the path, leaving Marva behind, weeping.

Aya's eyes misted up at the memory of Marva slouched in the studio doorway. The airline announced her flight would be boarding soon and that steeled her resolve. There was no going back now.

She had issues with trust since Bradley, and the past years with Desi had not helped. She couldn't be hurt again. She simply could not allow that pain. So what if she didn't know sexual pleasure? How many really did? Unintentionally, Desi had left a dirty residue in her bloodstream, and she couldn't contaminate Marley with it. Assuming he wasn't a whoring, lying son of an actual bitch.

How could she be with him, or anyone, now? No, she had to go take that trip of a lifetime and get out into the world again. How else for her to find topics to explore that would help her work through her issues? Besides, this time she could easily afford it. No more escaping through her credit cards.

This time she would not close herself off and pine for what was lost. She would find love again somehow, and not because she was lonely, desperate, or afraid. But because it was the right time with the right person. As much as it hurt her heart to ignore Marley all of these weeks, she had convinced herself it was the right thing to do.

Aya stood up to make one last trip to the washroom and noticed him. She could hardly believe the sight of what appeared to be a dishevelled Marley, racing through the terminal looking for something or someone. She stood as stiff as a board and wanted to disappear until his eyes locked in on hers. She could see love written all over his face—or could it be that she was imagining what she was longing to see?

As Marley approached her everything in the room moved in slow motion. He looked as golden and adorable as ever, wearing his usual ripped jeans with a T-shirt that could barely contain his bulging biceps. His dreads were reddish brown with several blond highlights now, and he was holding his plane ticket firmly in hand with a tan leather duffle bag dangling at his hip. He was panting when he reached her, beads of sweat streaking down his neck, yet he seemed energized.

"Marva didn't send me away this time. She told me where to find you and hoped you wouldn't be upset. I promised her I'd make it right."

What could she do now? Her legs would not move and she did not want to embarrass herself right there at the Virgin airlines gate. What was she so afraid of? Being happy, or of being disappointed yet again? Had he really lied to her as Desi said, or was that his last attempt to keep them apart? Could she really trust Marley, or anybody for that matter?

Then she had to consider what people would say: How they had been cheating and scheming while her cancer-ridden husband was off working so hard to feed his family. How bad it looked that she took off in less than a week after his entombment. How she had used him, made his life miserable, and given him very little in return.

She had taken the cash and run, leaving the Franklyns to fend for themselves; and that was hardly new. She had never been much involved in their lives in the first place and they had never complained, as they belonged to Desi alone. What did they expect her to do? She was not her mother and could not pretend to mourn her husband. She did have love for him, had not wanted him to suffer or wished him dead. She really had not. She simply had to get away from that situation.

As Marley held her in a bear hug, all of Aya's fears melted away. No more words were needed. This had to happen. She could not give up on this man who had opened up her world and heart so much. She had to give him a chance, only she would take things slowly as they had always done.

For they now had all the time in the world.

THE END
&
THE BEGINNING OF
Write Where I Started

Aya had clamped her eyes shut, held her breath, and gripped the armrest through the entire nine long minutes of severe turbulence at the end of her flight from Miami to the Caribbean island of her ancestry. She was furious with herself for not using the washroom when she had the chance and was about to wet herself right there on aisle 12, window seat A. Not the best way to begin her trip. She was convinced it was a sign of what was to come.

The gloomy quarter-mile drive up to Marva's was doing nothing to make her feel any better. As the taxi travelled the unfinished dirt road that wound along a maze of mango trees and through a crevasse in a limestone cliff, she tried phoning Marva once more and panicked when the ring tone went unanswered. She and Marva had grown close over the five years of Aya's marriage while Marva was her maid, but maybe she should have notified her family of her pending arrival? She had intended to sneak up to Marva's new place in the central uplands to get her thoughts together before facing all of her disappointed family's accusations. Of course, Marva would be full of her own questions to dodge, but she could only take on one issue at a time.

She rolled down the window, and the refreshing air of the balmy August evening soothed her frayed nerves. She decided to make the most of the peaceful drive under the starry skies and take in all the island smells she had not recognized she had been missing until now.

Aya had the taxi driver let her out in front of a dark and isolated home that she could barely make out in the half moonlight. She rolled her suitcase up to the covered porch and knocked on the door, which opened under her light pressure, and stepped into a foyer where she could hardly see two steps ahead. She was beginning to panic when she heard a large crash at the top of the stairs, followed by a holler from Marva, and darted through the darkness to rescue her friend.

She could not believe it when she reached the top of the landing to discover the bare-naked sixty-four-year-old woman rolling around on the ground with a huge, equally naked man.

"Marva!" Aya covered her eyes. "What the hell?"

The couple jumped up with a start, and the man leapt behind a potted fern to hide his dangling privates while Marva simply laughed and used her hands to cover her incredibly pert parts.

"Missus! Oh, Lordie! You come now? I forget all 'bout you. Earley, get out from behind there, ya blasted fool! The Missus ain't interested in anything you got!"

Aya turned her back to them, massaging her chest. Marva continued to snort uncontrollably as she turned on the lights, then directed her best friend to take a seat on the main floor while she made herself presentable.

Aya was in such a daze that she could hardly believe she managed to make her way down the stairs without collapsing. Had she really witnessed Marva sexing up some extremely well-hung and relatively handsome man? The same Marva who had closed up shop for decades and abhorred her own mother for her loose ways?

She sat gingerly at the bottom of the steps to ease her heart, which was still trying to settle down. Her cell went off, indicating a call from her lover. She answered it quickly.

"I made it here safely and all is good for now. I'll call you in a couple of days … No, I am not running away as usual. I'm trying to get myself sorted out, Marl. You agreed not to pressure me, remember? Aren't you tired of arguing? God knows we need this time away from each other. You know it too. Please, Marley … "

www.ingramcontent.com/pod-product-compliance
Lightning Source LLC
Chambersburg PA
CBHW030253100526
44590CB00012B/384